TEACHING LANGUAGE:
FROM GRAMMAR TO GRAMMARING

Diane Larsen-Freeman

The University of Michigan
and
The School for International Training

A TeacherSource Book

Donald Freeman
Series Editor

THOMSON
™
HEINLE

Australia • Canada • Mexico • Singapore • Spain • United Kingdom • United States

THOMSON
™
HEINLE

Teaching Language: From Grammar to Grammaring
Diane Larsen-Freeman

Publisher: James W. Brown
Senior Acquisitions Editor: Sherrise Roehr
Development Editor: Sarah Barnicle
Editorial Assistant: Audra Longert
Production Editor: Diana Baczynskyj
Senior Marketing Manager: Charlotte Sturdy

Manufacturing Manager: Marcia Locke
Compositor: Ethos Marketing and Design
Project Manager: Jessica Robison
Cover Designer: Ha Nguyen
Printer: Transcontinental Printing

Cover Image: Artville

Printed in Canada.
1 2 3 4 5 6 7 8 9 10   06 05 04 03

For more information contact Heinle, 25 Thomson Place, Boston,
Massachusetts 02210 USA, or you can visit our Internet site
at http://www.heinle.com

For permission to use material from this text or product contact us:
Tel: 1-800-730-2214
Fax: 1-800-730-2215
Web: www.thomsonrights.com

Library of Congress Cataloging-in-Publication Data

Larsen-Freeman, Diane—
  Teaching language: from grammar to
  grammaring/Diane Larsen-Freeman.
    p. cm—(TeacherSource)
  Includes bibliographical references.
  ISBN: 0-8384-6675-3
  1. English language—Study and teaching—
  Foreign speakers. 2. Language and languages—
  Study and teaching. I. Title. II. Series.

PE1128.A2L.348 2003
428'.0071—dc21

In memory of Elaine Larsen
and
Richard Hosking

Thank You

The series editor, authors, and publisher would like to thank the following individuals who offered many helpful insights throughout the development of the **TeacherSource** series.

Linda Lonon Blanton	University of New Orleans
Tommie Brasel	New Mexico School for the Deaf
Jill Burton	University of South Australia
Margaret B. Cassidy	Brattleboro Union High School, Vermont
Florence Decker	University of Texas at El Paso
Silvia G. Diaz	Dade County Public Schools, Florida
Margo Downey	Boston University
Alvino Fantini	School for International Training
Sandra Fradd	University of Miami
Jerry Gebhard	Indiana University of Pennsylvania
Fred Genesee	McGill University
Stacy Gildenston	Colorado State University
Jeannette Gordon	Illinois Resource Center
Else Hamayan	Illinois Resource Center
Sarah Hudelson	Arizona State University
Joan Jamieson	Northern Arizona University
Elliot L. Judd	University of Illinois at Chicago
Donald N. Larson	Bethel College, Minnesota (Emeritus)
Numa Markee	University of Illinois at Urbana Champaign
Denise E. Murray	Macquarie University, Australia
Meredith Pike-Baky	University of California at Berkeley
Sara L. Sanders	Coastal Carolina University
Lilia Savova	Indiana University of Pennsylvania
Donna Sievers	Garden Grove Unified School District, California
Ruth Spack	Tufts University
Leo van Lier	Monterey Institute of International Studies

TABLE OF CONTENTS

ACKNOWLEDGMENTS

Sometimes when I write, I feel as if I am a ventriloquist. I am the one writing, but the ideas of others come through. Although I cannot credit everyone who has helped shape the ideas I have written about in this book, there is no doubt that I have had numerous "teachers" over the years. And so, it seems appropriate here to first acknowledge my teachers, both formal and informal.

Therefore, let me thank Mrs. Rouse, whose first name I never knew, my high school English teacher, who showed me the power of grammar; Professor Gubbi Sachidananden, one of my first professors of Psychology, who inspired my lifelong fascination with learning, a fascination which led me later to undertake research in second language acquisition; Professor Kenneth Pike, one of my Linguistics professors, who helped me appreciate the systematicity of language and its interconnectedness to other aspects of human life; Professor of Applied Linguistics and friend, Marianne Celce-Murcia, with whom I have spent many hours happily attempting to resolve grammatical conundrums; Dr. Earl Stevick, Dr. Caleb and Shakti Gattegno, and my present and former colleagues at the School for International Training, who have shown me the power of teaching in a learning-centered way.

Then, there are the many "informal" teachers, too numerous to mention as individuals, from whom I have learned a great deal—especially my students at the School for International Training, where I have taught for 24 years. To them, I would add students with whom I have had contact for lesser periods of time: my first EFL students in Sabah, Malaysia, my first ESL students at the English Language Institute at the University of Michigan, Ann Arbor, my first graduate students at UCLA, and since my recent return to Ann Arbor, EAP and graduate students at the University of Michigan, and students I have taught in a number of short-term courses at summer institutes and academies over the years. My other "informal" teachers have been workshop participants and audiences in many parts of the world and friends and colleagues within the profession with whom I have enjoyed conversations in conference hotel hallways and over dinner. I cannot name them all here, but hopefully, some of them, at least, will recognize their contribution to the ideas I present in this book.

Second, I want to acknowledge those that had a more immediate impact on this project, beginning with Donald Freeman, for his invitation to write this book and for his guidance and his patience throughout its evolution. I am also grateful to the teachers who have contributed their voices to this book. Then, too, special acknowledgment should go to Nat Bartels, Patsy Lightbown, Michael McCarthy, Katie Sprang, Hide Takashima, and Elka Todeva, who have read portions of this manuscript and have generously offered me feedback. I am also grateful to Sherrise Roehr and Audra Longert, from Heinle, for skillfully moving the manuscript through the various phases of its production into a book.

Last, but not least, I owe an enormous debt of gratitude to my spouse, Elliott Freeman, who has always supported me with kindness and with grace. Given the recent loss of my mother and of my brother-in-law, to whom I have chosen to dedicate this book, Elliott's emotional support and untiring patience has meant even more.

Thank you all.

SERIES EDITOR'S PREFACE

As I was driving just south of White River Junction, the snow had started falling in earnest. The light was flat, although it was mid-morning, making it almost impossible to distinguish the highway in the gray-white swirling snow. I turned on the radio, partly as a distraction and partly to help me concentrate on the road ahead; the announcer was talking about the snow. "The state highway department advises motorists to use extreme caution and to drive with their headlights on to ensure maximum visibility." He went on, his tone shifting slightly, "Ray Burke, the state highway supervisor, just called to say that one of the plows almost hit a car just south of Exit 6 because the person driving hadn't turned on his lights. He really wants people to put their headlights on because it is very tough to see in this stuff." I checked, almost reflexively, to be sure that my headlights were on, as I drove into the churning snow.

How can information serve those who hear or read it in making sense of their own worlds? How can it enable them to reason about what they do and to take appropriate actions based on that reasoning? My experience with the radio in the snowstorm illustrates two different ways of providing the same message: the need to use your headlights when you drive in heavy snow. The first offers dispassionate information; the second tells the same content in a personal, compelling story. The first disguises its point of view; the second explicitly grounds the general information in a particular time and place. Each means of giving information has its role, but I believe the second is ultimately more useful in helping people make sense of what they are doing. When I heard Ray Burke's story about the plow, I made sure my headlights were on.

In what is written about teaching, it is rare to find accounts in which the author's experience and point of view are central. A point of view is not simply an opinion; neither is it a whimsical or impressionistic claim. Rather, a point of view lays out what the author thinks and why; to borrow the phrase from writing teacher Natalie Goldberg, "it sets down the bones." The problem is that much of what is available in professional development in language-teacher education concentrates on telling rather than on point of view. The telling is prescriptive, like the radio announcer's first statement. It emphasizes what is important to know and do, what is current in theory and research, and therefore what you—as a practicing teacher—should do. But this telling disguises the teller; it hides the point of view that can enable you to make sense of what is told.

The **TeacherSource** series offers you a point of view on second/foreign language teaching. Each author in this series has had to lay out what she or he believes is central to the topic, and how she or he has come to this understanding. So as a reader, you will find this book has a personality; it is not anonymous. It comes as a story, not as a directive, and it is meant to create a relationship with you rather than assume your attention. As a practitioner, its point of view can help you in your own work by providing a sounding board for your ideas and a metric for your own thinking. It can suggest courses of action and explain why these make sense to the author. You in turn can take from it what you will, and do with it what you can. This book will not tell you what to think; it is meant to help you make sense of what you do.

The point of view in **TeacherSource** is built out of three strands: **Teachers' Voices**, **Frameworks**, and **Investigations**. Each author draws together these strands uniquely, as suits his or her topic and—more crucially—his or her point of view. All materials in **TeacherSource** have these three strands. The **Teachers' Voices** are practicing language teachers from various settings who tell about their experience of the topic. The **Frameworks** lay out what the author believes is important to know about his or her topic and its key concepts and issues. These fundamentals define the area of language teaching and learning about which she or he is writing. The **Investigations** are meant to engage you, the reader, in relating the topic to your own teaching, students, and classroom. They are activities which you can do alone or with colleagues, to reflect on teaching and learning and/or try out ideas in practice.

Each strand offers a point of view on the book's topic. The **Teachers' Voices** relate the points of view of various practitioners; the **Frameworks** establish the point of view of the professional community; and the **Investigations** invite you to develop your own point of view, through experience with reference to your setting. Together these strands should serve in making sense of the topic.

To date, the various books in the **TeacherSource** series have examined the key elements of second language classroom education—from dimensions of teaching, including teacher reasoning, methodology, and curriculum planning, to dimensions of learning, including how second languages are learned and assessed, as well as various school models for effective instruction. At the core of all this work however, lie fundamental notions of subject matter: How do we understand *what* is being taught and learned? In other words, how we define language.

Diane Larsen-Freeman's *Teaching Language: From Grammar to Grammaring* goes to the heart of these questions to address language as the *what* of second language teaching. She weaves together an account which combines definitions of language as they have evolved in the English language teaching profession through the post-Chomskian era, with her own thinking. She outlines how she has moved literally from static descriptive ideas of grammar, based on rules, to more fluid and dynamic notions of reason-driven grammaring, which she defines as "the ability to use grammar structures accurately, meaningfully, and appropriately."

Larsen-Freeman's book is professionally steeped in a wide range of points of view, with equal measures of personal concern for language learning and language learners. Above all, she is passionate about language. She brings to its study the knowledge and tools of a respected applied linguist and a noted scholar in second language acquisition, as well as the know-how and practices of a widely traveled teacher educator and an effective materials writer. This variety of experience, and the plurality of purposes that underlie each area of activity, combine in what is unique to Larsen-Freeman's approach and her work. She clearly loves the order that is hidden in language and the potential explanatory power of frameworks—including her own form-meaning-use paradigm—to unlock that order. But equally, she recognizes the complexity of language and its chameleon-like potential to exceed boundaries, morph new forms, invent meanings, and to happen upon new uses. This facility and fascination with both the regular, predictable elements of language alongside its accidental and creative dimensions are what makes Larsen-Freeman the unique and powerful language practitioner that she is.

In this spirit, the reader of *Teaching Language: From Grammar to Grammaring* is left not with an encyclopedic group of definitions, but rather with a honed set of tools with which to approach language in language teaching. It is generative, exploratory work... as unruly as it is energizing.

This book, like all elements of the **TeacherSource** series, is intended to serve you in understanding your work as a language teacher. It may lead you to thinking about what you do in different ways and/or to taking specific actions in your teaching. Or it may do neither. But we intend, through the variety of points of view presented in this fashion, to offer you access to choices in teaching that you may not have thought of before and thus to help your teaching make more sense.

—*Donald Freeman, Series Editor*

Introduction

I have taken up in earnest Donald Freeman's invitation to write a personal account of the subject matter of this book. This is a book about language, especially grammar—what it is and what it is not—the product of one person's experience in her pursuit of a deeper understanding of her subject matter. As my education has been enhanced by the observations and teaching of many others, all that I present here did not originate with me—probably even less than I am aware of. This is to be expected. However, while there may be nothing new under the sun in our field, at the level of the individual, there remain many interesting avenues to be explored and new insights to be gained. All my professional life I have remained committed to furthering my own understanding and to contributing to our mutual understanding; in these pages, I hope to convey the excitement of the process of inquiry and discovery.

In 1996, I was asked to participate in a debate on the question, *Is teaching an art or is it a science?* In particular, I was asked to speak on behalf of the proposition that teaching is a science. Of course, few educators would argue that teaching is exclusively an art or a science; however, the debate proved to be a useful means through which to identify the relevant issues. I chose to make my case by suggesting that, as with good science, good teaching is best served when its practitioners cultivate attitudes of inquiry. This, then, is my ultimate hope for this book: that it will stimulate your curiosity to inquire into your own understanding of the nature of language and of grammar, and the nature of its learning and teaching.

However, curiosity is not sufficient. Therefore, I have built into this text questions and tools that will help you systematically inquire at the threshold of your own understanding. Each of the three main components of this book—Frameworks, Investigations, and Teachers' Voices—plays dual roles. The Frameworks serve both to relate what I have learned from my own experience and to offer you what I hope will be a fruitful way of looking at language, especially grammar. The Investigations invite you to begin to cultivate your own attitude of inquiry and to enrich your reading by connecting what you have read to your own experience. Finally, the Teachers' Voices both let you "listen" to the voices of others who have wrestled with some of the issues dealt with here, and encourage you to engage with colleagues in pursuit of deepening your own understanding. Indeed, if you read this book together with others and collaborate on the Investigations, that is all to the good.

Unlike much of my writing, this volume is not filled with a comprehensive inventory of academic citations. To complement the citations that are here, I have listed the works that I have consulted, or have been influenced by, in the section on suggestions for further reading at the end of each chapter. Also, in this book, I have curtailed my use of academic terminology. There no doubt still remains too much to suit all readers, but I have tried to be extremely selective in its use, believing that terminology should provide for convenient reference and links to other works, not add scholarly heft.

Finally, a word is in order about the focus of this book. It will come as no surprise to learn that teachers teach based on their conception of the subject matter. While the conception is often implicit, perhaps influenced by their own education as language learners or by the language textbooks they choose or are given to teach from, there is great value, it seems to me, for teachers to be able to articulate and examine their personal views of language and of grammar—views that, like mine, are doubtless influenced by their experiences both as learners and as teachers and by the views of their instructors, researchers, and colleagues. Thus, by the end of the book, I would hope that readers would be able to complete the following statements: "For me, language is..."; "For me, grammar is..."

I, too, will complete these statements in time. I will also put forth a grammar teaching approach that follows from my definitions. Although the examples in this text are drawn for the most part from English, the ideas and suggestions hold for all languages. I have been reassured in this regard by the many teachers of a variety of languages with whom I have been privileged to work over the years. For this reason, I will use the terms *target language* or *second language* or *foreign language* when generic reference is being made to the language being taught. I also intend to impute no special meaning to the words *learning* and *acquisition*, using them interchangeably sometimes, and at other times conventionally to distinguish tutored from untutored development.

We are ready to begin. To underscore the importance I accord to having you articulate your own views and begin to cultivate an attitude of inquiry, I will start right off with an Investigation. I will also use it as a way to introduce some of the terminology that you will encounter in the remainder of the text. It is my sincere hope that you will find your reading of this text an invitation to continue to explore language on your own, preferably in collaboration with others. I wish you well as you work to define your own personal approach to the teaching of language in general and grammar in particular.

1

DEFINING LANGUAGE AND UNDERSTANDING THE PROBLEM

THE IMPORTANCE OF DEFINING LANGUAGE

What Is Language?

What is language? You may or may not have thought about this question before, but it is an important question that anyone who is or wants to be a language teacher should consider. It is important because your answer to this question will inform your beliefs about language teaching and learning and what you do in the classroom as you teach language. As Becker (1983) put it, "Our 'picture' of language is the single most important factor… in determining the way we choose to teach one." It would therefore be useful to start off reading this book by answering the question for yourself.

1.1

Take a moment to think about what it is you teach: What is language? *Write your answer down. Then put your answer aside. I will ask you to come back to it from time to time throughout this book and to amend, expand upon, or reaffirm it.*

Here is a list of other language educators' answers to the questions about the nature of language, which I have culled and paraphrased from the literature of the past 100 years or so. I present them in the order in which they were first introduced to the field.

DEFINITIONS OF LANGUAGE FROM THE LITERATURE

1. Language is a means of cultural transmission.

2. Language is what people use to talk about the things that are important to them, for example, occurrences in their everyday lives.

3. Language is a set of sound (or, in the case of sign language, sign) and sentence patterns that express meaning.

4. Language is a set of rules through which humans can create and understand novel utterances, ones that they have never before articulated or encountered.

5. Language is a means of interaction between and among people.

6. Language is the means for doing something—accomplishing some purpose, for example, agreeing on a plan of action for handling a conflict.

7. Language is a vehicle for communicating meaning and messages.

8. Language is an instrument of power (those who know a language are empowered in a way that those who do not are not).

9. Language is a medium through which one can learn other things.

10. Language is holistic and is therefore best understood as it is manifest in discourse or whole texts.

Syllabus Units Corresponding to Definitions of Language

After reading these definitions, it should be clear why I chose to begin this book by asking you to define language for yourself. Despite some overlap among the ten definitions, each presents a view of language that may be realized in a language classroom in quite distinct ways. For instance, depending upon your view of language, you may choose different elements or aspects of language to foreground. To illustrate this point more concretely, the following are examples of syllabus units corresponding to each definition:

1. *Cultural transmission:* works of literature, poetry, history, and the vocabulary words and grammar structures that constitute them

2. *Everyday life:* talking about family, daily routines, situations (e.g., shopping, going to the post office)

3. *Sound and sentence patterns:* fixed and semi-fixed sentence patterns and sequences such as statements, questions, and negative statements, and sound (or sign) contrasts, intonation, rhythm, stress patterns that result in differences in meaning

4. *Rules:* rules of sentence construction related to permissible word combinations and word orders, for example, forming sentences, questions, negative sentences

5. *Means of interaction:* interactional language (language for interpersonal communication), that is, choosing and using appropriate language within a social context

6 *Means of doing something:* functions such as agreeing, disagreeing, proposing, clarifying, expressing preferences

7. *Vehicle for communicating meaning:* transactional language (language that functions primarily to communicate meaning), especially lexical items

8. *Instrument of power:* competencies such as finding a place to live, interviewing for a job, making medical appointments; sociopolitical skills such as negotiating with one's landlord, writing letters of protest, learning civic rights and responsibilities

9. *Medium:* content such as geography (learning about latitude and longitude, topographical features, climates), along with language learning strategies such as reading a passage for its gist, editing one's own writing, guessing word meaning from context

10. *Holistic:* reading and writing different texts, learning about rhetorical and genre patterns such as what distinguishes the language of narrative from that of expository prose in particular disciplines, working on the cohesion and coherence of language that hold a text together

The Link Between Definitions of Language and Theories of Learning

Not only may your definition of language influence your decisions about syllabus units, it may also shape your view of learning. Although there is not a unique connection between a particular view of language and a particular theory of learning, some theories of learning fit more naturally with certain definitions of language than others. For example, structural linguists, such as Bloomfield and Fries, who saw language as a set of sound/sign and sentence patterns (definition 3), promoted the audiolingual method's (ALM's) mimicry-memorization and pattern and dialogue practice. Consistent with their conception of language was the habit-formation view of language learning, in which it was seen to be the responsibility of the teacher to help students overcome the habits of the native language and replace them with the habits of the second language. Later, the psychologist B.F. Skinner's *behaviorist* perspective contributed the idea that what was important in establishing new habits was the reinforcement of student responses.

In contrast, those who, following Chomsky, saw language as a set of rules (definition 4) might embrace a *cognitivist* explanation for learning and expect students to formulate and test hypotheses so that they could discover and internalize the rules of the language they were learning. Those who defined language as a means of interaction among people (definition 5) probably subscribed to an *interactionist* view of the learning process—one that called for students to interact with each other, however imperfectly, right from the beginning of instruction, believing that such interaction facilitated the language acquisition process.

Associating Teaching Practices with Definitions of Language

In addition to foregrounding certain syllabus units and privileging certain theories of language learning, your choice of teaching practices might also follow from your definition of language. Of course, your definition of language does not prevent you from making use of a range of pedagogical practices; nonetheless, particular practices are consistent with certain types of syllabi. Indeed, each of the ten definitions of language above can easily be associated with common language teaching practices. To cite just an example or two for each:

1. *Cultural transmission:* translation exercises

2. *Everyday life:* situational dialogues

3. *Sound and sentence patterns:* sentence pattern practice and minimal pair discrimination drills

4. *Rules*: inductive/deductive grammar exercises

5. *Means of interaction*: role plays

6. *Means of doing something*: communicative activities and tasks, for example, asking for and giving directions, surveying class preferences

7. *Vehicle for communicating meaning*: Total Physical Response (TPR) activities in which the meaning of lexical items and messages is made clear through actions

8. *Instrument of power*: problem-posing activities in which students discuss solutions to their own real-world problems

9. *Medium*: content-based activities, through which students attend to some subject matter, for example doing math problems, at the same time that language objectives are being addressed

10. *Holistic*: text analysis activities in which students examine the features of texts that promote their cohesion, or process writing, whereby students produce successive drafts of their writing, receiving feedback after each draft

SOME CAVEATS

So far I have suggested that your definition of language has a powerful influence that extends beyond a conception of language and could affect your view of language acquisition and your teaching practice. However, before we proceed any further, some caveats are in order. First of all, many people's definitions of language are broader than any one of the ten that we have considered, overlapping with some of them, but not quite lining up with any one definition. Because language is as complex as it is, the ten definitions are not mutually exclusive.

Second, the coherence among language, learning, and teaching beliefs is often more theoretical than actual. This is because there are many important considerations in teaching. Primary among these is taking into account who the students are and why they are studying the language. An assessment of students' language needs and how they learn should inform the choice of syllabus units and teaching practices. We are, after all, teaching students, not just teaching language.

Marie Nestingen teaches Spanish in a high school in Central Wisconsin. Here is how she sees the matter of teaching students.

Marie Nestingen

> Reflecting back to my first years of teaching Spanish, I can definitely see how the pendulum swings of methods have influenced the way I think of language. And its swinging continues to affect my teaching as I continue to learn. [However] a huge factor for me in my teaching seems to be who my students are and why they are taking the class: their attitude towards a second language, their expectations, and their idea of what is involved in learning a second language play a factor in the class. I had one class of Spanish II students this year who seemed very adamant (more than previous classes) about learning the grammatical points. They wanted the rules! [However], in addition to the students' attitudes are the attitudes of their

parents. The question of why they are or need to take the class and/or learn a second language affects the choices I make as a teacher. I know it does.

As Marie says, students' reasons for second language learning affect teachers' decisions about what and how to teach. Having to prepare one's students to pass a particular standardized examination, for instance, can be a powerful influence on what one teaches. This is why I have been careful to use words such as *may*, *might*, *could*, and *likely* when I have been discussing the links among an individual's "picture" of language, theory of learning, and teaching practice. In language teaching, everything is connected to everything else. It is difficult to conceive of language apart from who one is as a teacher, who one's students and colleagues are, what the demands of the curriculum are, and so forth. Indeed, at the level of practice, most teachers are less likely to adhere to a narrow view of language, learning, or teaching. Most teachers, as well as the texts that they use, are more eclectic, interweaving a variety of syllabus and activity types into lessons.

A third caveat is that presenting definitions in chronological order, as I have chosen to do, makes the sequence seem orderly and lockstep, which is not the case. It is not as though at one time all teachers embraced one of these definitions of language, then suddenly abandoned it when another was proposed. It should also be recognized that, although I have presented the ten in the order in which they were first proposed during the previous century, many of these views persist today. Finally, I do not mean to imply that the stimulus for innovation was always a new definition of language, or that all change emanated from within the language teaching field. Change has often been inspired by new theories of learning or conceptions of teaching and has sometimes originated from advances in related disciplines such as linguistics, psychology, or education, or even technology.

To illustrate the impact of technology, one can attribute many linguists' and educators' recent fascination with multiword strings of regular construction, such as *and all that stuff*, to the fact that powerful computers and million-word corpora highlight the existence of, and facilitate the exploration of, such patterns of language use. Of course, examining language texts to identify patterns of language use is not a new enterprise in linguistics. It is simply that computers allow for principled collection, and systematic analysis, of huge numbers of texts. As a result, we have been able to appreciate how formulaic, as opposed to how completely original, our use of language is. And this appreciation has given rise to instructional approaches such as the lexical approach, which centers instruction on multiword strings and lexical patterns. The acquisition of such patterns can be accounted for by associationist learning, which highlights the brain's ability to process the huge amount of linguistic input to which it is exposed and, from it, to extract and retain frequently occurring sequences.

In all this, the point should not be missed that how we conceive language can have widespread consequences. Indeed, some have gone further than I in suggesting that "A definition of language is always, implicitly or explicitly, a definition of human beings in the world" (Williams, 1977: 21).

1.2

This would be a good time to read over your definition of language and determine if, in the light of the foregoing discussion, you want to make any changes to it. If you are doing this exercise with others, it would be useful to then discuss your definitions and any changes you may have made.

For histories of the field, see Kelly (1969) and Howatt (1984).

ACCOUNTING FOR THE SHIFTS IN DEFINITIONS OF LANGUAGE

Despite the caveats above, it is worth attempting to understand what motivated the shifts from one definition of language to another during the previous century. This is not the place to trace the history of the language teaching field, but simply to point out that a major contributor to the shifts was the dialectic between the function of language and its forms. In other words, some of the definitions follow from the conception of language in terms of its function—that is, accomplishing some nonlinguistic purpose (language as a means of cultural transmission, a way of discussing everyday life, a means of interaction, a vehicle for accomplishing some task, an instrument of power, a medium of instruction)—and others in terms of its linguistic units or forms (language as grammar structures and vocabulary words, sound/sign/sentence patterns, rules, lexical items, rhetorical patterns, genre patterns, multiword lexical strings and patterns).

It is essential to note that, regardless of whether a functional or a formal view of language is adopted, language teachers have commonly sought to develop in their students the ability to use the language, whether to develop spoken communication skills, to become literate, or both. Indeed, even those who have advocated a form-based approach to language teaching do so because they believe that mastery of its forms is an effective means of learning to use the language for some nonlinguistic purpose. For example, Robert Lado, an adherent of pattern practice drills, insisted that

> Nothing could be more enslaving and therefore less worthy of the human mind than to have it chained to the mechanics of the language rather than free to dwell on the message conveyed through the language (Lado, 1957 as cited in Widdowson, 1990).

Thus, the debate has not been about the goal of instruction but rather about the means to the end. At issue is the question of whether it makes more sense to teach others to use a language by preparing them to do so—systematically helping students develop control of the forms of language, building their competence in a bottom-up manner—or to have students learn in a top-down manner—learning to use another language by using it. In the latter instance, students' use of language may be halting and inaccurate at first, but it is thought that eventually students will gain control of the linguistic forms and use them accurately and fluently.

Now you may be thinking that the form–function dichotomy is a false one and that neither a bottom-up nor a top-down approach should be practiced exclusively, that both means should be integrated. Such an answer is in keeping with the laudable pragmatism of teachers. However, before dismissing the dichotomy, I think that we should recognize not only that the pendulum swing between function and form is characteristic of the field at large, but also that the same dynamic also takes place at the local level within our classrooms. We may include both foci—function and form—but we do not routinely integrate them. Typically, a teacher or a textbook will use both activities that are primarily communicatively focused and activities that primarily deal with the parts of language—yet these will occur in different lessons, or different parts of lessons, or in different parts of a textbook unit. In other words, even at the microlevel of a lesson, the two approaches remain segregated.

Understanding the "Inert Knowledge Problem"

I believe that including both means is an improvement over solely practicing one or the other; however, this approach is not without its problems. The first problem has to do with the uneven distribution of student energy. Few students sustain their enthusiasm for learning when the lesson focuses on the parts of language. Indeed, when students are asked to shift from a communicative activity to, say, a grammar exercise, there is often an audible response of displeasure. In spite of the fact that many students find it difficult to muster much enthusiasm for the study of grammatical rules, vocabulary items, and pronunciation points, most students acknowledge the value of studying them and willingly make the effort. Indeed, as we saw from Marie Nestingen's comments, some students will demand their inclusion if they are not part of what is regularly worked on in class.

Student ambivalence is not difficult to understand. First, although many students do not necessarily enjoy studying grammar rules, memorizing vocabulary, or practicing pronunciation points, learning the parts of a language is a very traditional language practice, one that many students have come to associate with language learning. Second, learning the parts gives students a sense of accomplishment; they feel that they are making progress. Third, learning the parts provides security. Students have something almost tangible to hold onto as they tally, for example, the number of vocabulary items that they have learned in a given week. Fourth, students believe in the generative capacity of grammatical rules, that knowing the rules of the language will help them to create and understand new utterances.

Although some of these beliefs could be challenged, for student-affective considerations alone, there is a reason to focus on the parts of language as well as its function. A greater concern remains, however. As many language teachers and learners will attest, what students are able to do in the formal part of a lesson often does not carry over or transfer to its use in a more communicative part of a lesson, let alone to students' using what they have learned in a noninstructional setting. Even though students know a rule, their performance may be inaccurate, or disfluent, or both.

Here is what Jane, an ESL teacher in a midwestern U.S. university intensive English program, has to say about her students.

Jane

> They oftentimes don't understand the rules. They just read a rule and go, "OK, I've read this since I was eleven years old. I've read it a million times back in my country and here." And they're still not using it right. They all know they need to use the third person singular "s" but half the class still doesn't use it. They use it in the grammar exercises, but they don't apply it while they're speaking or writing. (Johnston and Goettsch, 2000: 456)

It is easy to understand Jane's frustration. The third-person singular "s" on English present-tense verbs has been a challenge to many teachers and students, and no one is absolutely certain why this form presents such a learning burden. The fact is that even if students understand the explicit rule, they do not necessarily apply it. Indeed, as most teachers will attest, Jane's observation is not only true of the third-person singular verb marking in English; it also applies to many other examples, in English and in other languages. Long ago, Alfred North Whitehead (1929) referred to Jane's dilemma as "the *inert knowledge problem.*" Knowledge that is gained in (formal lessons in) the classroom remains inactive or inert when put into service (in communication within and) outside the classroom. Students can recall the grammar rules when they are asked to do so but will not use them spontaneously in communication, even when they are relevant. Besides the frustration that this engenders in students and teachers, I would imagine that it contributes to a great deal of attrition from language study. Students become discouraged when they cannot do anything useful with what they are learning.

It would be too ambitious to think that we can solve the inert knowledge problem, a problem that has plagued teachers and students for centuries. However, we can begin by rejecting the dichotomous thinking that has made the problem intractable. This will not be easy to accomplish.

1.3

To appreciate the magnitude of the change we will need to make, you only have to ask yourself what associations you make with the words grammar and communication. Do so now by completing the following sentences.

When I think of grammar, I think of...

When I think of communication, I think of...

Here is what other teachers have said when asked to freely associate with the words *grammar* and *communication*:

Figure 1.1: Teachers' Associations with Grammar and Communication

When I think of grammar, I think of …	*When I think of communication, I think of …*
• rules	• dynamic understanding
• parts of speech; verb paradigms	• the four skills
• structures; forms	• meaning
• word order in sentences	• accomplishing some purpose
• memorizing	• interacting
• red ink	• establishing relationships
• drills	• small group activities
• boring	• fun

Not everyone I have asked agrees with all these associations, of course. Some educators find the discovery of the workings of a language a joyful process, not a boring one. Even so, I think it should not be difficult to understand why forms (here, illustrated by *grammar*) and use (here, illustrated by *communication*) have so often been segregated in textbook pages and lesson segments. They appear to be completely different, a view embedded in dichotomous thinking.

CHANGING THE WAY WE THINK

If we aspire to build the bridge between forms and use that our students need in order to overcome the inert knowledge problem, to enhance their attitudes, and to sustain their motivation, we will need to change the way we think. I believe that it is our dichotomous thinking that needs to change, and I will illustrate the necessary change by considering grammar. Thus, for the remainder of this book, I will treat grammar as the forms of the form–function dichotomy, even though I acknowledge that there are more forms to language than grammatical forms. Let me be even more emphatic about this point. I certainly do not equate grammar with all the parts of language, let alone with communication. Two decades ago, in fact, in an article titled "The 'what' of second language acquisition" (Larsen–Freeman, 1982), I pointed out the multifaceted nature of communicative competence. I also acknowledge that choosing to focus on one subsystem of the whole has its risks. I have worried for some time about the tendency to isolate one of the subsystems of language and to study it in a decontextualized manner. Nevertheless, it is undeniably methodologically convenient, perhaps even necessary, to attend to one part of language and not to take on the whole in its many diverse contexts of use. At this point in the development of the field and in the development of my own thinking, the only thing I know how to do is to focus on one part while simultaneously attempting to hold the whole.

And I have chosen to work with grammar as the one part because it seems to me that it is the vortex around which many controversies in language teaching have swirled. Further, it is the subsystem of language that has attracted much attention from linguists, certainly ever since Chomsky, and in second language acquisition, ever since its Chomsky-inspired inception. Above all, I have chosen to write about grammar because I have always been intrigued by grammar and the paradoxes that surround it. It is at one and the same time an orderly system and one that can be characterized by many exceptions. Control of the grammar of a language can be empowering, but following its rules unswervingly can be imprisoning. The study of grammar is both loved and loathed.

In this book, I will be attempting to demonstrate that the associations in the right-hand column in Figure 1.1 are no less true of grammar than of communication. In the next chapter, I will introduce the changes in my thinking about grammar by challenging common conceptions concerning grammar. In chapters 3 to 7 I will present a view of grammar very different from those reflected in the left-hand column in Figure 1.1. In chapters 8 to 10 I will explore the acquisition of grammar in order to arrive at an understanding that will ensure the creation of optimal conditions for its learning and for unifying the form–function dichotomy. Finally, in the last chapter, I will offer an approach to teaching that builds on the insights gained from viewing grammar and its learning in a different way.

Suggested Readings

The particular views of language and common language teaching practices discussed in this chapter are associated with particular language teaching methods or approaches in Larsen-Freeman (2000a). Also, Wilkins (1976) discusses the difference between synthetic syllabi, where students are presented language units, usually structures, with which they synthesize or build up their competence, and analytic syllabi, where language is presented functionally, leaving it to students to analyze the language into its component parts. However, later, Widdowson (1979) pointed out that a syllabus organized by functions is also an example of a synthetic syllabus, not an analytic one. Graves' (2000) book in this TeacherSource series, *Designing Language Courses*, has a useful discussion on syllabus units. The dichotomy between formal and functional views of language presented in this chapter also exists in linguistics. See, for example, the introduction in Tomasello (1998) for a discussion. Finally, although more will be said later about multiword strings and lexical patterns in language, a seminal article in contributing to my awareness of the ubiquity of such patterns is Pawley and Syder (1983).

2

CHALLENGING CONCEPTIONS OF GRAMMAR

In this chapter, I will challenge some conceptions of grammar. I do so motivated by my conviction that we language educators have to change the way we think about the elements of language, particularly grammar, if we expect to help our students overcome the dual problems of their lack of engagement in learning the forms and their inability to call upon their knowledge of forms when they must put their knowledge to use.

I do not mean to imply, however, that all teachers are currently of one mind when it comes to conceptions of, and attitudes about, grammar and its teaching. Clearly there is no consensus about grammar teaching in the views of teachers surveyed by Eisenstein Ebsworth and Schweers (1997). The teachers surveyed were all experienced teachers of English teaching college-level students. Half of the teachers were from Puerto Rico and half were from the New York area.

> In Puerto Rico we respect tradition; we're careful about implementing new ideas just because they're new. Grammar has always been part of our language learning experience. We see no reason to abandon it totally. *(Puerto Rican teacher, interview)*

> I would not consciously teach grammar, no. Students can easily get bogged down with too many rules and exceptions. I use thematic units in teaching. I feel that using a whole language approach exposes students to a broad range of language. *(New York teacher, interview)*

> I usually try to teach English implicitly. But if there is something unclear or confusing, I supply a mini-lesson: explicit grammar with rules and lots of examples....The mini-lesson lowers the anxiety level. Often my students have been taught explicitly before, so some connection to what they are used to also seems to help. *(Puerto Rican teacher, questionnaire)*

> My own education included very formal language study including memorization, reading, writing, and grammar. Now I'm using a communicative approach, but I won't completely abandon the teaching that worked for me. Grammar helped me and I can see that it also helps my students. I have confidence in my own experience. *(Puerto Rican teacher, interview)*

> My students are adults who often know the grammar of their native language and benefit from this kind of meta-cognitive information. *(New York teacher, interview)*

I believe that substantial access to input in the English-speaking community explains the belief of many teachers and theorists in the U.S. that formal grammar presentation is unnecessary. *(New York expert, interview)*

My students want grammar; I believe they need it. *(Puerto Rican teacher, questionnaire)*

You can't start too early. If students learn correct grammar and practice it from the beginning, they will have a good foundation to build on. *(Puerto Rican teacher, interview)*

When I was working on my master's, we used to debate a lot about teaching grammar in our ESL classes. Everybody had studied some grammar. Personally, I enjoyed it. Some of us had a real love–hate feeling about it. Eventually, I guess we all have to make up our own minds about it. *(New York teacher, questionnaire)*

Even from this limited sample, we can see that teachers hold divergent beliefs and attitudes. Still, some themes emerge from more than one of these teachers' comments: the decision to teach grammar must take into account who the students are, what the students' experience has been, what the students want, what the teachers' experience has been, and what the teachers believe would be helpful to students. Interestingly, all the teachers who mention teaching grammar refer to teaching explicit rules, including exceptions, and giving a lot of examples. Before I share with you my thinking about some of these matters, please do the following Investigation, which will help you clarify your own beliefs about grammar.

Investigations

2.1

Please ask yourself the extent to which you believe the following assertions.

1. Grammar is an area of knowledge.

2. When we say something is grammatical, we mean that it is accurate.

3. Grammar has to do with rules.

4. Grammar is arbitrary.

5. One good thing about grammar is that there is always one right answer.

6. Grammar has to do with word order within sentences and structures, such as word endings or morphology.

7. Grammar is acquired naturally; it doesn't have to be taught.

8. Grammar structures are acquired in a set order, one after another.

9. All aspects of grammar are learned in the same way.

10. Learners will eventually bring their performance into alignment with the target language; error correction or feedback is unnecessary.

11. Grammar (teaching and/or learning) is boring.

12. Not all students need to be taught grammar. Children, for instance, do not benefit from formal grammar instruction.

If you found yourself wanting at the same time to both agree and disagree with some of these, that is not surprising. I have come to believe that these are myths and, as with all myths, there is likely an element of truth to each. However, if we continue to focus on what about them is true, we will never be able to meet the double challenge of engaging our students and helping them overcome inertia in using what they have learned. Therefore, while I acknowledge that these twelve statements are partially true, I will challenge them. I will be very brief here, elaborating in subsequent chapters of this book.

THE NATURE OF GRAMMAR

The first six statements have to do with the nature of grammar. Here are my thoughts about these six:

1. Grammar is an area of knowledge.

Grammar *is* an area of knowledge that linguists and language teachers study. However, if my students possessed grammatical knowledge for the language that I am teaching, but could not use the knowledge, I would not have done my job. Some psychologists (e.g., Anderson, 1983), therefore, have distinguished two types of knowledge: knowledge about the language system (declarative knowledge) and knowledge of how to use the language (procedural knowledge).

However, I think that it is more helpful to think about grammar as a skill rather than as an area of knowledge; this underscores the importance of students' developing an ability to do something, not simply storing knowledge about the language or its use. I have coined the term *grammaring* (Larsen-Freeman, 1992) to highlight the skill dimension of grammar. I also find this term helpful in reminding us that grammar is not so fixed and rigid as the term *grammar* implies. It is far more mutable. I will amplify on the **dynamism** of grammar in the next chapter.

When I ask teachers how many skills there are in language teaching, most answer four: reading, writing, speaking, and listening. The truth is that there are more than four, and one of my goals in writing this book is to convince you that grammar is the fifth skill (hence the title: *From Grammar to Grammaring*). When we view grammar as a skill, we are much more inclined to create learning situations that overcome the inert knowledge problem. We will not ask our students to merely memorize rules and then wonder why they do not apply them in communication. Skill development takes practice, and learning grammar takes practice. However, as we will come to see, it is not the sort of practice that involves a lot of rote repetition, which is boring, and which is not the most effective way to overcome the inert knowledge problem.

2. When we say something is grammatical, we mean that it is accurate.

Grammar *does* have to do with accuracy. However, for me, grammar is not only about accuracy of form. If a student of English says *It's a pencil on the table*, with the intended meaning *There is a pencil on the table*, I would say that the form is accurate but its meaning does not convey the student's intended meaning. The statement with *it* is used to show identity (*It's a pencil, not a pen, on the table*) whereas the sentence with *there* shows location. Grammar is not simply about form; it is about meaning as well.

Furthermore, there are other ways to indicate the location of the pencil. A speaker might have used the perfectly accurate sentence *A pencil is on the table*. Notice, however, that although this statement conveys more or less the same meaning as the sentence with *there*, it is not equally appropriate. Imagine, for example, that I was on the telephone, and I motioned to another person that I needed something to write with. It would not please me to be told *A pencil is on the table*, but *There is a pencil on the table* would be acceptable under the circumstances and (assuming that it was within my reach) would meet my need for a writing implement. In other words, grammar is also about appropriateness of use. It is not incorrect, but it is insufficient, to say that grammar has to do with accuracy of form; it relates to meaningfulness and appropriateness as well. In Chapter 4 I return to expand on the **complexity** of grammar in general, and on these three dimensions of grammar in particular.

3. Grammar has to do with rules.

"Grammar and rules" is, of course, probably the most common association, and in pedagogy, grammar rules—or perhaps better put, grammatical "rules of thumb"—certainly have their place. For one thing, they often provide students with security, something to hold onto. They provide useful guidance about how a language is structured. However, there are limits to their usefulness. For one thing, they deal mostly with accuracy of form, less so with meaningfulness, and rarely with appropriateness of use. For another, as teachers and students all too well know, rules have exceptions and are often quite abstract.

However, there are three additional reasons to justify my claiming that statement 3 is only partially true. First of all, it has become increasingly clear these days, with the use of million-word language corpora, that a great deal of our ability to control language is due to the fact that we have committed to memory thousands of multi-word sequences, lexicogrammatical units or formulas that are preassembled (e.g., *I see what you mean*; *Once you have done that, the rest is easy*) or partially assembled (e.g., NP + *tell* + tense + *the truth* as in "Jo seldom tells the truth"; "I wish you had told me the truth"). Clearly, then, if what we do when we use these formulas is retrieve the fully or partially assembled units from memory, not all of our grammatical performance can be attributed to the application of grammatical rules.

Second, at a more abstract level, there are grammatical patterns or constructions that signal the same grammatical meaning over and above the words that instantiate them and the rules of syntax that string the words together (Goldberg, 1999). For example, the ditransitive construction, where a verb is followed by two objects, has the meaning of "the subject (X) causes the object (Y) to receive something (Z)," as in "Pat faxed Bill the letter."

| Ditransitive | X causes Y to receive Z | Subj V Obj Obj | Pat faxed Bill the letter. |

Two other constructions tell us that X causes Y to move to position Z (the caused motion construction) or that X causes Y to become Z (the resultative construction).

| Caused Motion | X causes Y to move Z | Subj V Obj Obl | Pat sneezed the napkin off the table. |
| Resultative | X causes Y to become Z | Subj V Obj Xcomp | Pat ran Bill ragged. |

Goldberg (1999) points out that these constructions have a meaning unto themselves. In other words, I can change the verb in a ditransitive construction (e.g., *Pat paid Bill a visit; Pat gave Bill the message; Pat granted Bill his request; Pat sold Bill a bill of goods*)—and it will still have the meaning of "the subject causes the object to receive something." Furthermore, Goldberg asserts that no innate rules need to be posited to account for the existence of constructions in the grammar.

Third, even for language that might be considered generated by rules, the collocation of grammar with rule is not all that helpful for overcoming the dual challenge with which we are contending. Knowing a rule will not guarantee that learners will invoke it when needed. This is why I prefer to think of teaching rules *and reasons*. By "teaching reasons" I mean helping my students realize that there is an underlying logic to the language they are learning—that grammar is **rational.** I need to help give them access to the reasons so that they will not only understand the logic, they will also be able to use it to express themselves the way they want to and, conversely, to understand utterances that are spoken to them. If they understand the logic of the language, they will be able to understand both the rules and their "exceptions."

For instance, if students have only learned the rule that tells them that stative verbs in English do not take the present participle morpheme *–ing*, they may feel confused, or even deceived, when they hear someone use the present participle with a stative verb, such as:

I am loving every minute of this class.

And yet, most English speakers would agree that combining the present participle with a stative verb, as has been done here with the stative verb *love*, accomplishes the special effect of intensifying the emotion expressed by the verb, which makes it at least conversationally acceptable, and meaningful, in English. Chapter 5 in this text elaborates on the distinction between reasons and rules.

> When you say that the association between grammar and rules is only partially true, I think OK, but I also think about some of the Spanish students I had this year. For them, things had to be black and white—they wanted rules and didn't want to hear about exceptions. Other students in the class more easily went

Marie Nestingen

with the flow. They seemed better able to reason things and to grasp the exceptions. Personally, when I was first learning Spanish, I realize how rule-oriented I was. But the more I learned about Spanish (I am still learning!), the more and more I could understand the exceptions. So, I guess what I am coming to is that there may be a real difference in students' need for rules and their perception of them, based on who they are and their language level.

What Marie says makes a lot of sense to me. I am writing about grammar as an abstract system and Marie is thinking about grammar as embodied in the responses of her high school Spanish students. Clearly my discomfort in seeing grammar treated only as a set of rules does not matter to students who are trying to hold onto something while their linguistic feet are being pulled out from under them. Nevertheless, I persist. I want to understand the logic of the system, whether or not I ever use rules or reasons to teach my students, because I know that I can only be helpful to my students when I have first made sense of the subject matter for myself.

4. Grammar is arbitrary.

As I have just suggested, speakers use their knowledge of grammar for particular reasons. Grammatical resources are limited and precious. They are distributed in a nonarbitrary manner. Of course, the fact that language uses a particular form to convey a particular meaning may be arbitrary, at least from the vantage point of a single point in time. For instance, that English uses *-ed* to mark the past tense of regular verbs can be said to be arbitrary. The arbitrariness of the connection between sound and meaning was one of the important insights made by the Swiss linguist de Saussure. However, once a form has been settled upon to convey a particular meaning, then arbitrariness is less of an issue.

In order to experience the nonarbitrary nature of grammar, please do the following Investigation.

2.2

1. *Make a list of all the different places in the English language where* -ed *occurs—I don't mean in words such as* red *and* bed, *but rather as a grammatical marker or morpheme. I can think of eight.*

2. *Now that you have made your list, see if you can account for the use of* -ed. *In other words, what is the meaning of* -ed *in each item on your list?*

   Here are the eight that I thought of. I have identified the grammatical structure, given an example, and tried to ascribe a meaning or a function to the marker in each case.

Figure 2.1 The Meaning and Function of _-ed_ in English

Grammatical Structure	Example	Meaning
Past Tense	I walked to school yesterday.	Past time
Perfective Aspect	I have finished my homework.	Completeness
Passive Voice	The field was planted with corn.	Marks the receiver of the action
Conditional	If he finished his homework, he would go.	Hypotheticality
Indirect Speech	Diane said that she liked grammar.	Report
Adjective	I was bored by the lecture.	Marks the experiencer of the feeling
Question as Offer	Did you want something to eat? (The past tense with "do" is irregular.)	Politeness
Question as Inquiry	What sort of price did you have in mind?	Politeness

3.   _Upon initial consideration of this list, it would appear that the use of -ed is polysemous and quite arbitrary. But ask yourself now, what do all the items listed—yours or mine—have in common?_

My answer (informed by Knowles, 1979) is that they all signal some sort of remoteness—whether in time (the past tense of the first example); an action that has been terminated (perfective aspect as it is used in the second example); because it focuses on the receiver of the action, not the performer or agent of the action (passive voice); removed from reality (the hypothetical conditional); not a direct quotation but an indirect one, offered as a report of what has been said (indirect speech); because it marks the experiencer, removed from the cause (when used as an adjective); and since indirectness or distancing conveys politeness, it can be used with offers and inquiries to increase the politeness, as in the use of _do_ versus _did_ here.

In Investigation 2.2, I attempted to demonstrate that a grammatical resource of the language—in this example the morpheme _-ed_—has been distributed and utilized for a specific purpose, not on the basis of some whim. If we looked at language from a satellite or aerial photograph perspective, rather than from the ground, we would see the systematicity of grammar. Of course, it may make little sense to inform students of English that the morpheme -ed conveys remoteness or distance. This meaning is probably too abstract to be of use to them. Later in this text, we will see how the nonarbitrariness of language and grammar has pedagogic relevance. For now, my intention was simply to dissuade you of the notion that grammar is arbitrary, an issue I shall return to in Chapter 5.

5. One good thing about grammar is that there is always one right answer.

Teachers know this to be untrue, either intuitively or because they recollect the times when a student has asked if a particular way of saying something is correct and they have felt compelled to answer, "It is right if you mean...." Grammar is not the linguistic straitjacket it is made out to be. It is true that one meaning of the word grammatical has to do with whether or not a given utterance is consistent with normative conventions; for example, it is grammatical to use whom, not who, when asking a question about an object, not a subject:

Whom did you see?

However, although prescriptive grammars precepts such as this one have their place, normally, there is much more choice when it comes to decisions about which linguistic form to use to convey a certain meaning. Indeed, options abound, depending on psychological variables such as presupposition, focus, and emphasis, and social variables such as politeness, attitude, status, and register.

Are you going downtown after class?

Aren't you going downtown after class?

Are you not going downtown after class?

You're not going down town after class, are you?

You're going downtown after class, aren't you?

You're going downtown after class?

You aren't going downtown after class?

Going downtown after class?

I will have much more to say about **flexibility** and the grammar of choice in Chapter 6. Suffice it for the present to note that speakers of a language, although they must conform in part to the conventions of the language, have a great deal of choice in other ways, and that how they exercise that choice will influence how they and their ideas are perceived.

6. Grammar has to do with word endings and word order within a sentence and structures, such as word endings or morphology.

Grammar does have to do with the sentence and subsentence levels. Grammar is about word order in sentences (syntax) and word formation processes (morphology); it is also about using the correct function words. However, importantly, grammar plays a role in the construction and interpretation of texts. Grammatical resources are marshaled to contribute to the discourse coherence and cohesion, the interconnectedness of text. In other words, grammar is a **discursive** tool. I will take up this important function of grammar in Chapter 7, so for the time being, let me simply illustrate the discourse application of grammar.

For example, fill in the blanks in the following sentence with the English articles *a* or *the*:

_____ boy jumped over _____ stream.

At the sentence level you cannot be certain which article to use. Either *a* or *the* would be possible in both blanks. However, if you were asked to fill in the blanks for the same sentence in the text below, it should be clear which articles to use.

> A young boy was hurrying home from school and decided to take a shortcut through the woods. He entered the woods behind the school by climbing over a fence. He began to follow a familiar path. Later, _____ boy jumped over _____ stream.

You knew to write *the boy*, because the boy had already been introduced and thus needed to be marked with the definite article. You probably chose *a* before *stream* because the existence of a stream was not yet established in the discourse. While controlling the article system obviously requires knowledge of how grammar operates at the level of discourse, so do many other less obvious structures, as we will see in Chapter 7.

I would like to make another point here. If grammar is held to deal only with the morphosyntactic structure of sentences, then it may be unable to account for spoken discourse because, after all, people do not speak in sentences. Yet, of course, people do speak grammatically, so our definition of grammar will have to be broad enough to include speech. While there are clearly overlaps between a grammar of written sentences and a grammar of speech, there are differences as well. For example, given the pressure of real-time language use, English adverbials not normally found in clause final position occur there quite regularly:

> We have saved enough money almost.

It will be important, therefore, to be clear whether patterns in speech or in the written form of the language are being described.

THE LEARNING OF GRAMMAR

The next three statements apply to the learning of grammar.

7. *Grammar is acquired naturally; it doesn't have to be taught.*

It is difficult to refute the statement that grammar can be acquired naturally because such is the case with native language acquisition. More to the point here, many of us know of successful second language learners who have picked up the language on their own, that is, have learned it implicitly through immersion in an environment where the language is spoken. However, compelling counterevidence to this statement is the experience of all those learners who have lived for a long time in an environment where the target language is spoken all around them yet who have failed to acquire even its rudimentary morphology. So perhaps this statement is more a comment on language learners than it is on language learning.

To this qualification, Lilia Topalova would add that it also depends on the learning circumstances. Lilia, who taught English for 18 years in Bulgaria and spent 2 years in Ukraine as a teacher trainer, has the following to say concerning the statement that grammar is acquired naturally; it doesn't have to be taught.

Lilia Topalova

Well, maybe this is true if you are teaching English here in the United States. But I know it is not true of English learners in Bulgaria and Ukraine. My students, whose native language is very different from English, definitely have to be taught grammar. They really have very little opportunity to hear or speak English outside of class. And even in class, their opportunities to do so are limited. How would they ever learn grammar if I didn't teach them?

Thus, underlying statement 7 is the highly questionable assumption that what works well in natural environments is what should be adhered to in the language classroom. I have referred to this as *the reflex fallacy* (Larsen-Freeman, 1995), the assumption that it is our job to re-create in our classrooms the natural conditions of acquisition present in the external environment. Instead, what we want to do as language teachers, it seems to me, is to improve upon natural acquisition, not emulate it. We do want our teaching to harmonize with our students' natural tendencies, but we want our teaching to accelerate the actual rate of acquisition beyond what students could achieve on their own. As Lilia noted, the time to learn is so limited. Accelerating natural learning is, after all, the purpose of formal education. And helping our students learn faster than they would on their own may well call for explicit teaching and learning to complement the implicit learning that they naturally do. I will elaborate on one way this is accomplished when I discuss consciousness-raising in Chapter 8.

8. Grammar structures are acquired in a set order, one after another.

Second language acquisition (SLA) researchers have found evidence of developmental sequences for particular grammatical structures, such as questions. For instance, we know that ESL students begin learning yes–no questions with rising intonation, but without inversion. Later, they learn to invert. Still later, they overgeneralize inversion in embedded wh-questions—for example, "He asked what time is it?"—and must learn to "uninvert."

However, no acquisition order has been worked out for when questions are acquired as opposed to other structures in a language. And it probably never will be worked out, because it is not the case that learners tackle one structure at a time, first mastering one and then turning to another, like beads on a string. Even when learners appear to have mastered a particular form, it is not uncommon to find backsliding, where students' performance regresses, when new forms are introduced. The nonlinear nature of the language acquisition process will be taken up further in Chapter 8.

9. All aspects of grammar are learned in the same way.

I am not aware of anyone who boldly asserts that there is a single mechanism that would account for all aspects of grammatical structure acquisition. Even those who subscribe to an innatist Universal Grammar (UG) perspective, for instance, allow that the core grammar may be innate but that peripheral grammar may be learned through a different mechanism. However, it is the case that language teaching methods have sometimes been based exclusively on one view of the language acquisition process. Thus, for example, there was an affinity between audiolingualism and behaviorism, and between the cognitive code approach and cognitivism. Such affinities gave rise to general claims about the whole of language acquisition, that is, that language acquisition is a product of habit formation or of rule formation.

More recently, reprises of this theme have taken the form of claims about language acquisition resulting from setting/resetting of parameters (UG), or from the strengthening of connections in complex neural networks (connectionism), or from scaffolded interactions by a more proficient speaker of the language interacting with a less proficient one (Vygotskyan sociocultural theory). The problem is not that we have competing theories vying to explain the process; the problem is the expectation that all SLA will be explicable by a single process. With language as complex as it is, why should we expect that a single explanation will suffice? More will be said about this in Chapter 9 when I discuss how we can draw upon all these explanations to inform the design of output practice.

THE TEACHING OF GRAMMAR

The final three statements relate to the teaching of grammar.

10. *Learners will eventually bring their performance into alignment with the target language; error correction or feedback is unnecessary.*

Error correction may be unnecessary for those few gifted language learners who have the aptitude to learn a language on their own. In fact, from the perspective of an earlier model of UG theory, the presence of positive evidence alone—actual instances of particular grammar structures in the input—was seen to be sufficient for the parameters of particular principles to be set. Negative evidence—evidence that something was unacceptable—was thought to be unnecessary. However, such claims bring me back to the reflex fallacy. While positive evidence may be all that is minimally necessary for acquisition, our job as language teachers is to *maximize learning* by creating optimal conditions for it to take place. Receiving feedback on one's performance so that one can see what is acceptable and what is not is one of those optimal conditions. Therefore, we must think in terms of providing feedback in helpful ways, something I will discuss in Chapter 10.

11. *Grammar (teaching and/or learning) is boring.*

Grammar is never boring. What we ask students to do to learn it can be. Statement 11 is problematic on a number of counts. First, although I do not think that it is my job to entertain my students, I do believe that it is my job to engage them. It is at the point of engagement that most learning is likely to take place—when students are focused, relaxed, and attentive. Second, if grammar is presented as a system of static rules, students may not put in the time that they will need to master it. I will need to find a way to make grammar practice meaningful. Third, I will have to work on the attitude of (some of) my students. Just as I believe that teachers are well served when they cultivate attitudes of inquiry, I suggest that this is a good attitude to nurture in students. I cannot teach my students everything there is to teach about a language, and even if I could, language is always changing. What I can do is to give them the tools to learn. I will return to this point in Chapter 11.

For now, let me make the point about engagement by offering a simple contrast. When I started teaching, I had been trained to conduct pattern practice and structure drills. Thus, when I wanted to teach my students the inversion rule in English question formation, I would relate the details of my morning to my students and ask them to transform what I said into questions.

Diane: *I got up at 7.*   Students: *Did you get up at 7?*

I took a shower.   *Did you take a shower?*

I got dressed.   *Did you get dressed?*

I ate breakfast.   *Did you eat breakfast?*

And so on. Now, this could have been an engaging exercise if I had had an unusual morning, perhaps. But, more often than not, my mornings followed this predictable routine. There was not much student engagement in this transformation drill, I am afraid.

However, on one occasion, I asked my students to close their eyes. I allowed a few seconds to pass, then continued:

Diane: *Now open your eyes. I just changed five things about myself. Can you guess what they are?*

S1: *Did you take off your watch?*

S2: *Did you open a button?*

S2: *Did you take off your shoe?*

S4: *Did you comb your hair?*

I found that this exercise elicited a very different response from my students. While I had to help them a bit with the vocabulary, it turned out to be considerably more engaging than the first exercise. Understanding what makes it so proved to be very important in my teaching; I will discuss this further in Chapter 11.

12. Not all students need to be taught grammar. Children, for instance, do not benefit from formal grammar instruction.

The answer to the question of which learners benefit from studying grammar hinges on one's definition of grammar. While children, for instance, might not benefit from the study of explicit metalinguistic rules, there is no reason that they should be denied grammar instruction any more than any other segment of the language student population. Even though young children may be more receptive to implicitly "picking up" the forms of the language, they still should not be victimized by the reflex fallacy. We should always be looking for ways to facilitate the acquisition of language, and this includes helping children unlock its system. This question of for whom and when grammar instruction should take place will be further discussed in Chapter 11.

We have begun the important work of challenging some fundamental assumptions concerning grammar and disabusing ourselves of some of the more questionable ones. The twelve statements discussed in the chapter are partially true. But if we hope to liberate ourselves and our students from an unhelpful way of construing grammar, we must let ourselves be open to a different way of conceiving our subject matter. In the five chapters that follow I will elaborate in turn on the five attributes of grammar that have been introduced in this chapter: its **dynamic, complex, rational/systemic, flexible,** and **discursive** nature.

Suggested Readings

I discuss several of these grammar myths (and others as well) in a 1994 paper delivered at the Second Language Acquisition and Language Pedagogy Conference at the University of Wisconsin, Milwaukee (Larsen-Freeman, 1995). At the 1996 TESOL Convention, as a participant in a debate on the art and science of teaching, I was asked to defend the proposition that teaching is a science. I chose to do this by arguing that good practitioners, both scientists and teachers alike, are well served by cultivating attitudes of inquiry. See my remarks and those of the other debaters in the *Journal of Imagination in Language Learning* 2000 (Larsen-Freeman, 2000d).

3

THE DYNAMICS OF LANGUAGE (GRAMMARING)

For the purposes of teaching and learning a language, I suggest that it would be better to think of grammar as a skill or dynamic process, something that I have called *grammaring*, rather than as a static area of knowledge. Of course, the term *grammar* has many meanings, and certainly some of these can be homologous with knowledge. Linguists construct *descriptive grammars* by writing rules to account for the grammatical system of languages. Writers, especially, are admonished to conform to the norms of standard usage, the rules of *prescriptive grammars*, such as avoiding dangling modifiers. Some grammars are written to model *internal mental grammars*, what people know about their language. Teachers ask students to learn the rules in *pedagogical grammars*. However, if we language teachers make a simple equation between grammar and knowledge, then we run the risk of grammar's remaining inert, not available for use by our students.

Moreover, when grammar is taught solely as a body of knowledge—a collection of rules, norms, parts of speech, and verb paradigms—it is not surprising that the mention of grammar invokes a negative response on the part of many students. Most students find it hard to be enthusiastic about having to learn what appear to be arbitrary facts about a language, let alone sometimes being asked to learn them by rote. While I will have more to say later in this book about what sort of grammatical knowledge our students do need and how to teach grammar as a skill, for now I submit that there is another very good reason to entertain an alternative view of grammar, one that is less knowledge-centered. Indeed, not doing so obscures important truths about the nature of grammar and, more broadly, of language itself. It is these truths, expressly concerning the dynamic nature of language, that are addressed in this chapter.

3.1

The dictionary defines dynamic *as "characterized by continuous movement or change in time." In what ways do you think that language is dynamic?*

Now, besides thinking of grammar as a skill, there are at least four additional ways in which I think of grammar, or indeed of language itself, as dynamic. While I do not want to be guilty of conflating grammar and language, I do believe that my remarks about dynamics in this chapter apply both to grammar and, more generally, to language.

OVER-TIME DYNAMISM

The first way that grammar and language are dynamic is that they change over time. It is common knowledge that the language and grammar of today are not the same as the language and grammar of several centuries ago, even though English is undeniably the same language. For example, in an earlier state of the English language, the second-person pronoun *you* was defined by its opposition to *ye* (*ye* being a subject pronoun and *you* being an object pronoun) and to *thee* and *thou* (*thee* and *thou* being singular forms and *ye* and *you* plural forms). Later, *you* became a respectful way of addressing one person, like the modern French *vous* or the Spanish *usted*. Today, in modern English, *you* refers to both one person and to many and can function as either the subject or object in a sentence, not especially connoting respect. Languages are thus dynamic. Their state at one point in time stems from their development over time.

3.2

You have just been reading about language change and how many older second-person pronoun forms died out, leaving modern English with just the one form, you. As a result, you *refers both to one person (*What are you doing! *said with exasperation to a careless person) and to many people (*Thank you, *said to express gratitude to a group). What are some ways that English speakers of today compensate for the fact that the second-person pronoun* you *does not allow them to distinguish between singular and plural? In other words, what forms have been developed to refer in the second person to more than one person? And what do English speakers do without a distinctly respectful form of a second-person pronoun?*

Concern about language change has led some countries to feel that the best way to look after a language was to place it in the care of an academy. In Italy, the Accademia della Crusca was founded as early as 1582, with the object of purifying the Italian language. In France, in 1635, Cardinal Richelieu established the Académie française

> to labour with all possible care and diligence to give definite rules
> to our language, and to render it pure, eloquent, and capable of
> treating the arts and sciences.

There is a widely held belief that language change must mean deterioration, which leads to sloppy thinking. Older people observe the casual speech of the young and conclude that standards have fallen markedly. They place the blame in various quarters, from poor upraising to permissive schooling to pop culture. However, much teeth-gnashing could be avoided if the critics realized that language change over time is inevitable and rarely predictable or controllable.

3.3

Have you noticed ways in which English is changing these days? It will take a while longer for the changes to make their way into the written language, and still

longer for the grammatical system to be restructured, but there are changes underway in the spoken language that you may have noticed. Pick one of the following structures and, first, state the rule regarding its use. Then say how the structure is being altered in speech today. Can you appreciate how difficult it would be to try to incorporate these changes into a grammar in any definitive manner?

- The reflexive pronouns, especially *myself*
- The use of *more* for comparison with adjectives
- The modal-like form *had better*
- The interrogative/relative pronoun *whom*

Sometimes these changes come as a shock to language learners. It is easy to see how much more challenging the task of learning a language is when language is always changing. Michael Kozden, formerly an EFL teacher in Korea, found that his Korean colleagues were aware of the over-time dynamism of English and would look to him for what was acceptable.

Teachers' Voices

Michael Kozden

> Many of my fellow teachers believed that I, as a native speaker of English, had the final word on the way English was. They were aware that the grammar books they used were sometimes out of date. They would quiz me on the subject of changing forms in English. What struck me at the time was my insecurity in answering their questions. I, too, recognized that the language was changing, but I was reluctant to answer based on my intuitions alone. I really wanted to have a community of native speakers to confer with.

It is not always easy to draw a line between what is acceptable and what is not. What is the distinction between an error and a new form, which is the product of the dynamic and relentless process by which all new forms of language evolve? As Michael Kozden saw, acceptability of new forms is not individually determined; it is socially defined.

Frameworks

REAL-TIME DYNAMISM

While we might call such evolutionary changes *over-time dynamism*, the second well-known way that languages can be said to be dynamic can be referred to as *real-time dynamism*. To understand the second type of dynamism, it is helpful to think of the contrast between product and process. It is true that language can be described as an aggregation of static units or products—for example, parts of speech such as nouns and verbs—but their use requires activation, a real-time process. Language users must constantly scan the environment (an immediate one in speech, a more remote one in writing), consider their interlocutors/readers, and interpret what they are hearing/seeing in order to make decisions about how to respond in accurate, meaningful, and appropriate ways and then carry out their decisions in real time— that is, they must then somehow activate what they have decided upon. This clearly entails a dynamic process.

STASIS IN LANGUAGE DESCRIPTION

If language is dynamic in these two ways, why is it that linguistic descriptions do not reflect its dynamism? It would be worthwhile digressing for the moment to understand that the stasis in linguistic description is intentional. The Swiss linguist Ferdinand de Saussure, who has been called the founder of modern linguistics, determined that in order to define a proper object of study, the chaos of language in use would have to be stripped away. Saying "language is speech less speaking" (de Saussure, 1916, in Baskin, 1959: 17), de Saussure first isolated the category of *langue* (the abstract system of the shared code) from the category of *parole* (the individual utterances of speech) and declared the former the rightful object of linguistic investigation. In other words, he distinguished the underlying system that makes possible particular behaviors from actual instances of the behaviors, what I have been calling *real-time dynamism*.

Another position de Saussure took was to isolate the category of historical or diachronic linguistics from the category of contemporary or synchronic linguistics. In other words, he eliminated over-time dynamism as well. Remarking that "A panorama must be made from a single vantage point" (de Saussure, 1916, in Baskin, 1959: 82) and that "language is a system whose parts must be considered in their synchronic solidarity" (de Saussure, 1916, in Baskin, 1959: 87), he admonished linguists to ignore diachrony. Of course, de Saussure was well acquainted with the historicity and changing nature of language, but he determined that it was important to distinguish the facts about the linguistic system from facts about linguistic evolution. In order to reduce the noise or chaos of the dynamism of language, de Saussure encouraged the fixing of language as an idealization to facilitate its investigation (Harnett, 1995).

There was good reason for de Saussure's taking the position he did. After all, diachronic information is not especially relevant if we are to understand the system of a language operating at a particular point in time. If we want to describe modern English, for example, knowing that *you* is the second-person pronoun, singular and plural, is sufficient to describe its function in the pronominal system of modern English, without knowing anything about its earlier partnership with *ye*, *thee*, and *thou*. Similarly, in French, the noun *pas*, meaning *step*, and the negative adverb *pas* derive from the same source, but this fact is irrelevant to a description of how negation is expressed in modern French (Culler, 1976). To try to incorporate these historical facts into a description of the contemporary linguistic system would be adding unnecessary complexity.

It would also be overwhelming if linguists tried to account for all of the differences in the way individuals speak at a single point in time. When we talk about a linguistic system at a given time, we are abstracting common features from a very large number of idiolects, or personal dialects of individuals. Nevertheless, the linguistic system of a language exists to the extent that all the individuals understand one another, whereas individuals who speak a different language cannot understand them, or certainly not to the same degree. Since we want to represent this fact and speak of the system that these native speakers have in common, de Saussure advises that we study the linguistic system in a particular synchronic state. Thus, de Saussure fully appreciated the dynamics of language but, motivated by a search for the underlying system, proclaimed the synchronic system as the proper domain of linguistics.

The influential American linguist Noam Chomsky perpetuated the idealization of the language system by making a distinction between *performance* and *competence*. The former refers to "the actual use of language in concrete situations" (Chomsky, 1965: 4) and is not deemed the province of linguistics. Linguistics is, for Chomsky, primarily concerned with explaining homogeneous invariable competence, or the idealized speaker's knowledge of his or her language system. Chomsky's competence is not a social construct, as was de Saussure's *langue*, but rather psychological, a genetic endowment in each individual. Nonetheless, they both adopted a similar dichotomy of knowledge and behavior and proposed that it was the former that was within the scope of linguistic inquiry.

Later E-language (externalized) and I-language (internalized) (Chomsky, 1986).

Both these towering figures in linguistics, and many others in the field, have reached the same conclusion because they believe that, to have any hope of advancing the science of language, there would have to be an accounting of its underlying system, and its systematicity would not be apparent if the messiness of language change over time or language use in real time were to be included in the investigation. Besides, as all who have attempted to construct a grammar will attest, it is by no means clear how to write grammars that capture the dynamism of language. How do you turn a camera into a camcorder? For now, we may only be able to content ourselves with the awareness of the need for a new metaphor.

INTRODUCING DYNAMISM INTO LINGUISTIC DESCRIPTION

Not all linguists have limited grammatical competence to knowledge, however. Roman Jakobson, for instance, argued that linguists must study *parole*, and his work on the roots of sound change in synchrony led him to claim that synchrony can be both static and dynamic (Waugh, 1997). Then, too, anthropological linguist Dell Hymes (1972), in addition to expanding Chomsky's notion of (primarily grammatical) competence to communicative competence, included in competence not only knowledge but also the ability to use the knowledge, what I have been calling a skill.

Michael Halliday (1994) also observes that we would be well served by encouraging more dynamic models of language and of grammar. Working within a Hallidayan framework, David Brazil (1995) has attempted to produce a real-time description of syntax, an account of how people produce speech in real time. Brazil's Incremental Grammar focuses on a step-by-step construction of speech over time, building incrementally from one element to the next.

Another linguist, Paul Hopper (1988), objecting to Chomsky's depiction of grammar as a static object that is fully present at all times in the mind of the speaker, proposes instead that grammar is a phenomenon "whose status is constantly being renegotiated in speech and which cannot be distinguished <u>in principle</u> from strategies for building discourses" (Hopper, 1988: 118). As Hopper puts it, "Its forms are not fixed templates, but arise out of face-to-face interaction in ways that reflect the individual speakers' past experience of these forms, and their assessment of the present context, including especially their interlocutors, whose experience and assessments may be quite different" (1998: 156).

In the following table, adapted from Hopper (1998), the contrast is made clearly between a Chomskyan rule-based grammar, which Hopper calls an *a priori grammar*, and one that is *emergent*.

Figure 3.1 Contrasting A Priori and Emergent Grammar

A Priori Grammar	Emergent Grammar
Discrete set of rules	Regularity comes out of use in discourse; "sedimented" patterns
Logically and mentally detachable from discourse	Cannot be distinguished in principle from discourse
Prerequisite for generating discourse ("a cause")	Emerges in discourse ("an effect")
Sentence is unit	Clause is unit
Data supplied by intuition	Data come from actual discourse
A static entity, fully present at all times in the mind of the speaker	Regularities are always in flux and provisional and are continuously subject to negotiation, renovation, and abandonment
Essentially atemporal	A real-time activity
Homogeneous	Heterogeneous (many different kinds of regularities)
Analyzes all examples equally within the rule system; indifferent to prior texts	Investigates strategies for constructing texts that produce the fixing or sedimentation of forms that are understood to constitute grammar

Thus, from Hopper's emergent grammar perspective, "language is a real-time activity, whose regularities are always provisional and are continually subject to negotiation, renovation, and abandonment" (Hopper, 1988: 120). We can see from Hopper's words that he finds no incompatibility with the notion of grammar and the contingent, provisional disorderliness of its use in real time.

Not everyone sees grammar in perpetual flux the way Hopper does. Talmy Givón (1999), objecting to the absolutism of both Chomsky's a priori and Hopper's emergent grammar viewpoints, asserts that both views represent extremes. Givón maintains that the facts of grammar in natural language use tend to uphold a middle-ground position. Language must possess a certain rigidity for rapid speech-processing purposes, along with a flexibility that allows for change, adaptive innovation, and learning, not to mention the need to deal with contexts of high informational ambiguity and uncertainty. Thus, any model of grammar must be able to accommodate both rigidity and flexibility.

Also seeking a middle ground between the two positions, Adele Goldberg (1999) claims that the flexible, emergent quality of grammar is only apparent during initial grammar acquisition. "Once grammar is acquired, it is assumed that it has a highly conventionalized status, and that although minute changes in the system constantly occur, the system as a whole is fairly stable" (Goldberg, 1999: 200). While Goldberg's position seems quite sensible, note that it still dichotomizes stability and flux, just as Chomsky and Hopper did in their respective positions. Moreover, while Givón recognizes the need to accommodate both, he does not address the nature of the relationship between stability and flux. To do so, we must consider a third type of dynamism.

ORGANIC DYNAMISM

Thus far we have spoken of two notions of the term *dynamic*: change over time and language use in real time. There is yet a third type of dynamism that it would be worth our while to consider: the dynamic connection that is made at the intersection of the first two types. After all, when we say that language changes over time, what do we really mean? Language does not change of its own accord. On the other hand, changes in a language are not usually the product of willful attempts on the part of users to alter the code. This is not to deny that a user may from time to time deliberately strive to create linguistic innovations, as I have done by coining the term *grammaring*. The point is that individuals may not intentionally seek to change language, but they do so by their day-to-day interactions in using it. Rudy Keller (1985) observes that language is a phenomenon whereby change in the macrolevel system results from the microlevel behaviors of individuals unintentionally acting to bring about such consequences. Thus, the behavior of the system as a whole is the result of the aggregate of local interactions. I will refer to this third type of dynamism as *organic dynamism*.

Biologists know about organic dynamism because they know about the intimate connection between variation at one time and evolutionary change. The evolutionary biologist Douglas Futuyama has the following to say about the matter:

> …Variation is the heart of the scientific study of the living world.
> As long as *essentialism*, the outlook that ignored variation in its
> focus on fixed essences, held sway, the possibility of evolutionary
> change could hardly be conceived, for variation is both the product
> and foundation of evolution (Futuyama, 1986: 82).

Linguists recognize Futuyama's statement as the "Labov principle" (named for the sociolinguist William Labov), which attests to the link between (synchronic) variation and (diachronic) change. To put it in plain language, "the act of playing the game has a way of changing the rules" (Gleick, 1987: 24). James Gleick wrote this when he was describing what insights chaos theory yielded concerning naturally occurring systems, such as the weather and the rise and decline of animal species. I have applied many of these insights to language (Larsen-Freeman, 1997), feeling that language too is a naturally occurring system that, like the other systems with which chaos/complexity theory deals, involves dynamism, complexity, systematicity, flexibility, and interconnectedness. One of the promises of this way of looking at language, therefore, is that it connects real-time processing to change over time (see, for example, Smith and Thelen, 1993).

In short, the third meaning of *dynamic* makes no distinction between current individual use of language (real-time dynamism) and its evolutionary change (over-time dynamism)—they just occur at different levels of scale. As I am writing this and you are reading it, we are changing English. By analogy, at another level of scale, we are not only changing English, we are changing English in ourselves. "The act of using the language meaningfully has a way of changing the grammar in the user," as Karl Diller put it (1995: 116).

Charles Hockett has made a related comment:

> An individual's speech habits, at any moment, constitute a system
> which underlies and conditions what the individual says and how
> the individual interprets the speech of others; and every such
> episode of the use of language modifies the individual's system at

least a little. Quite clearly there is no such thing as a stable *état de langue* of the sort Saussure proposed, in either an individual or a community—or if there is, it is stable for only a fraction of a second (Hockett, 1987: 157–158n).

In sum, it is important to recognize that while freezing and homogenizing language, as de Saussure and Chomsky have sought to do, has its theoretical/methodological advantages and its adherents, it also has its liabilities and its critics. When linguists hypostasize language for the purpose of studying its systematicity, language becomes an idealized, objectified, atemporal "thing." In order to know it, we feel we have to describe it in terms of its parts. The result is that we come to think of language in a mechanistic fashion.

William Rutherford (1987) comments:

> The notion of language as a machine works satisfactorily for us in certain respects—language after all contains systems, and to probe the intricacies of any system is at least to impute to it the components that ostensibly comprise it. Yet there is another side of language that is not very machine-like at all, a side in which the edges become blurred or disappear altogether. Language is constantly in the act of change or growth.... Growth of course is quite unmachine-like, or alien to that which we can conceive of in purely mechanical terms. The apt descriptive term for growth then is not mechanic but organic. Thus, although language has characteristics that lend themselves to the machine metaphor, it has a great deal to it that also suggests very aptly the metaphor of organism (Rutherford, 1987: 36–37).

Others have said similar things. Humboldt (1949, cited in Robins, 1967) stressed that "a language is to be identified with a living capability by which speakers produce and understand utterances, not with the observed products of the acts of speaking and writing." Still earlier, commenting on what I have called *over-time dynamism*, (Schleicher, 1863, cited in Robins, 1967) went so far as to say that language is "one of the natural organisms of the world to be treated by the methods of natural science, one moreover that independently of its speakers' will or consciousness has its periods of growth, maturity and decline." In fact, it was Charles Darwin himself who alluded to the notion that languages evolve and diverge as species do.

3.4

Echoing some of the observations above, it has recently been suggested that languages should be treated as biological species to which the analytical methods of evolutionary biologists could then be applied (Pickrell, 2002).

What does it mean to say that a language should be treated as a biological species or as an organism? Have you ever thought about it this way? If so, what does this suggest for teaching and learning?

While not many people would embrace Schleicher's animism, it is appealing to me to view language in this way. While I have to be careful not to ascribe to a code a vitality of its own, since it is the people who use it who make it "come alive," it is nevertheless attractive to think of language as a natural phenomenon, a dynamic organism. Indeed, I was very moved the day that I realized that the structure of language and the structure of a natural entity such as a tree were both fractals. A fractal is a pattern that is self-similar at every level of scale. For instance, the structure of a tree consists of a central trunk with branches spreading out from it. When you focus on a single branch, you see essentially the same shape, with twigs emanating from a central stalk. At the end of the twigs are leaves with central veins and arteries radiating outward. Thus, each level of scale of a tree reveals the same basic shape. The same is true for language: It is self-similar at every level of scale. For instance, the ten most frequent words in a given text will be rank-ordered in the same sequence as in a much larger text which in turn will occupy the ten highest ranks in a word-frequency list of a much larger corpus of the language.

For other ways in which language is a fractal, see Larsen-Freeman, 1997.

The fractal image was very appealing to me, perhaps because I am a gardener. It is important to me to be in contact with the natural world. And, no doubt, the appeal of fractals was that they presented me with the opportunity to find common ground (pardon the pun) between my avocation and my vocation. In fact, I once went so far as to give a paper with David Nunan on "Grammaring and Gardening," where we discussed grammaring from the standpoint of gardening. There are many parallels between the two processes, such as preparing the ground, planting the seeds, watering, pulling weeds, pruning the plants, and so forth.

Being similarly inspired, Kim Murday, a teacher of Spanish at Carnegie Mellon University, once wrote in a paper for a course that I was teaching on dynamical systems theory and language/language acquisition:

Kim Murday

> The idea that language is a fractal, as much as any tree or [ecosystem], is a powerful reminder that we, and the results of our behavior (such as language), are part of nature (Murday, 2000).

THE DYNAMISM OF INTERLANGUAGE

Yet another application of dynamism may have occurred to you as you thought about the first Investigation in this chapter. What, after all, could be more dynamic than the developing **interlanguage** system of language learners who are open to learning a language, be it a first language or an additional language?

Second language acquisition (SLA) researchers who have attempted to write descriptive grammars of learners' interlanguage have found it hard to keep up with the moment-by-moment changes in the learners' systems. Even those who have resorted to employing variable rules (e.g., Stauble and Larsen-Freeman, 1978) and distribution tables (Heubner, 1979), which capture the variability of rule application in different linguistic contexts, acknowledge the difficulty of capturing the mutability of interlanguage. Significantly, though, such research has been predicated on a rather fixed view of language. It has been assumed that successful SLA is accomplished through the acquisition of the rules that bring the learner's performance into greater conformity with the target language. This perspective reflects an "acquisition metaphor" of learning (Sfard, 1998), that is, that human learning is conceived of as an acquisition of something, that "something" being an a priori category such as rules or units of language. Once rules or structures are owned or acquired, according to the acquisition metaphor, they may be applied, transferred (to a different context), and shared with others.

Since I have been entertaining a more dynamic view of language, a different metaphor of learning may be needed. Sfard offers the "participation metaphor." In the participation metaphor, rather than talking about acquiring entities, attention is given to activities. "In the image of learning that emerges from this linguistic turn, the permanence of <u>having</u> gives way to the flux of <u>doing</u>. While the concept of acquisition implies that there is a clear endpoint to the process of learning, the new terminology leaves no room" (Sfard, 1998: 6) for such.

This view leads to a much more dynamic concept of educational success. According to the participation metaphor, learning a language is conceived of as a process of becoming a member of a certain community.

> This entails, above all, the ability to communicate in the language of this community and act according to its norms.... While the acquisition metaphor stresses the individual mind and what goes "into it," the participation metaphor shifts the focus to the evolving bond between the individual and others (Sfard, 1998: 6).

Learning is taking part and at the same time becoming a part of a greater whole. What Sfard describes is very much in keeping with a Vygotskyan sociocultural view of language learning in which language use and language learning are not perceived as different processes. Indeed, from this point of view, the phrase *target language*, which is commonly used, is misleading, because there is no endpoint to which the acquisition can be directed. The target is always moving (Larsen-Freeman, 2000b; 2002d).

I hope by now it is clear why this chapter has been subtitled *grammaring*. To me the term *grammar* fails to capture the process nature of language—its dynamic character. It is fundamental to understand that language can be described both as a collection of products and as a process. However, since the product view has dominated in recent times, I have given the other side more attention in this chapter. Besides, I believe that "organism" is a better general metaphor of developing interaction among humans. As Rutherford (1987: 37) put it so well:

> Machines are constructed, whereas organisms grow. Machines have precision; organisms have plasticity. Machines have linear connections; organisms have cyclical interconnections. And, perhaps most important of all, machines are sterile, whereas organisms are fecund.

Suggested Readings

Much has been written about chaos/complexity theory since I first began reading about it in the early 1990s. Reading Gleick (1987) or Briggs and Peat (1989) is still a good way to start. Another accessible source is Waldrop (1992). More recent treatments of the theory abound. I have found Gell-Man (1994), Kauffman (1995), Kelso (1995), and Holland (1998) very informative. Some of the themes in this chapter have also been discussed within the ecology of language by Larsen-Freeman (2002d), van Lier (2002), and other contributors to Kramsch (2002). Also, although I have not yet had a chance to read it thoroughly, I have just received a new book by Herdina and Jessner (2002), who discuss a dynamic model of multilingualism.

4

THE THREE DIMENSIONS

In this chapter, I will begin by adopting a more conventional product view of language, that is, I will first analyze language into its component parts. However, my treatment of language parts will differ from customary practice in two ways. First, most analyses of language arrange the subsystems of language in an ascending hierarchy: phonemes, morphemes, words, syntax, and so forth. Such an arrangement is understandable, because phonemes are constitutive of morphemes, which are constitutive of words, and so on. Nevertheless, I have decided to present the parts in a nonhierarchical fashion because I wish to emphasize the dynamic interplay of the subsystems.

The second departure from customary practice is that I will treat the morphological and syntactic subsystems as a resource for making meaning in a context-sensitive manner. This will necessitate dealing with the complexity of grammar, demonstrating that there is much more of concern in the teaching and learning of grammar than whether or not students produce grammatical forms accurately. The complexity is partly captured by the fact that form is only one of three dimensions, all of which play a part in grammaring, as described below.

THE THREE DIMENSIONS APPLIED TO LANGUAGE IN COMMUNICATION

Form: Phonology/Graphology/Semiology, Morphology, Syntax

The first dimension, the forms of a language, consists of the visible or audible units: the sounds (or signs, in the case of sign language), written symbols, inflectional morphemes, function words (e.g., *of*), and syntactic structures. The sounds or phonemes of the language are accounted for by the study of *phonology*. *Graphology* is the study of graphemes, the minimal contrastive units in the writing system of a language. *Semiology* is the science that deals with signs or sign language. *Morphology* is the study of morphemes, the minimal meaningful units of grammar; in the form category, morphology is limited to inflectional morphemes (e.g., the *-ing* of the present participle) and to function words (e.g., *the*). A study of *syntax* determines what combinations of word and morpheme sequences are permitted and how they are sequenced in sentences.

Meaning: Semantics

The second dimension is meaning. *Semantics* is the study of meaning encoded in language; we will think of it here as the essential denotation of a decontextualized form, what we would learn about a particular form if we were to consult a dictionary. For instance, if an ESL student asked you what the word *cousin* means, you might say something like, "Your cousin is the son or daughter of your aunt and uncle."

Although the expression of meaning is distributed across all three dimensions, its prototypical units are words (lexemes), derivational morphemes such as *non-*, and multiword lexicogrammatical units—multiword strings that are semantically complete but have not fused into a single form, such as *and so forth*. Some language teaching syllabus developers might want to include general categories of meaning, called *notions*, in this dimension as well. Notions deal with, for example, space (location, distance, motion, size) and time (indications of time, duration, sequence).

It may be more helpful to think of **semantics** as the study of meaning potential, because we are well aware that the meaning of a word or lexicogrammatical string that is actually realized in communication may be quite different from its dictionary definition. For instance, *Good morning* is typically a pleasant and appropriate greeting in the morning when extended to family members and others. If, on a given occasion, I were to use *Good morning* to greet someone in the afternoon, you might point out that I had inadvertently committed a semantic error: I should have said *Good afternoon*. However, as I have just claimed, the meaning in a word or lexicogrammatical string is only a potential meaning. I could have deliberately used the same greeting of *Good morning* in the afternoon, fully aware of the time, but using it nonetheless to teasingly greet my teenage son, who had just arisen. Using the greeting as mild sarcasm illustrates the third dimension of language, pragmatics.

Use: Pragmatics

Pragmatics is not the meaning encoded in language, but what people mean by the language they use. The units of this dimension are social functions (such as promising, inviting, agreeing, disagreeing, and apologizing) and discourse patterns (such as those that contribute to the cohesion of texts).

Figure 4.1 Prototypical Units of the Three Dimensions

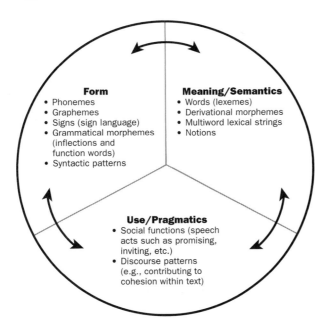

Form
- Phonemes
- Graphemes
- Signs (sign language)
- Grammatical morphemes (inflections and function words)
- Syntactic patterns

Meaning/Semantics
- Words (lexemes)
- Derivational morphemes
- Multiword lexical strings
- Notions

Use/Pragmatics
- Social functions (speech acts such as promising, inviting, etc.)
- Discourse patterns (e.g., contributing to cohesion within text)

Different Levels of Scale

One of the things that I find remarkable about this tripartite scheme is that although there are prototypical units that can be associated with each of the three dimensions, in order to arrive at a complete understanding of any one of the units, it must be described from all three perspectives, not just its "prototypical home." In other words, the same tripartite scheme can be applied at different levels of scale. Indeed, not to do so is to treat language in a very impoverished manner. Thus, being able to use grammar structures does not only mean using the forms accurately; it means using them meaningfully (semantics) and appropriately (pragmatics) as well. With the pie chart, and the following three questions, we can easily map the form, meaning, and use of any language unit:

Form: How is the unit formed?
Meaning: What does it mean (its essential meaning)?
Use: When and why is it used?

Meaning Units

Take, for instance, a vocabulary item—the noun *house*. An analysis of its form would include its pronunciation or sign, knowing that it has a diphthong vowel (/aw/), for instance. Part of knowing its form is also knowing its spelling. In the case of *house*, the silent *e* is noteworthy. Then, too, knowing that it is a common count noun would be necessary form information so that *house* could be used accurately in syntax. We might want to include other observations as well, such as that *house* takes a long or syllabic plural (*houses*), but this sketch should give you an idea of what is involved when we consider form.

Consulting a dictionary for its meaning, we would learn that *house* means a "construction intended to be used for human habitation" (*Webster's Third International*). This definition might have to be adjusted for students, especially those for whom no cognates exist, perhaps to something like "a place where people live."

But although knowing its form and meaning are important, having this knowledge is not sufficient for someone to be able to use *house* appropriately. In order to do so, the person must be able to distinguish *house* from *home*. He or she must know when to choose *house* as opposed to one of its near synonyms: *dwelling, domicile, residence, habitat, abode*. The person must know, too, how *house* is different from *flat, apartment, pad, digs, condominium*, and so forth. Of course, a student does not need to know all this the first time the word *house* is encountered; indeed a student may never know all the terms above. But it may not be long before a student has to complete some official document. When this time comes, it is not likely that the student will be asked for the address of his or her house, but might be asked this of his or her residence. Thus, to say that someone "knows a word" entails a great deal more than simply knowing its meaning.

This is true more generally of semantic notions such as temporality. I will not fully explicate this notion here, but I will use it to exemplify the point I made earlier when I wrote "meaning may be conveyed through all three dimensions." Temporality, for instance can be signaled through form: the use of verb tense-morphology. It can also be signaled lexically through adverbials, such as *today*, *in the evening*, and *afterward*. Finally, it can be conveyed pragmatically, simply by relating events in a text in the chronological order in which they took place.

Use Units

Similarly, one could take a prototypical unit from the pragmatic dimension—say, a social function of offering an apology for a slight transgression—and describe it using all three dimensions. First of all, we know that there are many possible exponents for this particular function:

I'm (terribly, very) sorry.
Pardon me.
(Please) Excuse me.

We can describe their general forms: statements with and without an intensifier, and imperatives with and without modulation, here achieved with *please*. Students would have to be able to pronounce all the sounds in these exponents, of course, but we will confine our comments on the phonology to those that may present special problems to all students. The essential meaning of these forms is to apologize for something we did or did or did not do or will or will not do when we were/are supposed to. Specifically, *excuse me* is a formula to remedy a past or immediately forthcoming breach of etiquette or other minor offense on the part of the speaker. *I'm sorry* is an expression of dismay or regret at an unpleasantness suffered by the addressee. Borkin and Reinhart (1978) have discussed how ESL students have to learn to use them appropriately. The following was elicited from a nonnative speaker of English, declining an invitation to the movies.

Excuse me. I'd like to go but I don't have time.

Native speakers whom Borkin and Reinhart consulted agreed that declining an invitation would be better accomplished with *I'm sorry*, and thus the use of *excuse me* is a pragmatic error.

Of course, the student's reply would be perfectly comprehensible, so this may not seem a very grave error. The point has been made that for many students of language, native speaker use is not the goal. This applies particularly to the use dimension because the use dimension deals with appropriateness, and when one is dealing with appropriateness one is forced to ask, "appropriate for whom?" Because appropriateness is socially constructed and context-dependent, in certain situations, adhering to native speaker conventions might be inappropriate for learners.

However, in situations of contact between native and non-native speakers of a language, pragmatic errors are insidious in that they often lead proficient speakers of a language to misjudge the intentions of less proficient speakers. Particularly if the speakers are fluent and accurate, listeners do not realize that a pragmatic error has been committed, instead misconstruing what was intended by the speaker and sometimes judging the speaker harshly as a result. Even though I work with language all the time, I myself have been guilty of making false inferences about the intentions of others.

One summer I was working with a group of teachers from a particular country. During the course of the summer program, these teachers developed a reputation among the native speakers of English for being quite rude. It was only after I was able to distance myself from the interaction that I realized that the evidence upon which the character of the teachers was being assessed (or assassinated?) was their "inappropriate" linguistic behavior. The teachers would often say *of course* to indicate agreement. *Of course* is a perfectly proper way to show agreement when one is responding to a request. If you answer *of course* to my request to help me move this table, your response shows your willingness to cooperate. However, saying *of course* to a statement of fact ("The square root of 144 is 12." "Of course.") implies that the speaker is not saying anything that the listener does not already know. There were other such responses that were interpreted by native speakers of English as a sign of rudeness. Only later, when I asked, did I find out that *of course* was taught to these English teachers as a direct equivalent of a form in their language that could be used to show agreement on all occasions. The point is that a pragmatic misstep can be judged harshly, and knowing when to use a particular form should not be treated as simple fine-tuning to be dealt with at advanced levels of language instruction.

Form Units

Interestingly, as I have illustrated earlier, the same three dimensions apply to all prototypical units, including those of form. For example, using the three questions in the pie chart, I compiled the following information about the form, meaning, and use of the existential *there* in English.

Figure 4.2 Form, Meaning, and Use of English Existential *There*

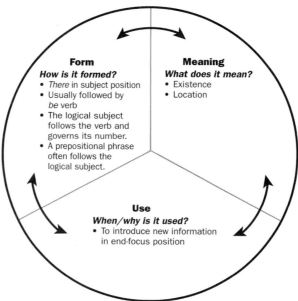

Using an example will help ground the following analysis:

There are Canada geese on the river.

There is an invariant form, occupying the subject position in the sentence. It is followed by a verb, usually a form of *be*, whose form in turn governs the form of the noun phrase that follows, or the logical subject. The logical subject is also typically indefinite—here, for instance, it is *Canada geese*, not *the Canada geese*. A prepositional phrase—here, *on the river*—often follows the logical subject.

The name of the structure, the *existential there*, gives us a clue about its meaning. It fits into the semantic category of asserting the existence of something or showing the location of something. It is used to introduce new information. The preferred position for new information is in end-focus position toward the end of the clause, and by using *there* to fill the subject position, the new information—in this case the whole proposition, Canada geese and their location—can be postponed until further in the sentence, in the preferred end-focus position.

Knowing this explains why, if I asked someone else for a writing implement while I was on the phone, I would be pleased to hear *There is a pencil on the table*, because I would have received the information that I needed in an appropriate form, but I would not be pleased to be told *A pencil is on the table*, because with this form comes the pragmatic implication that this is not new information and that I should not have had to be told. It would therefore be as much irritating as helpful.

4.1

Investigations

I asked Peter, a high school English teacher, to conduct a form, meaning, use analysis of the English possessive or genitive. I gave him the example Diane's book, *but asked him not to confine his analysis to this example. Using the questions and the pie chart, first try to do this yourself; then read Peter's answer below.*

Teachers'
Voices

Peter

Peter said:

Let's see. The form of the English possessive is "s", although with more than one possessor, it could be "s'" or just " ' ", like with "Chris' pen." In any case, it is attached to the possessor. Its pronunciation can also vary, of course, depending on the sound that precedes it. Here it is pronounced as a /z/. And, oh yes, regarding its syntax, the possessor precedes the possession—here, the book.

Its meaning is obvious, isn't it? It means ownership. Diane owns the book. Wait a minute. I can see that "Diane's book" is ambiguous. Diane could be the author of the book, and so I can say "Diane's book" about a book I possessed that you wrote. I suppose, then, that the "'s" can show authorship as well. As for its use, it is used when I want to show ownership or authorship, I guess.

Peter has made some important observations about the possessive in English. His description of the form is clear, and he saw the ambiguity of the *'s* in denoting ownership or authorship. There remains one point to clarify, though. Filling the use wedge of the pie does not entail simply listing occasions when a structure is used. Instead, it asks what is distinctive about the use of two or more structures with the same meaning. Remember, we had to work out the difference in use between There is a pencil on the table and A pencil is on the table. As I said earlier, use has to do with the distribution of forms.

For example, why would someone choose to say *Diane's pen* versus *her pen*? Both of these forms show possession by the same possessor. You might say that someone could use the form with the possessive adjective or determiner *her* when it was clear who was being referred to. While this is true enough, it is not the complete story. For instance, another factor in choosing to use the determiner versus the *'s* form to show possession is whether or not the possessor is present. So if I were conversing with two other people and one of them were to say to the other in my presence *I am reading her book*, meaning *Diane's book*, the speaker might be considered ill-mannered. In other words, when I am present, saying *I am reading Diane's book* would be more appropriate.

And what about the periphrastic possessive with *of the*, such as *the pages of the book*, rather than the inflectional possessive *the book's pages? The book's pages* may seem incorrect because human possessors are usually modified with the *'s* form; however, this generalization is by no means applied across the board. Many speakers of English would accept the *'s* with an inanimate possessor. They would find nothing remarkable if someone were to say *The book's pages are torn*. Then, too, it is possible to use the periphrastic possessive with a human possessor, for example, to speak of *the works of Shakespeare*, which a speaker might do to be more formal. More could be said about the possessive, but for our purposes here, the point is that there is more to knowing a grammar structure than how to form it.

Investigations

4.2

I have found that no matter how many examples I give of the three dimensions, people's comprehension is really aided by their actually doing an analysis themselves. Therefore, try to use the questions in the pie chart to analyze the English demonstratives: this, that, these, those.

Here is my analysis:

Form: *This* and *that* are the singular forms; *these* and *those* are the plural. They can be used as adjectives or determiners, in which case they precede the noun—e.g., *this pen*—or they can be pronouns, in which case they stand alone as noun phrases: *This is the answer to that.* Non-English-speaking students often have trouble with the pronunciation of the initial consonant in each of these terms.

Meaning: Demonstratives point to something in the situation. *This* and *these* point to proximate things, *that* and *those* to distant things. Notice that distance can be spatial (*This pen here rather than that pen there*), but demonstratives can also be used to convey temporal distance (*this week* [now] rather than *that week* [e.g., future]), psychological distance (*I prefer this wine to that one*), and sequential distance in a text (*That last point is more controversial than this one*).

Use: Here we need to be concerned with when the demonstratives are used for reference purposes and when they are not. For example, while it is accurate and

meaningful, it is not appropriate to answer a language teacher's favorite question (*What's this?*) using a demonstrative. Personal pronouns are preferred:

Teacher: *What is this?*   *What are these?*
Student: *It's a book.*   *They're books.*
         (NOT: This is a book.)   *(NOT: These are books.)*

It is also important to understand when demonstratives are used versus articles or personal pronouns in extended texts. In other words, the grammatical choices are not always within intact paradigms, such as the four forms of demonstratives. For instance, *this* gives more focus than *it* and thus is preferred for initial reference, even though both *it* and *this* refer to the same noun phrase—in this example, *warranty*:

> If you buy a newly built home, you may have trouble getting a mortgage unless it has a warranty such as the Buildmark Warranty from the National Housebuilding Council (NHBC). *This* covers most defects for ten years. *It* offers valuable insurance cover if the builder goes bust while the house is being built or if major structural faults develop (example from Hughes and McCarthy, 1998).

In other words, part of knowing a structure in language involves knowing both when to use it and when not to.

Distinguishing Meaning from Use

When I talk about these matters, teachers sometimes have trouble distinguishing meaning from use. Here is a conversation I recently had with Ed, a teacher who attended an inservice teacher education course that I was teaching.

Ed: I am having a hard time seeing meaning from use.

Diane: Yes. I can understand why. The two-headed arrows connecting the wedges in the pie chart are supposed to suggest the interconnectedness of the three dimensions. And some boundaries are more permeable than others.

Ed: Why is it important to make the difference then?

Diane: For several reasons. One is that I believe the dimensions are learned differently. Therefore, they should be taught differently. Also, the learning challenge that each presents to our students may be different. We need to be clear what the learning challenge is for a given grammatical structure. Consider modals in English, for instance. There are two types of modals: logical probability modals and social-interactional modals. Many modal verbs belong to both types. For instance, "may" can be used as a logical probability modal:

> It may rain tomorrow.

Or it can be used in its social interactional sense:

> You may leave now.

In the first example, "may" is being used to make a prediction, in the second to grant permission. Choosing among the logical probability modals for the right degree of certainty regarding one's pre-

Ed

diction is a meaning dimension challenge. Choosing the right way to request and grant permission depends not so much on meaning as it does on who is being asked and who is asking and what is being asked for. This represents a challenge in the Use dimension.

Finally, if the learning challenge is different for different structures, then presumably one would want to teach them differently.

Ed: OK. I guess that it will just take me some practice to see language this way.

Diane: Yes. I think it helps to use the wh-questions in the pie wedges as a tool to distinguish among the three dimensions: how is something formed, what does it mean, and, given two or more forms with the similar meanings, when or why is one used in one context versus another.

I have to confess to some uneasiness with Ed's question. I must step back from my own analytic proclivity and linguistic training to ask whether or not it really does make sense to distinguish meaning from use. Many treatments of language do not make the distinction. Indeed, it is commonplace to hear the binary oppositions, form–meaning and form–function, not the ternary one that I am making. However, it seems inadequate to me to say that what learners have to learn is to connect form to meaning because they have to learn when to use those form-meaning connections as well. Then, too, sometimes linguists talk about *pragmatic meaning*, noting that meaning cannot be determined apart from its use in context. While this again may be true enough, I feel learners do need to learn the meaning of linguistic units that transcends context. However, I do have to ask myself, just because I can make the three-way distinction, is it really worth the effort?

Clearly, this is a place where research is needed. Happily, this is beginning to take place. Jim Purpura's students at Teacher's College, Columbia University, for example, have been conducting studies to determine if the three dimensions are, in fact, independent constructs. And even if they are shown to be, the question still remains as to whether pulling them apart enhances pedagogical effectiveness.

The Three Dimensions are Learned Differently

See Eubank and Gregg, 2002 for references.

Despite being cautious, I will persevere at this point in claiming that a three-dimensional model of grammar makes sense. I believe that the three dimensions are learned differently and that therefore they have to be taught differently. For example, countless cases in the research literature attest to the existence of instantaneous learning, where very few instances of a particular phenomenon are needed for it to be learned. I think that this is often the case with semantics. A few instances of associating a lexical item or a grammatical structure with its meaning is sometimes all it takes. A colleague once told me that he learned the Japanese word for *pear blossom* from one exposure to it. Now, I would think that *pear blossom* is probably not very frequent in the input, nor especially communicatively useful. However, sometimes we can make such strong semantic bonds that they stick. On the other hand, I have had to practice particular syntactic permutations over and over again when I have studied a foreign language. Thus, when it comes to form, I think many instances may be necessary for mastery. Learning use requires that learners develop a sensitivity to context, which is different from associative learning.

As for pedagogical practice, again, it makes sense to me that certain techniques lend themselves more to teaching one dimension rather than the others. Take role plays, for instance. Role plays are ideal for working on pragmatics because the variables in role plays can be altered to help learners see and practice how context and interlocutor variables affect choice of form. Conversely, I do not think role plays would be especially suited for teaching the meaning or form of grammatical structures. Of course, it should always be acknowledged that the motivation for our choosing a particular pedagogical activity does not guarantee that students will use it for the same purpose.

Before concluding, we should remember that a great deal of our ability to control form consists of controlling unanalyzed multiword strings or formulas. These, too, can be—and for now I will say, should be—analyzed with the pie chart. For instance, earlier I made the point that knowing the phrase *of course* requires knowing its form, its meaning, and its use.

THE IMPORTANCE OF ALL THREE DIMENSIONS

In Linguistics

Knowledge that there are three dimensions, not one, enriches our understanding of language in communication. As Bourdieu (1991: 31–32) writes:

> The illusion of the autonomy of the purely linguistic order, asserted in the privilege accorded to the internal logic of language at the expense of the social conditions of its opportune use, opened the way to all the subsequent research that proceeds as if mastery of the code were sufficient to confer mastery of the appropriate usage, or as if one could infer the usage and meaning of linguistic expressions from analysis of their formal structure, as if grammaticality were the necessary and sufficient condition of the production of meaning.

As Bourdieu states, the primary concern of many linguists until recently has been form. The growing interest in cognitive linguistics, which sees forms as meaning-motivated, and functional linguistics, which sees forms as socially–functionally motivated, is testament to the broader view of language entertained by linguists these days. While clearly much remains to be discovered concerning linguistic form, knowing everything there is to know about how to form a grammar structure will not satisfy language teaching needs.

In Language Teaching

Of course, applied linguists are not immune to showing preference, either. It is the case that methods of language teaching commonly emphasize one or the other of these three dimensions.

4.3

Investigations

Think of language teaching methods with which you are familiar (or see Larsen-Freeman, 2000a). Now think about the way language is defined in each. It is often the case that a method has focused on one particular wedge of the pie, treating the other dimensions only incidentally or not at all. Which wedge of the pie does each method you have considered to focus upon? Which does it ignore?

It is also important to make clear that analyzing language according to the three dimensions by no means obligates teachers to present all this information to students, let alone to try to do so in a single lesson. We cannot and should not teach everything there is to know about the language we are teaching. It is important to be selective, a point that I shall return to later in this chapter. However, I do not think that we should be selective by ignoring an entire dimension. I further think that in order for teachers to know what to select, they need a sense of the whole of what there is to teach, and the pie chart can be a valuable tool for visualizing the whole.

A LINGUISTIC HEURISTIC PRINCIPLE

It is time to be explicit about an important heuristic principle in linguistics that I have been putting into practice: A difference in form always spells a difference in meaning or use. Therefore, if the form wedge of the pie chart is changed in some way in real-time use or over-time change, it will have the effect of changing one or the other of the remaining two wedges. Conversely, if the meaning or use wedges change, this will affect the form wedge. The system is **holistic**. This is what the double-headed arrows connecting the wedges in the pie are meant to depict. If grammar is a dynamical system—a view that I entertain in this book—the parts of a system mutually interact. Mutual interaction implies that they influence and co-determine each other's changes over time (van Geert, 1994). For example, consider these two sentences with different forms of *Nan*:

I can't imagine Nan's doing such a thing.

I can't imagine Nan doing such a thing.

In the first sentence, the *'s* marks *Nan* as the subject of a gerund *doing such a thing*. In the second sentence, without the *'s* marker, *Nan* is simply the object of the sentence, being modified by the present participial phrase *doing such a thing*. Some prescriptivist grammarians consider the second sentence to be erroneous— a malformed gerund. However, many English speakers these days consider such forms perfectly acceptable.

As our principle tells us, with the difference of form comes a difference in meaning. The gerund in the first sentence invites us to imagine the episode as a whole, whereas in the second sentence, with the object followed by a participle, the focus is primarily on *Nan*, not on the entire episode. The difference between the two is admittedly subtle, but it illustrates the fact that grammar is a tool of exquisite precision, allowing us to create forms in order to express delicate shades of meaning.

Here is what Pam, a university ESL teacher in a study by Yang and Ko (1998), had to say about shades of meaning with regard to modals, a structure I have just discussed. The class is going over an exercise on modals and discussing the sentence *You should get a call from him tonight*. Pam's student, Lee, asks, "Is the use of 'should' in this sentence common?"

Pam

Pam responds: Yes. I can say to my TOEFL class, 'Oh, don't worry. You should do well on the test. You studied really hard, you should do a good job. Or, you can say, 'You shouldn't have any problems finding a hotel.'

Lee then asks: "So the meaning of 'should' is similar to the meaning of 'must'? I know that 'must' can also be used to express certainty."

Here is Pam's reflection afterward.

> Basically, this question is about the meaning of "must" and "should." What's interesting to me is that Lee said that "must" can also be used to express certainty." It's like "Wait a minute," that is "must." Why does he think "should" is for certainty? "Should" is a little bit different from certainty. There's a misunderstanding between the levels of certainty. Like high probability and a lower level of probability. You do have to be careful because there's a conclusion that the student has already drawn and you have to be careful to address that confusion. That word "also"—that's what scares me. "Uh-oh [I think to myself], there's a strange conclusion there."

As Yang and Ko note, two things in Pam's reflection are significant. First of all, Pam demonstrates explicit knowledge of the meaning of the English modals *must* and *should*. Additionally, Pam shows that she understands the student's thought processes, pinpointing how the phrasing of the question shows exactly what the student is confused about. In other words, Pam has achieved a level of intersubjectivity with Lee that allows her to understand Lee's confusion and to define the learning challenge for Lee.

DEFINING THE LEARNING CHALLENGE

An important responsibility of teachers is to be selective about what they wish to present to students. It is impossible to present everything, and even if teachers had unlimited time and all was known about a given language, they still could not teach it all, because as we saw in the last chapter, language keeps changing. Instead, we must be judicious about what we choose to work on with our students. Let me offer an important principle in this regard, one that should be applied in tandem with use of the pie chart. I call this the *challenge principle*.

The **challenge principle** says that one of the three dimensions almost always affords the greatest long-term challenge to language students. It is important to remember that, with any given piece of language, all three dimensions of language are present. It is impossible to separate form from meaning from use. However, for pedagogical reasons, it is possible to focus student attention on one of these dimensions within the whole. Of course, for a given group of students, the immediate challenge may differ from the overall long-term challenge, depending on the characteristics of the students, such as their native language and their level of target language proficiency. However, it is possible to anticipate which dimension is likely to afford the greatest long-term challenge for all students, and it is important to do so, for being clear about the overall challenge will give you a starting point and suggest an approach that is consistent with the long-term challenge.

To illustrate this principle and its significance, consider the passive voice in English. First, we shall need to do a pie-chart analysis of the passive voice. Here is what one would look like.

Figure 4.3 Form, Meaning, and Use of the English Passive Voice

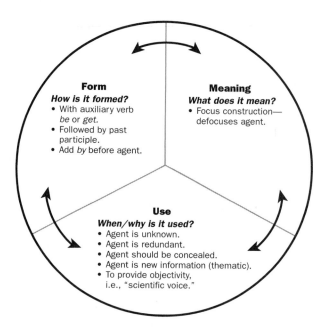

The next step is to ask ourselves in which dimension the long-term learning challenge lies. Is it how to form the passive, knowing what it means, or learning when to use it? (Of course, students will have to learn all three, although we do not necessarily have to teach all three.) Let us look at what learning challenges each wedge presents.

Students will have to learn how to form the passive voice, as I have said, but this should not create too much difficulty, since the passive is formed in English with the ubiquitous *be* and *get* verbs, which students have probably learned to conjugate correctly by the time the passive is introduced. Similarly, forming the passive requires that students use a structure they will have encountered before, namely, the past participle. This is not to say that students will not struggle with the various tense and aspect combinations for the passive voice; however, the problems should not be insurmountable because the combinations are regular.

The meaning of the passive should also not be difficult to learn. All languages have ways to shift the focus in an utterance, and the passive exists to do just this in English, shifting the focus from the agent of the action to the receiver.

This leaves us with the use dimension. Indeed, my experience has been that the greatest challenge is usually learning to use the passive voice appropriately. Learning when to use the passive voice versus the active voice for a sentence with more or less the same meaning is a formidable challenge. For example, which is the better way to complete this mini-text, with the active voice (a) or passive voice (b)?

Some of the Olympic athletes from the smaller countries, such as Korea and Romania, were truly remarkable. In fact,

(a) the Romanians won three gold medals in gymnastics.

(b) three gold medals in gymnastics were won by Romanians.

I would say that (a) is the better answer because the idea of *athletes from Romania* has already been introduced, and so they are known agents and thus natural subjects of the next sentence.

If the first sentence, however, had been about gold medals, *the Romanians* would have been unknown agents and the second version would have completed the text better:

Many medals were awarded to athletes from smaller countries. In fact, three gold medals in gymnastics were won by the Romanians.

If the challenge of the passive is indeed use, what, then, is the problem with presenting the passive to students, as it is often done, as a transformation of the active voice sentence?

Romanian athletes won three gold medals.

Three gold medals were won by Romanian athletes.

The problems are many. First of all, introducing the passive as a transformed version of the active implies that the latter is derived from the former. This is simply not the case. Worse, it implies that they are interchangeable. Nothing could be further from the truth. Use of the two is motivated by completely different reasons, and it is no help to students to mislead them when the challenge is figuring out when to use each. Finally, this approach leaves the impression that the agent preceded with *by* is very common in passive sentences. Once again, this is false. In fact, only about 15 percent of all passive sentences include the agent.

So we see that even if we are introducing the passive voice to students for the first time, it is important to bear in mind what their ultimate learning challenge will be, because that should inform how we proceed. The ultimate challenge of the passive voice is not form, as introducing the passive by transforming an active voice sentence would imply; although it is a grammatical form, it is not the form that presents the learning challenge. I trust the example with the passive serves to make the point that we must be clear about our students' learning challenges— and, of course, be prepared to switch if we discover, once we engage them in a particular activity, that we have anticipated their challenge incorrectly.

4.4

Investigations

Consider the following English grammatical structures. Which dimension do you think presents the greatest long-term challenge for each: how it is formed, what it means, or when and why to use it, as opposed to another structure with a similar meaning?

(a) the present perfect "tense"
(b) phrasal verbs
(c) indirect, or reported, speech
(d) *too* vs. *very* as intensifiers

The point should be clear: although we are dealing with forms, it is not always form that presents the greatest long-term challenge.

Using the Pie Chart for Professional Development Purposes

It may be discouraging at first to realize that one's knowledge is inadequate to address all three dimensions. However, it would certainly be contrary to my intentions to leave readers feeling overwhelmed. Instead, it should be enough to recognize that it is important to be able to fill in all three wedges for anything we teach. Not being able to do so for a particular wedge of the pie can help provide direction for where we need to work to fill in the lacunae in our own understanding. I have certainly found this to be the case in my own professional development. I attempt to assign what I know about a particular structure to the three wedges of the pie, only to discover that there are certain pie wedges where I have very little to say. This tips me off that there is research to be done to fill my own knowledge gaps.

Sometimes, when I have talked about the pie chart to teachers who are not native speakers of the language they teach, they despair most about the use wedge of the pie. Since they lack the intuitions of native speakers, and since they themselves were not necessarily taught about the pragmatics of grammar, they feel it is hopeless to think that they will be able to do an adequate job with their own students. Such a feeling is certainly understandable. However, there is some comfort to be derived from knowing that they themselves have learned a great deal of the pragmatic conventions governing a structure, even if only implicitly. Besides, once one accepts that grammaring involves knowing when to use a structure, in addition to knowing how to form it and what it means, then one has no recourse. One has to accept that there will always be something to learn about one's subject matter.

This is how Cindy Gunn (1997: 60), a teacher from British Columbia who was teaching EFL in Japan, put it:

Teachers' Voices

Cindy Gunn

> This paper has examined one way that helped me as a teacher of EFL students become better prepared to meet my goal of teaching grammar in a communicative classroom. This was done by looking at grammar through the pie chart lens as suggested by Diane Larsen-Freeman and then defining the challenge for my students. The pie chart allowed me to learn while preparing to help my students. For myself, and possibly for other teachers as well, this may be the most useful part of the pie chart, as John Cotton Dana eloquently points out: "Who dares to teach must never cease to learn."

And to my way of thinking, Dana's comment can be just as much a promise as an injunction.

Suggested Readings

Cognitive and functional linguists are interested in the meaning and use dimensions of grammar structures. A good introduction to cognitive and functional approaches can be found in Tomasello (1998). This is an anthology with chapters written by some of the leading cognitive linguists. Of course, Halliday (1994) and Langacker (1987; 1991) fit this category. Also, in Celce-Murcia and Larsen-Freeman (1999), we have analyzed the major grammatical structures of English from the perspective of form, meaning, and use. Larsen-Freeman (2001) contains additional teaching suggestions for the three dimensions.

5

RULES AND REASONS

GRAMMAR RULES AND REASONS

Grammar and rules are undoubtedly synonymous in the minds of learners and teachers—in fact, in the minds of most people. This is not surprising, of course, because linguists hypothesize about rules, theorists highlight them, applied linguists write or interpret them, textbooks feature them, teachers present them, and students memorize them. The association between grammar and rules is powerful because the partnership has been fruitful.

Rules have served the learning of language by capturing generalizations about morphosyntactic regularities in a language, such as that the finite verb is clause final in a German subordinate clause. They represent generalizations that are helpful for learners, telling learners of Spanish, for example, that masculine nouns end in -*o* and feminine nouns end in -*a*. Rules also allow materials developers to work with "right-sized" chunks of language, to help students deal in an orderly and systematic way with the grammar of the target language. They provide a modicum of security to language learners—they give them something to hold onto in the vast rush of noise that is the new language. Finally, they also vest a certain amount of authority in the source of rules—the materials and the teacher.

5.1

Have you found rules helpful in your teaching or learning of language? How do you work with rules in your teaching? Do you give them to your students or do you have students figure them out? Do you state, or do you have your students state, the rules explicitly? Do your students memorize explicit rules? Do they do practice exercises with them? If you do a variety of things with rules, what makes you choose to work with rules one way sometimes and another way at other times? What are the pluses and minuses to working with rules in the way you do?

Most language teachers work with rules in some way, even if the rules are not stated in formal metalinguistic terms. And most learners find learning about them satisfying. Jennifer Monahan Roca, who teaches English in a Massachusetts high school, speaks for many teachers and learners when she offers this anecdote as an example of her experience with rules.

Jennifer
Monahan
Roca

Once a student asked me, "Why can't I write 'more easy'?" My response was that with certain adjectives you add "-er" instead of "more." She understood this, but she wanted to know why. I had to tell her that I didn't know why. I searched my grammar books and discovered that any adjectives with one syllable and any adjectives with two syllables, one being a _____y, take the "-er" or "-ier" ending. All other adjectives with two or more syllables take "more." I explained this to the rest of the class. They were amazed. I could see the lightbulbs going on in their heads. So I truly feel that if you offer reasons for the rules the students will feel more confident with the language.

I can relate to Jennifer's experience. I have watched the lightbulbs go on in my students' heads. Watching the dawning of awareness in my students is one of my most inspiring moments in teaching. And giving students a rule does in fact offer a type of explanation for a linguistic phenomenon, which can turn on the lightbulbs. However, when I use the word *reasons* in conjunction with *rules*, as I have done in the title of this chapter, I have in mind something deeper than a generalization about the language. The rule about *-er* and *more* with adjectives in English captures an important, though changing, generalization about how the language works; it does not, however, explain why the language behaves in this way.

The Reason for the Rule

Now, maybe it is because I am by nature inquisitive, and I have always been curious about language—after all, I have made understanding it part of my life's work. However, to my way of thinking, it is important for learners not only to know the rules, but also to know why they exist. I am not referring to how the language came to be; I am referring to what I call the "reasons" underlying the rules. Rules have to do with *how*, reasons with *why*. If one understands the *why* underlying the *how*, one appreciates how much more rational grammar is than it is normally given credit for being. I think it is important for learners to know the reasons because this knowledge is empowering. It helps make the acquisition of a language less rote, less mechanical. After all, our learners are thinking human beings; why not tap their cognitive powers and help them engage with the language they encounter, help them cultivate an attitude of inquiry?

Furthermore, rules tend to be limited to generalizing about the form of language, but grammatical forms have meanings and uses as well, which students also need to learn. And proficient speakers of a language will override rules of form when they are motivated to express certain meanings or are influenced by certain conditions of use. If second language students know the reasons why a rule exists, they may also know when it is possible to "violate" it in the service of meaning or use, just as proficient speakers of the language would do. For instance, they will know, as we have seen, that it is possible to use the present progressive with a stative verb in English, even when the rule about form says that this is not so. A *rule* of English grammar proscribes using the progressive with stative verbs. The *reason* for the rule is due to the semantic incompatibility between processes depicted by the progressive, which typically involve change, and unchanging states embodied in stative verbs. Thus, English does not permit:

*He is owning a car.

because, in English, ownership is considered an unchanging state. Of course, he could sell his car, in which case he would no longer own it. But at the time of the utterance, ownership is conceived of as a state.

However, certain states are interpretable in the present progressive, especially if there is an assumption of change in the degree of relation between the subject and object of the verb. Thus, while *love* is also classified as a stative verb in English, English speakers will say

I am loving this class.

because they mean to convey the changing, intensifying nature of the relation. If there is an assumption of change, the semantic incompatibility between the progressive and stative verbs is diminished.

Knowing the reason for a rule also gives language students an understanding of the logic that speakers of another language use. It may help students learn to see the world as the speakers do. This may not only facilitate students' internalization of language, it may also contribute to their understanding of difference in the world, that is, it may help them understand different worldviews, different ways that speakers of other languages construct experience in the world. For some learners, it may provide access to enhanced cultural understanding, which may be their purpose or their reward for studying a language in the first place.

While I have been careful to acknowledge that rules have their place in language teaching and learning, I think that there are drawbacks to associating grammar strictly with rules. Rules are static descriptions of, or prescriptions/proscriptions about, the forms of language, when, in fact, grammar (language) is anything but static. Furthermore, the generalizations that rules attempt to capture are never broad enough to prevent exceptions. These are not necessarily due to the fact that the rules are poorly formulated, but rather that grammar is flexible, allowing for the expression of new meanings—a vital quality, because we humans are meaning-making beings.

Linguist John Haiman (1985: 260) points to

> a fundamental difference between the laws of physics and the laws
> of language. The law of gravity is not modified by use: no matter
> how many times we throw a ball into the air, it will fall to the
> ground with the same acceleration. Rules of grammar, on the other
> hand, are modified by use (i.e., languages change)...

The final problem is not a linguistic one. It is political, having to do with the distribution and the withholding of power. It can be asked, "Who owns the rules?" "Who makes them up?" The answer to these questions is not "language students." This is a problem if we truly want our students to feel that they own the language. I think one solution to this problem is to help language students understand the internal logic of the language that they are studying so that they will be free to express the meaning that they want in accurate and appropriate ways.

COUNTERING THE ARBITRARINESS OF RULES THROUGH REASONS

Rules of form often seem sterile and arbitrary to students. An example is the English rule that, when the existential *there* fills the subject position in the sentence, the determiner preceding the noun phrase following the verb (the logical subject) must be indefinite:

> There is a snowstorm coming.

In other words, the rule tells us that *snowstorm* requires the indefinite *a* in this sentence because the existential *there* is serving as a surrogate subject.

5.2

Can you figure out the reason underlying this seemingly arbitrary rule, which accounts for the use of a *before* snowstorm?

Now, upon first consideration, the rule requiring an indefinite article in this sentence might seem rather sterile and arbitrary. It certainly appears to be the result of a rather convoluted set of conditions. It turns out, though, that the answer is not at all arbitrary. As I pointed out in the previous chapter, the function of *there* is to introduce new information, information that is being introduced into the discourse for the first time. In this case, the coming of a snowstorm is the new information. And, in English, new information is marked with an indefinite determiner. If someone were to say

> There is the snowstorm coming.

he or she might be reminding listeners of the snowstorm (i.e., *We had better not plan to drive to Denver because, remember, there is the snowstorm coming*), and thus the snowstorm would not be new information. Alternatively, if it were possible to perceive an expected snowstorm developing at a distance, someone might be able to say

> *There* is the snowstorm coming.

But notice that in this instance, *there* receives stress, and thus its meaning has been changed by this change in form. The *there* in this sentence is not the existential *there* but is rather the locative adverbial *there*. We know this because not only is *there* stressed in this sentence, the sentence would also likely be accompanied by a gesture pointing in the direction of the approaching storm.

I am convinced that it would be helpful for English language learners to understand the reasons for the form-based rules—in this case, to understand that the function of *there* is to introduce new information into the discourse, and because of this function, English requires that information in the predicate be marked as new. Not everyone would agree with me, however. Here is what Monika Floyd, a teacher of beginning-level ESL in Massachusetts, has to say about the matter of rules and reasons.

Monika Floyd

From my experience in the classroom and my own L2 acquisition process, being aware of grammar rules and their exceptions is vital for the understanding and production of language. I surely concede that there are reasons for the rules and that there is logic in the language. But what's the point in expanding on the fact that there is a third person singular "s" in the present tense? Let the beginner have his rules; save reasons for the advanced.

I understand Monika's position. I note that Kathryn, a teacher of advanced level English language students at a Midwestern university, makes a similar point, observing that "It's not so much how you do it, it's why you do it, I think, for students, when you're talking about grammar, at least at this level" (Johnston and Goettsch, 2000: 456).

USING REASONS IN LANGUAGE TEACHING

Nevertheless, I maintain that helping students understand why things are the way they are is as important a part of teaching grammar as is showing students how things are done. Of course, I would not go into a class of advanced students, let alone beginners, lecturing about reasons, any more than I would lecture about rules. Still, it seems to me that reasons have their place in language instruction at all levels, even if the reasons only inform the choices that I make as a teacher.

For instance, if I were teaching *there* to beginners, I would want to choose or craft an activity carefully so that the function of *there* was made clear. Therefore, knowing that *there* introduces new information, which is marked with an indefinite article, would help me avoid teaching *there* in a misleading way, such as bringing in a picture, putting it in front of the classroom, and asking students to make statements with *there* about things they observe in the picture. This activity would be misleading because when the teacher and the students are looking at the same picture, the function of *there*, to introduce new information, is not on display. I can get students to practice the form of sentences with *there* using this activity, but I am misrepresenting the use of the structure. On the other hand, if I used two similar, but not identical, pictures and had the students all look at one while I, the teacher, looked at the other, we could legitimately use statements with *there* to introduce new information, describing the pictures and attempting to identify the contrasts between them.

A follow-up activity to this one might involve having students work in pairs with two different pictures, contrasting them in a similar manner. I might conclude this pair of activities with a consciousness-raising activity by pointing out—or having students induce for themselves—that the function of *there* is to introduce new information, information that is not known to the listener or reader, and that all the grammatical forms used in conjunction with this structure support this function. To me, this provides a more satisfying way of teaching *there* and counters the arbitrariness of the rule governing the form of the noun phrase following the *be* verb.

ACCOUNTING FOR "VIOLATIONS" OF FORM-BASED RULES

I take Monika's point, though. Clearly, there are rules that capture form-based generalizations about English that are useful as rules of thumb, especially for beginning-level learners. As she says, one simple, helpful rule that students of English are given early in instruction is the rule of subject–verb agreement. In English, as in many other languages, the verb must agree in number and person with the subject. Of course, in English, this rule only applies in the present tense unless it is the *be* verb. But since the *be* verb is usually introduced to beginners, it is commonplace to furnish the rule of subject–verb agreement in some form to students, either as a statement or as a verb paradigm.

I am here.

He/She/The cat is here.

We/You/They/The cats are here.

Again, I am not questioning the wisdom of this practice, something that I myself have done. However, I do want to illustrate the consequences of providing students with deterministic form-based rules or paradigms only, because at some point students will hear or read sentences such as

Ten miles is a long way to hike.

where the singular verb is preceded by an overtly plural subject, and

My family are all coming for dinner.

where an overtly singular subject is followed by a plural verb.

Such sentences demonstrate that the system is more flexible than an absolute form-based rule would suggest. Both of the above sentences are perfectly accurate, of course. Putting them in this form tells us that the speaker has opted to see *ten miles* as comprising a hike and, therefore, as a single entity, and, conversely, to see *family* as a collection of individuals. Clearly, then, semantic considerations can often override formal constraints.

5.3

There is a rule of tense harmony or tense concord with reported or indirect speech in English that requires the verb in the complement clause to be in the same tense as the verb in the main clause.

The man **said** that the weather **was** going to be good.

While this rule is adhered to for the most part, it can be "violated" for certain purposes. What do you think are the motivations of speakers of English who produce the following?

He said that you divide the numerator by the denominator.

He said that his name is Paul.

She mentioned that she will be taking the day off today.

To cite a final example, many teachers tell their students that, in English, the adjective precedes the noun.

The yellow field

Again, this is a good rule of thumb, especially helpful to students whose native language requires adjectives to follow the nouns they modify:

*The field yellow

But notice that, in English, it is also possible for the adjective to follow the noun it modifies:

The field yellow with goldenrod

While we understand the prenominal adjective to refer to a characteristic enduring quality of the field, the position following the noun is reserved for adjectives depicting a more temporary quality, resulting from a specific cause.

The point of all this is, of course, that rules tend to be stated and conceived of in deterministic ways, when in actuality many, although not all, are more probabilistic, flexible even, bending when it comes to expressing meaning.

DEALING WITH THE ARBITRARINESS

Another limitation of rules that was alluded to earlier is their apparent arbitrariness. Nothing could be truer of the way in which verbs that take infinitives and gerunds as objects in English are usually presented. Often students are referred to long lists of verbs that take infinitive complements, verbs that take gerund complements, and verbs that take both types of complements, and are then told to memorize the lists. For example:

Figure 5.1 Verbs Taking Infinitive and Gerund Complements

Verbs That Take Infinitives	Verbs That Take Gerunds	Verbs That Take Both
aim	admit	begin
dare	appreciate	continue
expect	defend	forget
hope	deny	hate
intend	enjoy	try

However, this approach puts a great deal of the learning burden on students of English and is of no help to them when deciding on a given occasion whether to use an infinitive or a gerund with a verb from the third column. Instead of seeing the verbs as equivalent except for the complements that they take, it is helpful to have students understand the reason for the categories of verbs. Linguist Dwight Bolinger (1968) offers a semantic explanation. The infinitive tends to go with events that are hypothetical, future, unfulfilled; conversely, the gerund goes with events that are real, vivid, fulfilled. In other words, one can only *aim to go* because at the time of the utterance, the *going* has not yet taken place. On the other hand, one can *admit going* because with a verb that takes a gerund, one assumes that the *going* has occurred.

With verbs that take both an infinitive and a gerund, a meaning difference can be perceived, depending on which complement follows the verb. Compare, for instance,

He tried to go, which suggests that he did not succeed in going, with *He tried going*, which suggests that he did indeed go but left for some reason. Even with emotive verbs, a slight difference in meaning can be detected. For instance, if the speaker is engaged in the activity at the time—say, dancing—he or she is more likely to say *I hate dancing*, rather than *I hate to dance*. While this distinction is admittedly subtle, and not failproof, it can be an aid to students who are trying to decide which form conveys the meaning they intend, or how to interpret something someone else had said to them.

Jane, who teaches an advanced ESL class, makes the point this way.

Jane

> So I sort of assume that they know a certain level of all this, but maybe they have forgotten or never understood it when they first learned it. They maybe just memorized the rules and studied for the test and took the test.... They just maybe never understood why there was a possessive gerund or why it was like this (Johnston and Goettsch, 2000: 455).

To remove the burden of rote learning from my students, I want them to know *why*. There is, after all, a great deal of systematicity to grammar.

REASONS ARE BROADER BASED THAN RULES

Because of the systematicity of grammar, reasons are broader based than rules. They apply to more phenomena than single syntactic structures. For example, English has a rule that states if the direct object is a lexical noun and the verb is transitive, phrasal, and separable, speakers have a choice as to where to put the direct object—before the particle of the phrasal verb or after it.

She looked *the word up* in the dictionary.

She looked *up the word* in the dictionary.

However, when the direct object is a pronoun, it must come between the verb and particle, not after the particle:

She looked *it* up in the dictionary.

*She looked up *it* in the dictionary.

This condition does seem arbitrary. However, if we start from the premise that there is an underlying reason, we will come to see that this condition is far from arbitrary and has to do with the information status of the noun phrase. As we saw in the previous chapter, a fundamental fact about English word order is that the preferred position for new information is toward the end of a clause. Again, this is called *end focus* or *end weight*. Given a choice, and unless some extra nuance of meaning is intended, English speakers will choose not to put a pronoun in clause-final position, since pronouns are by definition not new information. In order to use a pronoun, its referent must be clear from the context, for example, through prior mention. Thus, the pronoun *it* is old information and should not occupy clause-final position.

A rule is often given to English learners that claims that the indirect object can- not immediately follow the verb when the direct object is a pronoun and the indirect object is a noun:

*We sent John it.

Conversely, when the indirect object is a pronoun and the direct object is a noun (especially a nonspecific one), the indirect object is likely to precede the direct object:

We sent him a package.

Can you find a reason for this rule?

The observations in Investigation 5.4 can be explained, as we have just seen, by noting that pronouns refer to old information and are therefore not likely to be put in end-focus position. This is not to say that an indirect object that is a pronoun can never occupy the position at the end of a clause, but when it is placed there, a different interpretation would probably be made—for example, a contrastive one.

We sent a package to him. (not her)

Furthermore, with verbs that allow two different word orders with direct and indirect objects:

Meredith gave Jack advice.

Meredith gave advice to Jack.

the choice, as you may have guessed, is determined by what speakers want to give end focus to. In a full-sentence answer to the question *What did Meredith give Jack?* the first would be appropriate. The question *To whom did Meredith give advice?* would be answered by the second version.

The fact that English speakers tend to put new information at the end of a clause thus accounts for word order phenomena in a wide range of syntactic structures. This fact is much broader than a rule that only applies to one syntactic structure, evidence of the systematicity of grammar. Moreover, there is a pragmatic explanation for it. By ordering information from old to new in a clause, speakers or writers are orienting their listeners or readers to the new information being presented.

Incidentally, it may seem arbitrary from a present-day (synchronic) perspective that certain verbs—such as *give*—allow the direct and indirect object alternation patterns while others—such as *explain*—do not:

Meredith explained the situation to Jack.

*Meredith explained Jack the situation.

This is less arbitrary than it seems, however. Although it is admittedly difficult to know which verbs allow both patterns and which do not, the difference has to do with the source language from which the verbs were borrowed into English. In general, Germanic verbs permit both sequences, verbs of Romance origin do not.

LEARNER SECURITY, TEACHER AUTHORITY, AND THE POLITICAL QUESTION

It is important to underscore that part of the attractiveness of rules for language learners is learners' need for security. Deterministic rules—what we have been calling rules of thumb, such as subject–verb agreement—have their place. However, the first time students encounter an instance where the rule is violated, a good deal of their security is undermined. On the other hand, one can build a great deal of confidence in one's students when they themselves can figure out how a part of the system works.

Here is what Kathryn, the teacher of advanced ESL students whom I introduced earlier, has to say about this matter.

Kathryn

> They have a tendency to think that anything that looks like a preposition is a preposition and that it's too overwhelming for them to handle prepositions in general so we've found it somewhat comforting to students to separate out which are prepositions and which are particles attached to a verb, so they can have some sense that there is some logic somewhere in this whole system. There's a comfort factor here for students. By the end of the term, they generally say they start to feel somewhat more confident that they can manage these words that they had a feeling they couldn't manage before. Because particles and prepositions, all kinds of adverbials, all look the same to them, they don't know what to do with them. That's what I am after in this (Johnston and Goettsch, 2000: 460–461).

Teachers, like Kathryn, know the power their students feel when they learn to figure out for themselves the reasons underlying the grammatical forms. Encouraging students to be curious, to see that there is a logic to the language they are learning, and giving students the tools to understand it and to make it their own—these are the things I like to do when I teach. I believe that these practices will serve their learning well, long after they leave my classroom. And that is *reason* enough.

Suggested Readings

Givón's (1993) two volumes offer a good resource for meaning and use insights into English grammar structures, as does Celce-Murcia and Larsen-Freeman (1999). For a discussion of the given–new distinction as applied to reading and writing, see Vande Kopple's and Fries' chapters in Miller's (1997) anthology. Also, see Larsen-Freeman (2000c) for another rendition on the theme of rules and reasons working together.

6
THE GRAMMAR OF CHOICE

Speakers of a language will choose certain grammar structures in keeping with the meaning they wish to express. However, it is not only the intention to express a particular meaning that motivates speakers to use a particular structure. In fact, when the meaning is held more or less constant, speakers still face socially or discursively motivated grammatical choices. The discussion of such choices involves the dimension of use.

The use dimension is often neglected in materials and in instruction. To my way of thinking, this is most unfortunate. I hope to compensate for this situation by dedicating two chapters to matters of language use, this one to social factors and the one that follows to discourse factors.

THE "ONE RIGHT ANSWER" MYTH

One of the enduring myths about grammar is that there is always one right way to convey a particular meaning. Contrary to this myth, which presumably arose in the context of prescriptive grammar and discrete point grammar tests, teachers know that there is often more than one right answer to a question about grammar. In fact, they frequently find themselves hedging when their students ask them if a particular way of saying something is "right." A very common teacher response to such a question is: "It depends."

Meg teaches English in a community college in the United States. When she heard me say that it is common for teachers to answer students' question about correctness with "It depends," she interjected:

> Yes. It is true. Just yesterday, this student from Venezuela asked me if it is possible to say "If I *was* rich," rather than "If I *were* rich." I know sometimes people say this and so I said, "Well, I have heard people say 'was,' but it is better to say 'were.'" The student wasn't satisfied though, and he said, "Yes, but which is correct?" I found myself saying what I always say on such occasions, "Well, it depends. If you are talking to someone informally, then you might say or hear 'was,' but if you are taking the TOEFL, you'd better use 'were'." That was the best that I could do, but I know that it was not a very satisfying answer. I also worry about saying too much. "How much do they really need to know?" I often wonder.

Meg

While we have all experienced Meg's desire to give an authoritative answer, we should not fail to appreciate that Meg's reply reflects an important understanding of the contingent and complex intersection of grammar and context. The choice of which grammar structure to use depends on the context or the purpose for which the language is being used. However, we can also appreciate the student's consternation, his or her concern with having to get it right. "Getting it right," it turns out, does not always involve an exclusive solution. But in the drive for uncertainty reduction, sometimes teachers want absolute answers as much as students.

Here is what Barb, a student in a teacher education course, had to say when she was asked, "What do you do when you are asked a question and you don't know how to answer it at all?"

Teachers' Voices

Barb
and
Pam

> *Barb*: In a classroom full of Asian people who expect that you know your subject matter, it is difficult to say "I don't know" and you might lose the respect or the credibility from your students. So I think it would make me very very nervous when a student asked me a question and I do not know the answer. If I didn't know the answer, maybe I shouldn't be a teacher (Yang and Ko, 1998).

And now here is what Pam, an experienced teacher, offers on the matter of not always knowing the "correct" answer:

> *Pam*: You know what has helped me? I'll say, "You know in many cultures you lose face if you don't answer the question." I say, "In our culture it's better to admit that you don't know the answer. You'll lose more face if you give the wrong answer, than if you say 'I'll find out for you.'" I talk directly about the fact that different cultures look at it differently. Sometimes by just talking about that, it clears the air and they don't disrespect you (Yang and Ko, 1998).

That the students want to know and the teachers want to give them the correct answer is understandable. Barb's concern, and Pam's strategy for handling a student's question when she does not know how to respond, both make sense. However, teachers and students also need to know, if they don't already, that grammar is not a linguistic straitjacket. It is much more flexible. There is rarely one right answer to a grammar question. There is a lot of latitude in the forms that we use, which is why I have elected to title this chapter *the grammar of choice*.

Frameworks

BASING CHOICES ON SOCIAL-INTERACTIONAL FACTORS

Further, the choice is not stochastic. There are reasons for our choices. We often base our choices on social-interactional factors, those factors that have to do with the interpersonal relationships we establish and nurture.

Our students will be judged for the way they say something as much as for the forms they use or the meaning they express. Sometimes the judgment may even be harsher because the judge is unaware that his or her assessment is based on linguistic factors, not character. I can recall working in a department where the secretary used to complain about the rudeness of the international students. A little investigation showed that the students would often couch their requests in the form of statements such as *I want a schedule* or *I need a catalogue*. While they were able to communicate their requests and have them met, their linguistic behavior made them appear rude. A simple lesson on using the modal form *would like*, accompanied by *please*, would have made a world of difference in the impression they made.

Mindful of the work of Leslie Beebe (1995) on rudeness, I, for one, recognize that sometimes language students need to be rude, or at least assertive. I therefore would not want to encourage my students to be courteous conformists who are robotically polite. As Beebe (1995: 167) notes, "students do have to get power/control and express negative feelings, but in appropriate ways." Furthermore, I am not recommending that we judge our students' performance against native speaker norms, nor is it likely that all students will aspire to conform to such norms. It is the students who must (and will) decide how they wish to position themselves as speakers of a given language. They will need to understand that, as speakers or writers, they have choices to make, and that those choices have consequences, so that they can learn to use the language in a way that honors their intentions. Besides, students need to be able to draw inferences about the intentions of others. To the best of our ability, therefore, we should help students understand the linguistic options available. Thus, an understanding of when or why to use a particular grammatical form should be part of teachers' understanding of grammar so that they will avoid giving students easy answers in the moment that contribute to confusion later on.

CAVEATS TO TEACHING PRAGMATICALLY APPROPRIATE CHOICES

There are several important caveats to all this. First, as a teacher, I do not want to be prescriptive about the behavior of my students. I am not in the business of giving my students guidance on how to behave appropriately. Nonetheless, it seems to me that I should be giving my students information about how they might be perceived if they exercise particular linguistic options in particular contexts. I need to ensure that my students have knowledge of what is normal and customary in such contexts. However, besides knowledge of social convention, they also need to know

> the ways such conventions can be circumvented or subverted by individual initiative. Uses of language are, in one respect, necessarily acts of conformity. But they are not only that: they are also acts of identity whereby people assert themselves and manipulate others. Pragmatics is concerned with how people negotiate meaning, but also how they negotiate social relations (Widdowson, 1996: 68).

This leads me to my second caveat. It is impossible to anticipate how someone will be perceived by others in the moment. Clearly, perceptions are not influenced only by linguistic performance. At best, all that we can do is call our students' attention to the norms of linguistic usage. We cannot be sure that these will be operational in all exchanges, nor can we be sure that everyone would agree on the conventions by which we abide, since norms are not conveniently homogeneous. We can, however, help our students to become sensitive to differences among forms in general as a way to make them aware of the possible implications of their choices. Even when students are studying a foreign language that is not the language of the environment, pragmatics is an issue. After all, they still need to understand how to interpret what is said or written by others, beyond what the words themselves literally mean.

A final caveat regarding teaching about appropriateness in grammatical choice is to acknowledge that it is always possible to alter the meaning and certainly the pragmatics through paralinguistic or extralinguistic means. A speaker can use the most polite lexicogrammatical form imaginable, but if his or her voice is dripping with sarcasm (such as with an exaggerated *puhleeze*), we know that the politeness is ironic. Or if a student is fluent and accurate in a language but has not mastered the interactional norm of maintaining eye contact with her interlocutors, then she may be misjudged all the same.

Of course, while it could be argued that a learner should attempt to understand and practice the sociocultural mores of the society in which he or she is a guest, there may be no cause for learners of a language to adopt the interactional norms of its speakers in order to use the language in most of the situations in which they find themselves. Learners of a foreign language often do have to pass discrete-point grammar tests, containing items for which there is "one right answer." Then, too, in the case of English—a world language in the process of being set adrift from its cultural moorings—there is even more reason to question whether the interactional norms of English speakers should be adhered to at all. For instance, English is increasingly used by non-anglophone Europeans to communicate with each other. Although they may be curious about the interactional patterns of English speakers, knowing them may be of little help when French meets Italian. In such cases, perhaps norms of appropriateness different from those of native speakers of English are warranted. Thus, all we can do is talk about norms and help raise our students' consciousness regarding what pragmatic factors may be at stake.

In this chapter, I will not attempt a thorough inventory of all the pragmatic factors that can be signaled by a change in form. A further qualification is the reminder that the use dimension involves an active process of fitting the language to the context. All I can do here is look at language excerpts, snapshots of decontextualized language, and assign possible social implications to the use of the forms. To illustrate the impact of grammatical choice on interpersonal interaction, I will briefly touch upon the parameters of attitude, power, and identity. This important topic of grammatical choice will also be taken up in the next chapter, when I explore the consequences of exercising choice in the construction of text.

PRAGMATIC FACTORS SIGNALED BY A CHANGE IN FORM
Attitude

6.1

Consider the following short dialogue from Riddle (1986):

Anne: Jane just bought a Volvo.

John: Maureen has one.

Anne: John, you've got to quit talking about Maureen as if you were still going together. You broke up three months ago.

What is the cause of Anne's chiding John? How could John have avoided the scolding if he had wanted to?

One pragmatic effect of grammatical choice is that we convey a particular attitude depending on the grammatical forms (among other things) that we choose to use. In Investigation 6.1, John could have stated the same propositional content using the past tense, even though the case may be that Maureen still owns the Volvo. If he had done so, he might have avoided the rebuke from Anne because his use of past tense would have made his relationship with Maureen appear more psychologically distant. Either the past tense or the present tense is "correct" here, but deciding which to use, while not necessarily a conscious choice, can clearly have an impact on one's listener. It all depends!

Here is another example of the use of tense to indicate attitude. This time the example comes from Batstone (1995: 197):

> Smith (1980) argued that Britain was no longer a country in which freedom of speech was seriously maintained. Johnson (1983), though, argues that Britain remains a citadel of liberty.

Batstone points out that the use of the past tense with Smith and the present tense with Johnson has nothing to do with their chronology; rather, the author is indicating that Smith's argument is not worthy of current interest, whereas Johnson's argument is held to be of continuing relevance. Of course, the writer's lexical choices reinforce this interpretation; it is not all in the grammar. For instance, had the writer used demonstrated, rather than argued, to describe the position taken by Smith, our perception of the writer's attitude toward Smith might have been different.

Sarah Kipp-McGowan, who teaches language arts to deaf adolescents using American Sign Language, recognizes the link between language use and attitude, and the importance of making her students aware of what is appropriate.

> I do address issues of "spoken" (signed) language and use in my classroom. Our students need to finesse the cultures of two worlds and cultures: the culture of the Deaf community and the culture of the hearing world. For this reason, and because adolescents are inherently struggling with, and challenging, appropriate use of language, I provide much feedback to my students about the type of language use that is appropriate within the classroom. They need reminders at times about how to "appropriately" (by my standards) respond to staff and peers. Terms used or attitudes conveyed within peer discourse are often not appropriate within the more formal setting of a classroom. Therefore, this aspect of language becomes a daily, incidental element of instruction.

Sarah
Kipp-McGowan

Importantly, Sarah reminds students about issues of appropriateness as defined by her own standards. As I mentioned in Chapter 4, sometimes teachers who teach a foreign language that is not native to them are concerned that their intuitions about what is appropriate are not reliable. It seems to me quite natural to have such feelings. I know that when I was teaching Indonesian, I was aware of my limits when it came to giving my students information about appropriate use of grammatical structures. However, we can only teach what we know, although we can make it our professional responsibility to expand our knowledge. Teachers who teach a foreign language can also derive comfort from the fact that sharing a native language with their students, which they often do, makes them more sensitive to their students' expectations in terms of the social norms of language use.

Power

I have already acknowledged that knowing a language can be empowering, and hence that there is a political dimension to language proficiency. At a more concrete level, the continuous choices that speakers face in exploiting the potential of the grammatical code can also hinge on issues of power. This is an extremely important awareness when it comes to the grammar of choice, because when you are teaching the social aspects of use, you always have to remember that appropriateness is relative to a particular time, place, the social status and relationship of the interlocutors, and so forth. Neglecting to teach this reality could lead to our teaching language use only as an act of conformity, inadvertently perpetuating inequalities in language use, such as explaining to students that in the language we are teaching, women have to defer to men (Norton Peirce, 1989).

Critical discourse analysis is concerned with issues of power imbalances in society, and those who practice it examine language for the subtle, yet influential, way in which power can be conferred on certain participants at the expense of others. Stubbs (1990 as cited in Batstone, 1995), for instance, finds it significant that in South African newspaper accounts dealing with events surrounding the release of Nelson Mandela, agency was often ascribed to Black South Africans by making them the subject of the clause when reporting acts of violence. Here is an example from a newspaper report:

Jubilant Blacks clashed with police...

The same propositional content could have been conveyed if the roles of the subject and the object had been reversed (i.e., *Police clashed with jubilant Blacks...*). Since such texts are not ideologically neutral, it seems that the order chosen was intended to assign responsibility to Black South Africans.

The point is that as language teachers, we should never forget that issues of power and language are intimately connected. For example, it is unfair, but nevertheless true, that native speakers of a language are permitted to create neologisms, as I have done with *grammaring*. Such a coinage, however, might have been corrected if a nonnative speaker of English had been its author. Of course, the very issue of who a native speaker is is socially constructed. And when it comes to English, native-speaker status becomes more nuanced, given the evolving World Englishes. Teachers of English must decide which norms to teach and to accept.

Identity

The final area that I shall take up in this limited examination of pragmatic considerations of grammatical choices is the rather large one of identity. Henry Widdowson (1996: 20–21) has written that "although individuals are constrained by conventions of the code and its use, they exploit the potential differently on different occasions for different purposes.... The patterning of a person's use of language is as naturally distinctive as a fingerprint." Widdowson's observation relates to how we use language to establish and maintain personal identity. There are a number of contributing factors to identity development that may influence the patterns of grammar use.

For example, Roger Putzel (1976) administered the Myers-Briggs personality type indicator to a group of male graduate students at UCLA, whom he also interviewed. He later transcribed the interviews and correlated the patterns of language use with the results of the personality tests. Putzel found a number of significant correlations between the grammar the students used and their personality type. To offer just one example, Putzel found that extroverted students used modal forms such as *I am going to* more often than introverts, who favored *I should.*

To cite another factor, it is well known that language use is age-graded. Adolescents in particular are known to adopt a special argot to distinguish themselves from the adults they have not yet become. Currently, one pattern of usage is to use the preposition *like* as in the following:

Emily: He told me like...

This is not as indiscriminate a use of a preposition as it may appear to any adult eavesdropper. The *like* actually has several functions. The one illustrated here could be the functional use of distancing the speaker from what he or she is about to report.

Many other identity factors influence the forms we use: our origin, social status, group membership, and so on. Certainly most language teachers have to wrestle with the question of which dialect of the language they are going to teach. In some cases the choice is clear; teachers are expected to teach the standard dialect. An example would be the situation in Italy, where different people in different geographic areas speak different dialects but children in school learn standard Italian, which is used for national communicative purposes and to foster national identity. Some teachers in North America seek to have their students become bidialectal, so teachers are extremely careful to treat the grammar in a child's dialect not as less than, but simply as different from, the standard dialect. The students' dialect is more useful in certain social situations, less so in others—just as is the case with the standard dialect. As many language teachers will attest, it is important, though not always straightforward, to distinguish an error from a dialect feature.

And, as we are always reminded, languages are in a state of flux themselves. Even powerful governmental agencies like the Académie française generally cannot make language flow in a predetermined direction. "In 1994, for example, France's National Assembly enacted the so-called *Loi Toubon*, a law named for its champion, the French culture minister Jacques Toubon. The law called for a ban, enforceable by fines of up to US$1,800 and by prison terms, on the use of foreign words in business or government communications, in broadcasting, and in advertising, if "suitable equivalents" existed in French. (A committee had previously been established to draw up suitable equivalents where none existed in French; the committee's work has resulted in the coining of 3,500 new French words, mostly to replace borrowed English-language ones.) [However, eventually,] France's Constitutional Council, the country's highest judicial body, weakened the law, applying it only to government documents" (Murphy, 1997). Attempts to prescribe language use almost always prove futile.

As I indicated at the outset of this chapter, I have only chosen some of the ways that social issues impact grammar use. I have also pointed out that many other systems of language play a role here. Certainly, one's accent is usually a good indication of one's place of origin, lexical choices mark membership in different discourse communities, and so forth. Further, sometimes what is *not* said is as clear a mark of, say, attitude as what *is* said. Silence is ambiguous in this regard. It can be the silence of those who feel they have no voice, or the willful withholding of information or refusal to participate of those who feel that they do have a voice. For example, a teacher who writes a letter of recommendation for a student in which the teacher's highest praise is for the student's penmanship or regular attendance leaves the recipient of the letter to infer a great deal about the student—not all of it favorable!

Not all of the distinctions discussed here should be taught, of course. A lot of these distinctions are acquired by students without their being explicitly included on a syllabus. If students are studying a language in an environment in which it is spoken outside the classroom, they will probably have already encountered a great deal of linguistic variety. Then, too, they may already have chosen the particular group of speakers of the language with whom they would like to identify or disidentify. When the need for instruction arises, teachers can inform their students, for example, that a particular form is associated with a particular regional dialect, without teaching the form for production. Yet, there are distinctions among the ones I have illustrated that do enable students to express meaning in a way they would choose, and that would therefore be candidates for instruction. Much of the initial instruction might be of the consciousness-raising sort, where students are made aware of the choices they have.

See Chapter 8 for a discussion of consciousness-raising activities.

In conclusion, far from being a linguistic straitjacket, grammar is a flexible, incredibly rich system that enables proficient speakers to express meaning in a way appropriate to the context, to how they wish to present themselves, and to the particular perspective they wish to contribute. While accuracy is an issue in grammar, so are meaningfulness and appropriateness of use. A better way to conceive of grammar for pedagogical purposes, then, might be a grammar of choice.

Suggested Readings

For elaboration on attitude, power, and identity and a discussion of other types of pragmatic difference, see my chapter (Larsen-Freeman 2002a) in *New Perspectives in Grammar Teaching*, S. Fotos and E. Hinkel, eds. Close (1992) discusses grammatical choices governing the meaning and use dimensions of grammar, although he does not make a distinction between them. Cook (1999) explains why nonnative learners should not be held to native speaker norms. An article entitled "The decline of grammar," written by Geoffrey Nunberg and published in the magazine *Atlantic Monthly* in December, 1983, drew one of the greatest volumes of reader response ever. Mark Halpern's article, entitled "Language: A war that never ends" in the same magazine in March, 1997, continues to fuel the controversy between prescriptivist and descriptivist grammarians.

7

THE GRAMMAR OF DISCOURSE

The fact that we have grammatical options helps us negotiate social relationships. We can choose certain grammar structures over others to express our attitudes, to allocate power, and to establish and maintain our identities, among other things. Understanding the choices that people exercise helps us interpret the intentions of others. As important and overlooked as these choices are, there are several other areas of choice in grammar that need to be considered in order to fully explicate appropriateness in the use dimension. These areas are united by the fact that they all involve the *grammar of discourse*.

To learn about the grammar of discourse, we will examine **texts**, the coherent product of the discursive process. A text is any stretch of language that functions as a whole unit, no matter how brief, even something as short as *No smoking*. However, in this chapter we will be concerned with texts of multiple sentence or utterance length because it is with these that the dynamics of language use can be especially appreciated.

In order to make a full accounting of the article system in English, we needed to consider the use of articles at the suprasentential level. It is not hard to think of other structures that fit into this category. Considerations of when to use personal pronouns, demonstrative determiners and pronouns, and the existential *there* often transcend individual clause or sentence boundaries and depend upon context and **co-text** (the linguistic context). However, there are many other pervasive, yet less commonly realized, linguistic dependencies among sentences or utterances in texts.

See
Chapter 2.

THE ROLE OF GRAMMAR IN TEXTS

In this chapter we will focus on choices that are made to enhance the processability of texts—options that are exercised to assist the listener or reader in interpreting what is being expressed. This will involve an examination of the co-text, the language environment surrounding the structure under scrutiny. One of the reasons that grammar appears arbitrary is that we only look at it at the sentence level. When we adopt a broader perspective we come to realize that there is a lot less arbitrariness than appeared at a narrower perspective. We begin to see the patterns in texts in the way that we can see weather patterns from an aerial photograph or a satellite transmission—patterns that cannot be appreciated from a ground-level perspective.

By elevating our perspective to the level of discourse, we will be able to see five additional roles of grammar, that is, how grammar structures:

1. work to organize a text, to make it *cohesive*;

2. connect ideas, thereby improving the *coherence* of a text;

3. contribute *texture*, making a text whole;

4. work together to create *discourse patterns*; and

5. fulfill *discourse functions*.

7.1

The following seven sentences come from a paragraph that has been scrambled. Unscramble them to restore the paragraph to its original form. Then examine why you put the sentences in the order that you did. What linguistic clues helped you?

1. When all her friends were applying for college admission, my sister went job-hunting.

2. Thus, her grades weren't the reason.

3. You know, she may never go to college, and I guess that's OK.

4. My sister has never wanted to go to college.

5. She did so well that she had many offers.

6. When she was in high school, she was always a good student.

7. She accepted one of them and has been happy ever since.

GRAMMAR AND THE ORGANIZATION OF DISCOURSE

Did your unscrambled paragraph look like this?

> My sister has never wanted to go to college. When she was in high school, she was always a good student. Thus, her grades weren't the reason. When all her friends were applying for college admission, my sister went job-hunting. She did so well that she had many offers. She accepted one of them and has been happy ever since. You know, she may never go to college, and I guess that's O.K.

Even if you did not reproduce this paragraph exactly as I did, your version was probably very close. This may have seemed an easy task, but do not let its ease be deceptive. Stop a moment and consider that from the seven sentences in this paragraph there are 5,040 possible sentence sequences (7x6x5x4x3x2x1). Now are you impressed that we reconstructed the paragraph identically, or at least similarly? In addition to any connection that we were able to make among the propositions, we were enabled to do this by the number of linguistic devices in the paragraph, devices whose purpose is to organize texts.

Units of spoken or written language have an organizational structure of their own. Putting the second or third sentence in this paragraph into initial position would have created an anomaly. We can no more move sentences around in a paragraph (unless we alter them in some way) than we can move words around in a sentence without making other modifications. There is, then, a grammar of discourse.

7.2

As a graduate student I took a course called Experimental Syntax with the eminent linguist Kenneth Pike. One of the heuristic procedures that Professor Pike used in the course was to have us rewrite a paragraph, making the necessary changes to the syntax of sentences in order to preserve the meaning of the original text. This procedure revealed a great deal about the grammar of discourse. Try it yourself. Reorder the sentences of the paragraph in Investigation 7.1 and see what changes you need to make in order to have the paragraph retain its meaning.

Cohesion

Halliday and Hasan (1976; 1989) have pointed to a number of linguistic mechanisms that give cohesion or structure to a text. Each of the following was represented at least once in the paragraph in Investigation 7.1.

- **Reference**
  My sister has never wanted to go to college. When *she*... (*She* refers to *my sister* and contributes to the cohesion among sentences.)

- **Conjunctions**
  ...she was always a good student. *Thus* (*Thus* makes explicit the causal relationship between the second and third sentences.)

- **Substitution**
  ...my sister went job-hunting. She *did* so well ... (*Did* substitutes for *job-hunted.*)

- **Lexical Cohesion**
  ...job hunting. ...*offers.* (We understand *offers* in the context of job-hunting.)

Other common mechanisms that were not illustrated in the paragraph include:

- **Ellipsis**
  A: Who didn't want to go to college?
  B: My sister. (*My sister* elliptically signals *My sister didn't want to go to college.*)

- **Continuatives**
  Still, my sister never wanted to go to college.

- **Adjacency pairs**
  A: Why didn't your sister want to go to college?
  B: She wanted to be independent.

  (An adjacency pair is simply two conversational turns that work together. For example, we expect a question to be followed by an answer, an offer to be followed by acceptance or refusal, etc.)

- **Parallelism**
  My sister didn't want to go to college. Her friends didn't want to get jobs.

In addition to the above cohesive devices, Halliday and Hasan also discuss theme–rheme development and given–new information, which I will elaborate on the following page.

Perhaps it is clear now why I have chosen to call this chapter "the grammar of discourse." Grammar structures contribute greatly to the processability of texts, enabling others to follow or interpret what is being said or written without the speaker's or writer's being overly redundant. However, it is not only cohesion among sentences that a discourse grammar fosters; it is also coherence among ideas.

Coherence

English has fairly fixed word order in sentences; still, variations are possible. For example, here are three of the possible word orderings for a single proposition:

> The Yankees beat the Red Sox despite the fact that Pedro Martinez struck out a record number of Yankee batters.

> Despite the fact that Pedro Martinez struck out a record number of Yankee batters, the Yankees beat the Red Sox.

> The Red Sox were beaten by the Yankees despite the fact that Pedro Martinez struck out a record number of batters.

Again, then, we see that we are dealing with the matter of choice. Of course, I am not suggesting that it is free choice, because presumably one of these will fit better with a certain co-text than the others. For instance,

> What happened to the Red Sox yesterday?

With this as the opening question in a conversation, I would say that the passive, the third sentence, fits best, although the cohesion would be further improved with the use of a co-referential pronoun, *they*, in subject position.

This example illustrates another concept helpful in understanding the organization of text. The concept is the distinction that Hallidayan systemic–functional linguistics, following the Prague School of Linguistics, makes between *theme* and *rheme*. The theme provides the point of departure and offers a framework through which to make sense of what follows in the rheme. A common pattern of development in texts is to first introduce new information in the rheme of one clause, then treat it as given information in the theme of a subsequent clause. *Given information* is that which is assumed by the writer or speaker to be known by the reader or listener. This assumption is made either because the given information has been previously mentioned or because it is in some way shared between the writer/speaker and reader/listener. *New information*, on the other hand, is "newsworthy"—not something the writer/speaker can assume that the reader/listener knows.

Look at this adjacency pair:

> What happened to the Red Sox yesterday?

> They were beaten by the Yankees despite the fact that Pedro Martinez struck out a record number of batters.

In the second sentence, *they* is the given information—information that has already been introduced in the co-text by the questioner. It is made the theme of the reply through the use of the passive voice. The new information is what happened to the Red Sox. We are told this in the rheme of the passive voice sentence.

7.3

Return to your version of the unscrambled paragraph in Investigation 7.1. See if you can see linguistic dependencies of the theme–rheme variety among the sentences.

This pattern of development in this paragraph is often referred to as the Z-shaped pattern of discourse. Why do you think it is given this name?

I have already called attention several times to the tendency to place new information toward the end of a clause, called *end focus,* which presumably aids listeners/readers by directing their attention to the new information. In some informal conversations (data from Hughes and McCarthy, 1998: 272), information is even provided in a slot before the theme, presumably stemming from a sensitivity to what the listener does not know.

> It was strange cos one of the lads I live with, Dave, his parents were looking into buying that pub.

> This friend of ours, his son's gone to Loughborough University.

While such a sentence may appear "ungrammatical," providing some introduction to a new theme is a characteristic pattern in the spoken language of many languages and, according to Hughes and McCarthy, is "presumably a reflection of the exigencies of face-to-face interaction and the real-time nature of talk."

Texture

One way to create texture, a feeling that the text is a coherent whole, is through the use of verb tenses. Veteran language teachers know that the challenge of learning verb tenses is not how to form them (although students do need to know how to do so) and is not what they mean (although students need to know this, too); it is knowing when to use the tenses that is problematic—especially when to use one over another in a particular co-text. The problem is exacerbated by a teaching strategy that presents the tenses one by one without showing students how each fits into a system. The problem is compounded because often new tenses are introduced at the sentence level, obscuring the system operating at the suprasentential level.

7.4

Here is a composition written for pedagogical purposes by Tom Kuehn, an ESL teacher at Portland State University. How would you assess the writer's use of verb tenses?

> I don't know what to do for my vacation. It will start in three weeks. I saved enough money for a really nice trip. I already went to Hawaii. It will be too early to go to the mountains. I worked hard all year. I really need a break.

Now this composition would be considered grammatical by many, and a teacher of English might be pleased if her English students wrote this well. After all, each individual sentence is well formed, the use of tenses is temporally consistent and meaningful. However, Tom created this composition to exemplify a disjointed text. Several factors contribute to its lack of texture, but one of them is that the tense usage violates the maxim that texture is enhanced when we adopt a particular perspective on an event and adhere to that perspective until we are given license to depart from it. If the author of this paragraph had stayed within one axis of orientation—say, for example, the present—the discourse would have been less disjointed and more coherent. Here is Tom's rewrite with a fixed present axis of orientation:

> I don't know what to do with my vacation. It starts in three weeks. I have saved enough money for a really nice trip. I have already been to Hawaii. It is too early to go to the mountains. I have worked hard all year. I really need a break.

While there are still some stylistic infelicities, when you compare the two versions, you see that a number of persistent questions that students have about tense usage can be answered. For instance, the question of when to use the present perfect and when to use the past is at least partially answered by saying that when a writer has adopted a present time frame as the axis of orientation, the present perfect is the appropriate tense, even when, as is the case here with the trip to Hawaii, the event has been completed.

Then, too, the question often comes up of when to use the simple present versus the simple future to express future time in English. You can see that the simple present is being used in the second version to refer to a future event because the writer is viewing it from the vantage point of the present. Questions about tense usage such as these are difficult to answer if you think about tense/aspect as purely a sentence-level phenomenon.

Co-occurring Structures in Discourse

Sometimes a discourse-level perspective can also clear up other grammatical conundrums. For example, consider the difference in English between *used to* and *would*. Again, if we confine our observations to the sentence level, it is difficult to tell them apart; they are both modal forms, they both have a shared meaning of past habit. If, however, we adhere to the heuristic principle that changing the form changes the meaning or use, we should be looking for a difference in use. Although the difference is elusive at the sentence level:

> I used to worry a lot when I was younger.

> I would worry a lot when I was younger.

it is easier to discern at the level of text.

Suh (1992) noticed that the temporally more explicit *used to* tends to mark an episode boundary or set up a frame for a past habitual event, whereas the more contingent form *would* or *'d* supplies details or elaborates the topic, with the simple past also occurring as an alternative to *would*. In the following example from Terkel (1974: 32), cited in Celce-Murcia and Larsen-Freeman (1999), a speaker is complaining about the discrimination he faced as a child in the United States. Notice that *used to* sets the frame, and the details are supplied with *would*:

> The bad thing was they **used to** laugh at us, the Anglo kids. They **would** laugh because we**'d** bring tortillas and frijoles to lunch. They **would** have their nice little compact lunch boxes with cold milk in their thermos and they**'d** laugh at us because all we had was dried tortillas. Not only **would** they laugh at us, but the kids **would** pick fights.

Discourse Function

Another function of tenses in discourse, beyond marking temporality, is to distinguish the main story line from less important information. It has been observed that, in a discourse narrative, certain sentences provide background information while others function in the foreground to carry the main plot. These sentences are often distinguished from each other by verb tenses. For instance, in the following (not very inspired) narrative, the past tense is used for the foregrounded information, the present tense for the background:

> Yesterday I went to the market. It has lots of fruit that I like. I bought several different kinds of apples. I also found that plums were in season, so I bought two pounds of them.

In this short text, the foregrounded past narrative is interrupted by the second sentence with a present tense verb. This second sentence provides information—a statement about the market—that is general background information to the story.

Another example of a discourse function is illustrated by the use of the present perfect as a discourse "bridge." In the following excerpt from a newspaper article, notice how the present perfect (*All that has changed now*) helps form a bridge from the way Chattanooga was a few years ago to the way it is today:

> "Downtown was basically a ghost town," said Rich Bailey, director of the local chamber of commerce's news bureau. "That was a result of economic changes all across the country. Historically, Chattanooga was a manufacturing town, and many of the manufacturers left the city. We had entire blocks with almost empty buildings and parking lots. It was scary."
>
> *All that has changed now.* The air is much cleaner, the warehouses have either been torn down or renovated to accommodate the new businesses, and the Tennessee River waterfront that had once been used for slag heaps and empty coke furnaces is today lush, green and vibrant. (*The Brattleboro Reformer,* July 7, 1999)

Examining the grammar of discourse shows us its function in shaping texts and improving their processability. Further, it suggests that facts about grammar that are elusive at the sentence level—such as the use of the present perfect—begin to make much better sense and are easier to teach at the level of text. As a further demonstration of this, Hughes and McCarthy (1998) point out that the past perfect, which occurs in the last sentence of this excerpt (*that had once been used...*), is often used for discourse-level backgrounding, providing an explanation for the main event, which it does here with a description of Chattanooga prior to its rehabilitation.

A final example of grammar structures that have discourse functions involves the use of *actually*. This is a single adverb in form, and consulting a dictionary tells us that it means *fact* or *reality*. Notice, though, its use at the beginning of the following telephone conversation, an excerpt I have borrowed and modified from Clift (2001):

Ida: *Hello.*

Jenny: *Hello, Ida. It's Jenny.*

Ida: *Hello Jenny. How are things? All right?*

Jenny: *Yes. Fine. Yes. I am ringing up about tomorrow* actually. *I'll do coffee tomorrow morning.*

In this extract, we see that *actually* initiates a topic, the reason for the call. Its function is best understood as part of one turn in a series of turns to organize the structure of the conversation.

SPOKEN GRAMMAR VERSUS WRITTEN GRAMMAR

As this last example is from a conversation, at this point, it would be worth considering to what extent the grammar of written texts differs from that of spoken texts. The grammar of speech is often seen against a written grammar backdrop. It probably makes more sense to see the grammar of speech in its own right than as something less than written grammar. The new electronic availability of spoken language corpora has allowed us to more easily investigate the formerly elusive nature of spoken language. In so doing, certain features of spoken texts become obvious. For instance, face-to-face interaction, where a context is shared, permits a great deal of ellipsis, where parts of a sentence are "omitted" since they can be retrieved from the context. In the following short conversation, I have put the elided material in parentheses:

Joe: *(Do you) Wanna go to the movies?*

Jim: *Sure. (I want to go to the movies)*

Joe: *Which one? (do you want to see)*

Jim: *(It) Doesn't matter.*

As can be seen in this brief exchange, the basic organizational unit of most conversations is short, averaging six words, presumably to relieve pressure on working memory. This is true even when a speaker's turn is much longer, where short chunks are chained together in a simple incremental way for ease of processing. This occurs especially in narratives, where the chunks correspond with intonation units (Chafe, 1987):

You know   I was on my way here   when I ran into Dan.

Earlier in this chapter, I mentioned Hughes and McCarthy's data that show that speakers have a tendency to encode information before the theme in a clause to aid the listener's processing of what is being said. "Tails" (Carter and McCarthy, 1995) that occur at the end of a clause are presumably motivated by the same reason. For example:

Do I stir it first, the tea?

As fascinating and important as these and other characteristics of spoken text are, they provoke the worrisome thought that a spoken grammar and a written grammar constitute two different systems, both of which need to be taught to language students. However, I derive comfort from Leech (2000), who tentatively adopts the position that spoken and written grammars share the same grammatical repertoire, but with different frequencies. Besides, as Leech points out, since features of spoken grammars tend to be found among different languages, students may already possess strategies for handling speech that they can apply to the target language.

See McCarthy, 1998 and Leech, 2000.

CONTEXTUAL ANALYSIS AND CORPUS LINGUISTICS

Now would be a good time to digress a little and explain how I became interested in discourse grammar. The initial stimulus for my interest was my recurring experience with my ESL students. They would produce texts where something was not quite right, but it was sometimes difficult to pinpoint what was wrong, or identify ways to improve it. Later, while working with my colleague at UCLA, Marianne Celce-Murcia, I became interested in contextual analysis, a methodology for studying grammar use in context. Marianne, our students, and I would pore over issues of news magazines, listen to radio talk shows, and skim novels, looking for sufficient instances of a particular grammar structure to show how this structure behaved. Needless to say, it was tedious—though usually rewarding—work.

These days, the rewards can be obtained with much less tedium. Huge corpora of oral and written texts of different languages have been amassed as computer databases that are made available for research purposes. The corpus revolution has meant that researchers have ready access to attested instances of language, enabling them to, among other things, construct performance grammars. Corpus linguists can make use of concordance software to locate and display many instances of the particular pattern, lexical item, or grammar structure that they wish to study. In some cases, corpora of language learner texts are also available. When this is the case, contrastive interlanguage research can take place.

For instance, Lin (2002) found her Hong Kong Chinese students writing paragraphs such as the following:

That's means more graduate students feels hopeless. A lot of graduate students are difficult to find job from 1997–1998. A lot of graduate students need about three months to find first job. Then, some graduate students cannot find first job after?

Lin focused on problems such as the one in the second sentence, which she diagnosed as the common problem of students failing to use an anticipatory *it*. Lin then went to a learner corpus at the Hong Kong Polytechnic University; it consisted of 160,000 words, mainly argumentative essays and reports of students' writing. She compared this to in a corpus from the production of native English speakers, known as LOCNESS (Louvain Corpus of Native English Essays). Through this comparison, she discovered that the Hong Kong students significantly underused *it* compared with native English speakers. Using a concordancing software program, she produced the following three groups of concordances, partial sentences from student essays:

sults show that graduates are **hard** to seek their "perfect job"

s in the black market will be **hard** to control as those criminals

nal factor makes the disabled **hard** to find a job is the economic

ed into the community becomes **difficult** from social public to the ind

lous society. This makes them **difficult** to integrate into the communi

refore, the disabled are very **difficult** to find a job is the economic

her practices the skills were **easy** to be forgotten. Tabl

d that the graduates were not **easy** to have a job which is mush

of the disables, they are not **easy** to do some daily works in the

These concordances showed Lin that many errors related to the underuse of *it* stemmed from students' failure to use an anticipatory *it* with certain common adjectives. For example, the second sentence in the student's paragraph above could be corrected by rewriting it as:

It was difficult for graduate students to find jobs from 1997–1998.

Lin attributes the lack of anticipatory *it* use to the fact that Chinese discourse structure calls for maintaining topic continuity by repeating the topic (topic chaining). In order to maintain a flow of ideas inside a paragraph, the writers transferred a typological feature of Chinese into their English interlanguage, repeating the topic of their paragraph at the beginning of each sentence.

The example of Lin and her Chinese students also speaks to the issue of *intersubjectivity*, in this case, the importance of a teacher's establishing just what it is that the student is trying to express, and why. Lin's knowledge of Chinese helped her in this regard. The importance of understanding "where a student is coming from" is key to helping students express themselves in the manner they intend and in a manner that will assist the listener or reader to interpret their intentions.

The use choices I have discussed in this chapter are important ones. I am certainly not proposing that a discourse grammar should replace a sentence-level grammar, for there are insights into grammar that a sentence-level view affords; however, it is an incomplete view, and sometimes one that is even contradicted at a higher level. The higher level—what I have referred to as an aerial photograph view of grammar—shows the dynamic interplay between expressing one-self and taking into account the way such an expression will be interpreted by one's listener or reader. In this way, a grammar of discourse is constitutive—critical to both text building and text interpretation. Thus, a grammar of discourse reveals the pattern in the path, in the same way that an eddy in a stream is only visible in the flow of water.

Suggested Readings

Work by Celce-Murcia has done much to advance our understanding of the role of grammar at the discourse level. Early on, she wrote of her contextual analysis approach to understanding grammar use (Celce-Murcia, 1980). Since then she has written a lot about grammar and discourse, for example, Celce-Murcia (1991) and (1992). Hughes and McCarthy (1998) is another good source in this regard. Larsen-Freeman, Kuehn, and Haccius (2002) discuss the English verb tense/aspect system and its operation at the level of discourse. Much is being written about corpus linguistics these days (Sinclair, 1991). Good sources for teachers are Partington (1998), McCarthy (2001), and Tan (2002). Biber, Conrad, and Reppen (1998) provide an introduction to corpus linguistics. Hunston and Francis (2000) have written a corpus-driven "lexical grammar."

A number of electronic corpora are available, usually accessible for a modest fee. For a list of corpora of natural spoken English discourse, see Leech (2000). The one with which I am most familiar, the Michigan Corpus of Spoken Academic English (MICASE), a 1.8-million word corpus of oral academic English, is a resource that has been made available without cost on the web by researchers at the English Language Institute, the University of Michigan (www.hti.umich.edu/m/micase). For discussion of a corpus of international English, see Seidlhofer (2001) and for discussion of a corpus of learner English, see Granger (1998) and Granger, Hung and Petch-Tyson (2002).

8

LEARNING GRAMMAR: INSIGHTS FROM SLA RESEARCH AND CONSCIOUSNESS-RAISING

I have spent the last five chapters viewing grammar in a rather unconventional way. No matter how edifying it is to see grammar as a dynamic, complex, rational, flexible, and discursive interconnected system, we still have to answer the "so what?" question: Does seeing it so help our students to learn any better? Whatever our students' purpose is in studying a language, one fact, to which all teachers can testify, remains: There will never be enough time to do all that could be/should be done to help guide students' learning. Of course, my students' and my goals may include more than my students' learning of language. For instance, one of my goals might be to help my students cultivate more positive attitudes toward speakers of the target language. Another might be to motivate my students to want to persist in their study in order to attain higher levels of proficiency. I might seek to help my students increase their awareness of their own language or to enjoy literature written in the target language. No matter what the goals, we are still held to the same standard: Did we achieve our goals to the degree we sought in the time we had available?

This is why I believe it is a myth that grammar can be learned on its own, that it need not be taught. While some people can pick up the grammar of a language on their own, few learners are capable of doing so efficiently, especially if they are postpubescent or if their exposure to the target language is somehow limited, such as might be the case where a foreign language is being acquired. Furthermore, very few learners, even if they have the opportunity to live in a community where the target language is spoken, would learn the grammar as efficiently outside the classroom as they can within it. The point of education is to accelerate the language acquisition process, not be satisfied with or try to emulate what learners can do on their own. Therefore, what works in untutored language acquisition should not automatically translate into prescriptions and proscriptions for pedagogical practice for all learners.

This cautionary note also applies to what we know about native language acquisition or even about the second language acquisition of young learners. While there may be characteristics common to all language acquisition, it is not hard to make a case for a fundamental difference (Bley-Vroman, 1988) between, on the one hand, first language (L1)/early second language (L2)/bilingual acquisition and, on the other hand, older learner/adult L2 acquisition. It is plausible, for instance, that adult second language acquisition depends more upon general problem-solving strategies than upon any specific language acquisition capacity of the sort that has been posited for young language acquirers.

Having said this, I would add that it would nevertheless serve us well to know as much as possible about natural, untutored—as well as tutored—language acquisition in order to better understand how learning may unfold. Indeed, I mean the term *grammaring* to reflect not only a dynamic view of grammar—its over-time evolution and real-time processing, and its sense of being an ability to use structures accurately, meaningfully, and appropriately—but also the dynamic process of its development. Thus the focus of the next three chapters will be on the development of learners' grammar. The specific foci of the three chapters will be "the big three": consciousness-raising (helping to raise students' awareness about grammatical features), practice, and feedback. In this chapter I will briefly review what second language acquisition (SLA) research can tell us in general about the development of learners' grammar. Then I will discuss various proposals from the research community for raising the consciousness of grammar students. In the next chapter I will consider what insights we can gain from research from other disciplines concerning the matter of output practice. And in the third chapter in this sequence on learning, Chapter 10, I will discuss feedback.

Before proceeding, one comment is in order. The language acquisition research I will consider in these chapters takes place in a context different from the one in which you are teaching. Ultimately, it is the particular needs and responses of the students with whom you work and the conditions under which you work every day that will significantly shape your practice. I do not, therefore, see research as the ultimate arbiter of pedagogical practice, though I do see it as giving us one way to interpret the needs and responses of students. Sometimes research findings confirm what experience tells us; at other times they challenge it, not permitting us to get complacent in our thinking or overly routinized in our practice.

It would be impossible to review all the literature that pertains to the acquisition of grammar as, due to its theoretical implications, this issue has been prominent on SLA research agendas for many years. I have therefore been highly selective, simply highlighting some of the relevant themes in the SLA research literature. Finally, since teachers often ask me for insights from SLA research, I have chosen to organize the presentation according to questions that teachers have posed to me.

For other reviews, see Pica, 1994; Doughty and Williams, 1998; Lightbown, 2000.

1. WHAT DOES SLA RESEARCH SAY ABOUT THE PROCESS OF GRAMMAR ACQUISITION IN GENERAL?

Overall, most language acquisition researchers operate under the assumption that grammatical development begins when learners entertain hypotheses about features of the target language. If the researchers' theoretical commitment is to Chomsky's universal grammar (UG), then the "hypotheses" would be seen to arise from an innate UG, consisting of a set of core principles common to all languages, and parameters, which vary among the world's languages. Since Chomsky believes that L1 input is too incomplete and fragmentary to enable children to induce a grammar, the innate principles (increasingly abstract in Chomsky's [1995] minimalist program) are thought to guide the L1 acquisition process. Then, with exposure to language, the parameters of a given principle would be set. (See example below.) Second language learners, on the other hand, would come into contact with a target language with hypotheses about its parameter settings based on the settings for their L1. Their job would be to reset the parameters for the L2 when necessary.

See Larsen-Freeman and Long, 1991 for a discussion of the different types of theories.

Alternatively, if the researchers' theoretical predisposition is more to an environmentalist/empiricist, rather than an innatist UG perspective, hypotheses would not come from an a priori UG but would be generated by learners' analysis of the target language input.

In both cases, the learners would then proceed to subject the hypotheses to the cognitive process of *inferencing*. If the hypotheses about the L2 are derived from L1 parameter settings, the inferencing is said to be *deductive*. In other words, learners approach the L2 with a set of hypotheses about its parameters that either are confirmed by some structural feature in the L2 input, or are not confirmed. If not, the parameter setting would have to be adjusted for the L2. For example, there is a binary parameter in UG that exists because the languages of the world can be divided into two categories: those that allow the subject of a sentence to be dropped when understood from the context (e.g., Spanish *está contenta*, "is happy") and those that do not (e.g., English, *She is happy*.). A Spanish-speaking learner of English would, upon being exposed to English, infer that the (pro-drop) setting of this parameter is different in the second language than in the first and "reset" this parameter for English. This should be relatively easy to do unless the L2 parameter is more marked than that of the L1—that is, unless it is more complex and/or is infrequent among the languages of the world.

Instead of starting with the parameters and deductively seeking confirmatory or disconfirmatory evidence of their settings, empiricists would claim that the inferencing is *inductive*, that is, learners come with no built-in hypotheses; instead, they infer generalizations about the target language on the basis of specific examples. For example, after some exposure to Spanish, a student of Spanish might hypothesize that there are two markers for singular common nouns in Spanish: *la*, which seems to correlate with nouns that end in *-a*, and *el*, for nouns that end in *-o*. The student might go on to "test" this hypothesis by trying to put *la* before other singular nouns ending with *-a*. This hypothesis would be confirmed for many nouns, but if the learner tried it with a noun such as *día* (the Spanish word for *day*), the learner would come to realize that the hypothesis needs to be modified, for *día* takes *el*, not *la*. At this point the learner might either revise the hypothesized rule or correctly infer that *día* is an exception.

Of course, no one believes that learners are scientists, consciously doing all this analysis. Sometimes learners may have explicit hypotheses that they are testing; at other times they may not. Sometimes they may pay attention to relevant evidence—that is, linguistic data; at other times they may not. But overall, from an empiricist's perspective, it is assumed that learners are engaged in construction of the L2 grammar rules, based on inductive inferencing from target language forms.

Inferencing is also the cognitive process used by researchers as they attempt to understand language learners' behavior. When such behavior includes *overgeneralizations* of rules, such as English learners' producing *eated* or *sleeped*, researchers infer that learners have made a generalization based on exposure to many regular English verbs, which are marked with an *-ed* for past tense; that they are trying out these "interlanguage rules" in practice; and that, ultimately, they will notice discrepancies between their own performance and that of others, causing them to reject or adjust their rule for past tense formation.

2. IS THE SLA OF GRAMMAR ALWAYS A MATTER OF FIGURING OUT THE RULES?

A newer approach, called *connectionism*, also relies on inductive inferencing to model learners' performance, but it rejects an account that claims that it is rules that are being induced. Connectionists have developed computer models of networks, which are held to be analogous to the neural networks in the brain. The networks consist of interconnected nodes. The nodes are taken to represent neurons, which are connected with one another through synapses. The computer models are "trained" by receiving massive amounts of target language input. As the language data are taken in, certain connections in the networks are strengthened. Connection weights are thus tunable; they fluctuate from second to second. At any given time, the weights are settling into or moving away from certain states. At any point in the "training" of these computer networks, the distribution of weighted connections represents the network's current map of the structure of the target language.

The networks are *self-organizing*, meaning they organize themselves in response to positive evidence, that is, the patterns in the input. However, some connectionist models use other learning algorithms, such as back propagation, in which connections are weakened when incorrect outputs are produced (i.e., they are "corrected"). In any event, although there is no conscious hypothesis formation of rules occurring, the networks model bottom-up inductive learning, mapping patterns that are present in the input and increasingly approximating the target in response to more and more input.

Another fascinating characteristic of such networks is that sometimes additional strengthening of connections results in output containing overgeneralization errors of the *eated* sort, even though such forms are not present in the input. In other words, the computer simulations appear to be producing rule-governed behavior, even though they do not follow rules—that is, they are not programmed to follow rules. Connectionists have even been able to model the *U-shaped learning curve*, known to exist for English past tense formation, whereby learners' performance on both regular and irregular verbs is initially accurate, then reaches its nadir when learners overgeneralize the regular *-ed* ending to irregular verbs, and finally is restored to accuracy as the learners incorporate the irregular verb forms into their interlanguages. Plunkett and Marchman (1993) have pointed out that the U-shaped function reflects a dynamic competition between regular and irregular past tense verb endings in English.

> As the number of verbs in the competition pool expands across the course of learning, there are shifts in the relative strengths of regular and irregular forms. The U-shaped dip in the learning curve occurs around the point in development in which there is a change in the proportional strength of regular *-ed* compared to other mappings. Thus, sharp changes in behavior can be due to the natural evolution

of a nonlinear system even when the external forces are constant (Elman et al., 1996: 202–203).

Other dynamic systems also experience this dynamic instability or bifurcation point. Referred to in *Chaos/Complexity Theory* as the "camel's back phenomenon," at some point in time "the last straw" is placed and the system undergoes a perturbation. Since such systems are self-organizing, the chaos subsides and new order emerges; the interlanguage has been restructured. A speaker's grammar is thus seen not as a fixed body of rules but rather as "a statistical ensemble of language experiences" (N. Ellis, 2002) that changes every time a new utterance is processed—usually slightly, but on some occasions dramatically.

But connectionism does not merely help to model emergent approximations to the target language. Unlike behaviorists, connectionists are interested in cognitive processes, not just responses to stimuli (Gasser, 1990; McCarthy, 2001). For instance, it is known that "in connectionist networks, items of new information are more easily incorporated when analyzed as variations on known information; new patterns are automatically assimilated to old patterns as much as possible" (Goldberg, 1995: 71). Shirai (1992) therefore suggests that connectionism can illuminate crosslinguistic transfer. When new languages are encountered, the existing representations of L1 or other previously learned languages are activated to reshape the incoming L2 data.

As attractive as connectionist models are, they clearly do not explain all human acquisitional experience. No computer can be programmed to reflect human agency or intentionality. Computers are basically passive; they are not goal-directed. There is no computer program that only selectively attends because it is daydreaming about the upcoming football game and not focusing on the language input. While they provide good models of implicit learning, they do not take into account attention. Because of this, they are slow to learn. Nevertheless, the results so far are intriguing and provide support for a claim I made long ago that frequency in the input is an important factor in second language acquisition (Larsen-Freeman, 1976). It pays to stick around! By the way, none of this redeems the practice of merely subjecting students to abundant comprehensible input, for the reason I gave earlier. It is still our professional responsibility to seek the most efficacious way to acquire a language, and merely providing learners with comprehensible input is not likely to be it (see #7 that follows).

3. WHAT ABOUT PATTERNED SEQUENCES OR LEXICOGRAMMATICAL UNITS?

Connectionist modeling may be very useful in accounting for the acquisition of multiword strings/sequences or lexicogrammatical patterns, especially if Bolinger (1975) is correct that language, rather than being subserved by a rule system, is produced on the basis of "a large, capacious and redundantly structured memory system" (Skehan, 1994: 181).

Well before the advent of computer-driven corpus linguistics, it had become increasingly clear that native speakers of a given language control thousands and thousands of fixed and semi-fixed patterned sequences that behave as single lexical units. Fixed expressions in English, such as "at any rate" and semi-fixed open expressions such as "I'm not at all sure that…" have been credited with contributing a great deal of fluency to English native speaker speech (Pawley and Syder, 1983). In other words, according to Pawley and Syder, every time we speak, our utterances are not created anew by the application of rules, but are at least partly composed of these meaningful, unanalyzed chunks of language, which are retrieved holistically from memory, saving time in planning and carrying out syntactic operations.

Of course, while retrieving patterned sequences from memory might explain real-time language processing, not everyone would accept that acquisition of fixed patterned sequences accounts for all language acquisition. Surely, for example, there must be some generative mechanism that supports linguistic innovation. Although the position is somewhat controversial, some SLA researchers contend that a likely scenario is that learners acquire a stock of fixed and semi-fixed chunks of language, which they later analyze to discover generative grammatical rules (Wong Fillmore, 1976). In the case of first language acquisition, it is possible that the stock of patterned sequences becomes the material on which universal grammar operates (Peters, 1983).

In other words, grammar acquisition may be first characterized as a period of lexicalization, in which learners use prefabricated sequences or chunks of language, followed by a period of syntacticization, in which learners are able to infer a creative rule-governed system. The sequence may conclude with a period of relexicalization, in which learners, like native speakers, use patterned sequences to produce accurate and fluent speech (Skehan, 1994). This sequence may not characterize the learning of all L2 learners, though. It is possible, for example, that some second language learners, having satisfied their communicative needs, will stop at the lexicalization stage. Then, too, more analytically inclined learners may push quickly into the syntacticization phase, while more memory-oriented learners may tend to treat language more in terms of chunks.

This is not to suggest that these processes are mutually exclusive in language users. In fact, some believe that both memorization and rule-governed processes operate. For instance, positron emission tomography (PET) scans have shown different patterns of brain activation for human subjects asked to produce past tense of English regular and irregular verbs (Jaeger et al., 1996). From this finding, the researchers draw support for Pinker and Prince's (1994) dual-systems hypothesis, which proposes that regular past tense is computed by rule and past tense forms of irregular verbs are computed by activating some aspect of lexical memory.

However, some believe that a dual mechanism account is unnecessary and argue against its application to SLA (e.g., Murphy, unpublished manuscript). The fact that different areas of the brain are activated offers no insight into functional differences. Besides, Jaeger et al.'s methodology is flawed, it is claimed. And even if there is a processing difference between regular and irregular forms, it may have less to do with the regular–irregular difference and more to do with their different frequencies of occurrence in the input (Seidenberg and Hoeffner, 1998). Indeed, research by N. Ellis and Schmidt (1998) suggests that both regular and irregular forms can be accounted for by associative memory using a simple connectionist model.

In sum, there may be a lot of truth to the statement that what we humans do is "push old language into new" (Becker, 1983), or retrieve chunks of language from our memories of discourse and reconfigure them in novel, principled ways. How we do this, of course, is the big question.

See Hatch's (1974) distinction between *rule formers* and *data gatherers* and Peters' (1977) *gestalt* versus *analytic* as depicting different learning styles.

4. How are patterned sequences reconfigured to produce new forms?

Just how are new forms to be reconfigured from an acquired stock of patterned sequences? No one knows for sure, but perhaps the philosopher C. S. Peirce's concept of *abduction* offers an explanation. I first learned about abduction in a talk given in 1990 by John Oller at the Georgetown University Round Table on Languages and Linguistics. I listened very keenly to what Oller had to say that day because it seemed to me even then that abduction might represent a missing link in the hypothesis-testing model of SLA. After all, with deduction, hypothesis space is defined from the start by a set of principles. With induction, while patterns in the input are revealed, there are no built-in principles to explain why the data pattern as they do, and Chomsky has argued that, given time constraints, a learner cannot possibly test all possible explanations. Therefore, to my way of thinking, a different type of inferencing would seem to be needed to complement induction—and this could be abduction. The function of abduction is to identify the explanations that are most likely to be fruitful in accounting for a given pattern of data. Abduction involves after-the-fact reasoning in order to determine why something happened as it did. Learners of a language, for example, attempt to make sense of the input forms, fitting the new forms into the network of interrelated constructions or patterns that constitutes their knowledge of language (Goldberg, 1995: 71).

8.1

The following are illustrations of deduction, induction, and abduction, based on Yu (1994). After reading the examples, see if you can understand why Yu writes that abduction creates, deduction explicates, induction verifies.

Figure 8.1 **Illustrating Deduction, Induction, and Abduction**

Deduction	*Induction*	*Abduction*
All As are Bs.	A1, A2, A3...A100 are B.	The surprising phenomenon X is observed.
C is B.	A1, A2, A3...A100 are C.	Among A, B, and C, A is capable of explaining X.
Therefore, C is A.	Therefore, B is C.	Hence, there is reason to pursue A.

An example may help your understanding of abduction of new forms from patterned sequences. Data from a study by Myles, Hooper, and Mitchell (1998) show that their subjects, students of French, began by learning a number of set formulas or patterns. One such pattern was *j'aime*, the contracted form for the English *I like*. Since it was a fixed pattern, the students would use it correctly to refer to themselves, but incorrectly overextend or overgeneralize it to refer to others. For example, they would say *Richard j'aime le musée* (*Richard I like the museum*) for *Richard likes the museum*. Eventually, most of the learners, although not all, "unpacked" the *j'aime* chunk. Presumably they encountered other patterns that did not conform to their knowledge/use of the language. There was thus a disconnect between what they were saying and the patterns they were hearing. In order to make sense of the input, they had to entertain the most plausible explanation to account for the data. The need to establish explicit reference (third person, in particular) apparently triggered the breakdown of the chunk and the acquisition of other subject pronouns by analogy.

5. MY STUDENTS' LANGUAGE SEEMS TO BE CONSTANTLY FLUCTUATING; ONE DAY THEY SEEM TO HAVE IT, THE NEXT DAY THEY DON'T.

A common observation in SLA research is that the language that learners produce, their *interlanguage* (IL), changes rapidly. Thus, ILs exhibit a high degree of variability. Sometimes learners use one form for a given meaning, sometimes another, although both may be non-targetlike. This does not mean, however, that ILs are constructed arbitrarily any more than are other natural languages. For instance, certain UG-oriented SLA researchers find evidence of learners adhering to the abstract principles of universal grammar, although researchers are not of one mind with regard to how accessible UG principles are to second language learners as compared to first language learners (cf., for example, Hawkins, 2001 with White, forthcoming). Other researchers find that learners systematically rely on their knowledge of their L1 to compensate for their underdeveloped L2 proficiency. Still others seek and find evidence that learners are testing hypotheses and systematically applying particular learning strategies when they produce the target language.

8.2

Examine the following data from a Hmong-speaking adult learner of ESL studied by Huebner (1980, cited in Larsen-Freeman and Long, 1991). The assumed glosses appear in parentheses following the learner's utterances. What hypothesis do you think the learner may be testing?

Waduyu kam from? (Where are you from?)

Waduyu kam Tailaen? (How did you come to Thailand?)

Waduyu kam? (Why did you come?)

Waduyu sei? (What did you say?)

Does it make sense to you to consider the SLA process one of hypothesis formation and testing? Why or why not?

Besides its variability and its systematicity, another striking feature of learners' IL is its *nonlinearity*. Although we sometimes treat interlanguage metaphorically as a path traversed by learners journeying from the L1 to the L2, learners' grammars do not, of course, develop in such a linear fashion. Learners do not tackle structures one at a time, first mastering one and then turning to another. Even if we have evidence that learners have "acquired" a rule, there is no guarantee that they will apply it consistently.

Furthermore, even when learners appear to have mastered a particular aspect of the target language, and even when they sustain the same degree of effort, it is not uncommon to find backsliding occurring when new forms are introduced. For instance, it has been commonly observed that students of Spanish who know the preterite tense reasonably will regress in their performance on the preterite when they first encounter the imperfective. It is not until the learners have sorted out the differences between the two, and their internal grammars have been restructured to capture the difference, that their performance improves. Assuming, then, that the conditions of learning are propitious, accurate formation of the target structure is eventually restored. Such being the case, we might characterize the learning as more wavelike than linear stagelike.

The following is a quotation from an article in the *Science News*. It describes the learning in general of children, but it could just as easily be describing SLA:

> Traditional developmental researchers want to narrow down children's various attempts at solving specific problems. In experiments to explore learning, these scientists weed out such variability so that they can discern typical, age-specific thinking strategies. Such studies portray kids as moving, one step at a time, from simpler to more complex types of thought.
>
> On closer inspection, this developmental staircase vanishes like a statistical mirage.... Microgenetic [looking more closely at particular children's performance in an attempt to detect the origin of a given form or strategy] evidence shows that children usually make mental advances by riding "overlapping waves" of learning strategies.... At any one time, some strategies are cresting, some are waning, some are gaining renewed force, and new ones are forming just below the surface of conscious deliberations (*Science News*, March 17, 2001, p. 172).

This is no less true of SLA. At any one time a learner's interlanguage may include many overlapping forms. Such is the case, for example, in the development of English negation, where learners may be using *he no go, he don't go,* and *he doesn't go*—all at the same point in time. However, if we were to inspect the overall genesis and use of these forms, we might discover that the second type of negation was predominant, with the first and third representing earlier and later strategies, what have been called *trailing patterns* and *scouting patterns*, respectively. Or we might find that the learner is experiencing tension between a lexicalized phase (*he don't go* on analogy with the chunk *I don't know*) and a syntactic phase (where through abduction the learner has analyzed *don't* into its component parts of *do + not* in its third person singular present tense form). Still another possibility is that the communicative task demands too much of learners' attention for them to be able to perform syntactic operations, so they rely on their lexical knowledge to get by in the moment. In any event, the variation exhibited in learners' production at one point in time may encapsulate the variation of the same learners over time.

Paradoxically, although the overall language acquisition process is nonlinear, there remains evidence of common developmental sequences for specific aspects of grammar to which all learners adhere. In addition to the attested sequence for English negation, there have been many others in English and other languages. For instance, word order in German sentences was widely studied in the 1970s and 1980s by German researchers (Meisel, Clahsen and Pienemann, 1981). Such researchers found a developmental sequence to which learners of German adhered. They didn't abandon one interlanguage rule for another; they accumulated rules, adding new ones while retaining the old. Here are three of the attested stages.

Verb separation—nonfinite verbal elements are moved to clause-final position in a number of linguistic contexts, for example, *Morgen Abend rufe ich dich nochmals an.* (Tomorrow evening call I you once again up.)

Inversion—finite verb form precedes the subject of its clause in certain linguistic contexts, for example, *Wann gehen wir ins Kino?* (When go we into the cinema?)

Verb-end—finite verbs are placed in final position in all subordinate clauses, for example, *Ich trank das Glas Milch als ich den Brief schrieb.* (I drank the glass of milk while I the letter wrote.)

It is important to note that instruction can accelerate the overall rate of acquisition, but developmental sequences seem to be impervious to instruction. For instance, R. Ellis (1989) found that students learning German word-order rules applied the rules in their interlanguage in the sequence established above, no matter how much instructional emphasis each was given.

As the learners proceed through developmental sequences, the learning process is gradual. As we have seen, learners do not master forms with their first encounter. Even if they start using the form soon thereafter, its use might not coincide with its target language function. For this reason, we have been urged to view learners' interlanguage as a developing system in its own right, a *basic variety* (Klein and Perdue, 1997), not as a deficient form of the target language (Bley-Vroman's [1983] *comparative fallacy*). Acquisition is a gradual process involving the mapping of form, meaning, and use. Form–meaning–use correspondences do not simply first appear in the interlanguage in target form. Unfortunately, sometimes non-target forms remain in a "frozen" form in learners' interlanguage, the result of **fossilization**, which I will discuss further in Chapter 10.

6. WHAT CAN MY STUDENTS LEARN FROM EACH OTHER?

So far in this chapter I have discussed many considerations affecting individual language acquisition. This is understandable, given the psycholinguistic origin of the field. Also, from your reading so far, it should not surprise you to learn that I majored in psychology as an undergraduate student. Even then, I was intrigued by the question of how people learned. Nevertheless, I have also been aware of the social-contextual dimension of the language acquisition process for a long time due to work by Tarone (1979), Beebe (1980), and others. Of course, I have long believed that language acquisition takes place through some sort of interaction, and indeed some of the leading "psychologically oriented" theorists make interaction their centerpiece. As Hatch has often been quoted as saying, "one learns how to do conversation, one learns how to interact verbally and out of this interaction syntactic structures are developed" (1978: 409). Hatch cites *vertical structures,* such as the following from L1 data, as evidence in support of this proposition:

Child: *Kimby*
Mother: *What about Kimby?*
Child: *Close*

The typical vertical structure is a joint construction, here of a mother and her child. The child nominates a topic, the mother seeks elaboration, and the child responds. As the child's ability progresses, the child's initial turn is longer including both topic and comment; thus the child's ability to construct an utterance moves from "vertical" collaboration to "horizontal" autonomous production.

Vygotsky's sociocultural theory, which has had increasing influence on SLA research, is even more explicit about the essential role of social interaction. Vygotsky (1989: 61) asserts that "social interaction actually produces new, elaborate, advanced psychological processes that are unavailable to the organisms working in isolation." The metaphor of *scaffolding* is used for the means by which this is brought about. Through social interaction, knowledgeable participants (teachers or fellow students) can create supportive conditions where students of lesser proficiency can participate, even solve a problem that they could not solve on their own. According to Wood, Bruner, and Ross (1976) (in Donato, 1994: 40–41), the supportive conditions include:

1. recruiting interest in the task
2. simplifying the task
3. maintaining pursuit of the goal
4. marking critical features and discrepancies between what has been produced and the ideal solution
5. controlling frustration during problem solving, and
6. demonstrating an idealized version of the act to be performed.

Through their participation in a scaffolded interaction, students of lesser proficiency can extend their current skills and knowledge to higher competence (Donato, 1994: 40). In other words, they can jointly construct with their more knowledgeable partner a *zone of proximal development* (ZPD), "the distance between the actual developmental level as determined by independent problem solving and the level of potential development as determined through problem solving under adult guidance or in collaboration with more capable peers" (Vygotsky, 1978: 86).

The following data, extracted from a Japanese lesson for elementary school students, illustrates scaffolding (Takahashi, 1998: 399). The English translation for the Japanese utterances is on the right:

Japanese	English
T: Hai. ([Teacher] shows a picture of a man eating an apple.)	T: Here you go.
S1: Denisu wa ringo o tabemasu. Masu!	S1: Dennis eats an apple. Eats!
T: Denisu wa ringo o tabemasu, ii desu ne. Mary? (Calling on S2, named Mary.)	T: Dennis eats an apple. Good. Mary?
(Teacher shows a picture of a boy who is thinking about eating an apple.)	
S2: Denisu wa ringo o tabe...	S2: Dennis an apple...ea
T: Tabe...?	T: Ea...?
S2: Tabemasu.	S2: He eats.
S3 (directed to S2): Tabetai. Tabemasu. Tabemasen.	S3: He wants to eat. He eats. He doesn't eat.
(S2 is silent.)	
(Teacher begins singing the "I want" song.)	T: Remember this song? Tai, tai, tai.
T/Ss: Ta tai, tai, nomitai, tabetai, hon yomitai, netai, kaitai, terebi mitai.	T/Ss: I want, I want, I want to drink, want to eat, want to read, want to buy, want to watch TV.
T: Haaaai, tabetai! Ii desu ka? Tabetai.	T: Goooood! He wants to eat! All right? He wants to eat.
Ss: Tabetai.	Ss: He wants to eat.
T: Tabetai, hai, Mary?	T: He wants to eat. Here you go. Mary?
S2: Denisu wa ringo o tabetai.	S2: Dennis wants to eat an apple.
T: Hai, ii desu ne!	T: Yes. That's great!

In her initial turn, S2 (Mary) begins to use the same verb form as S1. However, the teacher is showing a different picture, so she should no longer be using the verb form for *eats* but the form for *wants to eat*. S3 apparently intends to remind Mary of verb conjugations that they have learned before. When Mary still does not respond, the teacher and the students sing a song that features the *want to* form of many verbs. After assistance from the teacher and students, Mary produces the correct form of the verb. Takahashi states that although Mary's actual developmental level did not allow her to accomplish this linguistic task, guidance from her peers and her teacher allowed her to outperform her present competence (see Cazden, 1981). In this way, learning and teaching were realized as a co-constructed process within the child's zone of proximal development, and teacher and peers, rather than being suppliers of input, are cast in the role of joint constructors of the arena for development. In sum, the origin of the individual's higher mental functions is situated in the dialectical processes embedded in the social context (Vygotsky, 1978 in Donato, 1994: 45–46).

7. WHAT DOES THE EVIDENCE SAY ABOUT THE VALUE OF TEACHING GRAMMAR IN ACCELERATING OR COMPLEMENTING THE NATURAL PROCESS?

One influential SLA researcher, Stephen Krashen (1981; 1982), would answer this question by saying that explicit grammar instruction has very little impact on the natural acquisition process because studying grammar rules can never lead to their unconscious deployment in fluent communication. This position has been referred to as the *non-interface* position because of the claim that there is little or no interaction between conscious, *explicit learning* and *implicit learning*, or acquisition that takes place without conscious operations. According to Krashen, the only way for students to acquire grammar is to get exposure to comprehensible input in the target language, finely tuned to their level of proficiency. Krashen believes that if the input is understood and there is enough of it, the necessary grammar will automatically be acquired.

Many other researchers dispute this claim. In support of the argument for the necessity of attention to linguistic form, Long (Schmidt, 1994: 176) cites the fact that adults often fail to incorporate basic target structures into their interlanguage, despite their prolonged exposure to comprehensible input. Another consequence is premature stabilization of their interlanguages. After conducting a meta-analysis of research studies conducted during the last twenty years, Norris and Ortega (2000) conclude that focused L2 instruction results in large target-oriented gains, that explicit types of instruction are more effective than implicit types, and that instructional effects are durable. Since it is central to the focus of this book, it is worth highlighting the work of Lightbown and Spada from among the studies reviewed. They found that teachers who integrate grammar lessons into their communicative teaching are more effective than teachers who never work on grammar or who do so only in decontextualized grammar lessons (Spada and Lightbown, 1993; Lightbown, 1998). Finally, White (1987) also counters Krashen's claim by proposing that it is actually *incomprehensible* input that stimulates the necessary grammar building, not *comprehensible* input. When the learner cannot parse the input, a restructuring of the grammar to account for the input is motivated.

It is particularly telling that in the case of immersion students in Canada, who have abundant opportunity to receive comprehensible input in French, the students' performance nevertheless falls short of what one might expect. While the children make great strides in French, they still commit some fundamental morphosyntactic errors, calling into serious question the assumption that just being exposed to the language is sufficient to enable students in classroom situations to acquire accurate production skills. An explanation for the basic morphosyntactic errors committed by immersion students is that the students have created a classroom dialect from the self-reinforcing nature of peer interlanguage. As a counterpoint to what has just been discussed about the benefits of peer–peer interaction, this explanation would argue against the unremitting use of such interaction.

Indeed, Higgs and Clifford (1982), drawing on their many years of teaching foreign language, warn that unmonitored practice of inaccurate language forms can actually cause fossilization. Learners acquire certain ungrammatical forms in their interlanguage that are extremely difficult to dislodge. Thus most SLA researchers concur on the need to teach grammar. However, they advise doing so by "focusing on form" within a meaning-based or communicative approach in order to avoid a return to a "focus on forms" approach in which language forms are studied in isolation (Long, 1991).

Incidentally, although I welcome the calls and the empirical support behind efforts to focus on form within a communicative approach, I do feel that the term "focusing on form" is misleading because its shorthand suggests that teaching/learning grammar is all about teaching/learning form, which, I believe, underestimates what is involved in the acquisition of grammar especially, although not exclusively, by ignoring the dimensions of meaning and use.

8. WHAT PEDAGOGICAL PRACTICES FOR GRAMMAR TEACHING ARE SUBSTANTIATED BY RESEARCH FINDINGS?

Very few form-focused practices have been thoroughly substantiated. This is in part because the research remains in its infancy. It is also because it is thought better to be cautious than to return to a pure focus on forms. Nevertheless, in the interest of raising awareness concerning researchers' agendas, I will discuss some pedagogical practices that I have culled from the research literature.

Significantly, much of SLA research has centered on consciousness-raising practices as opposed to grammar production activities. Rutherford and Sharwood Smith (1988) were among the first SLA researchers to discuss the long-held assumption that raising students' consciousness about target language rules facilitates language acquisition. In doing so they left the definition of *consciousness-raising* broad enough to embrace a continuum ranging from mere exposure to grammatical phenomena at the one end to explicit pedagogical rule articulation at the other. Within this broad range, a variety of practices have been investigated.

Promoting Noticing

In a study of his own acquisition of Portuguese in Brazil, SLA researcher Richard Schmidt observed that he was not able to assimilate a new linguistic item until he first noticed it (Schmidt and Frota, 1986). In other words, in order for the new item to become intake, he had to first attend to it in the input.

Karen Stanley, an ESL teacher in a community college in the United States, describes the various levels of awareness she experienced in her acquisition of items in a new language:

Karen Stanley

1. I am unaware of an item.
2. I become aware of an item (either through being told about it or through noticing that someone else's production is different from my own).
3. In production, I catch myself right after a non-use situation, and self-correct.
4. In production, I catch myself in the middle of production, and self-correct.
5. I catch myself before production, and produce the "correct" form.
6. I produce the pattern without thinking about it at all.

I do not mean that these "stages" are clearly separate from each other. Depending on stress, time available, fatigue, etc., these different "points" overlap; I regress so to speak. [However,] I still clearly remember the first time I became aware that the Greek subjunctive had sprung out of my mouth without my thinking or being aware of it until afterward, and I was so shocked at my success that I had to go back and check to see that the automatic usage had, indeed, been correct. It had been. I felt triumphant.

For example, see McLaughlin, Rossman, and McLeods (1983), Tomlin and Villa (1994), Simard and Wong (2001).

Few learners are as in touch with their learning processes as Stanley. Nevertheless, her experience speaks to the power of noticing in SLA. Unfortunately, the terminology surrounding *noticing* is particularly murky in the SLA literature, with some using *noticing* interchangeably with *awareness, consciousness, detection,* and *attention.* Still, although there is disagreement over how many types of attention there are, most SLA researchers acknowledge the value of promoting noticing, some even considering it a necessary condition to convert input into intake in order for learning to take place (Schmidt, 1990).

Thus focusing on form is said to be of benefit because it helps guide learners' particular attentional resources. Now, there are a number of ways in which this can happen. For example, simply presenting students with a traditional explanation of some grammar structure might prime their subsequent noticing. *Priming* makes a second instance of a phenomenon more readily accessible without necessarily bringing its learning back to conscious attention (Stevick, 1996). Another way this is talked about in the SLA literature is using the term "trace." When learners notice a structure, they are said to store a trace, which will help them to process the structure more fully at a subsequent time (R. Ellis, 1993a). Less explicit, less obtrusive means of focusing students' attention on form are to underscore, use boldface, use different fonts, use color, and so forth to heighten the saliency of some particular grammatical feature in written texts, thereby presumably drawing learners' attention. Also fitting into this category is an *input flood,* that is, exposing learners to texts with particularly high frequencies of the target structure. Of course, all teachers can do is enhance the input (Sharwood Smith, 1993); they cannot guarantee that learners will actually notice and take in what the teachers have in mind.

Consciousness-Raising Tasks

I have already discussed exposure under the heading of ways to promote noticing. The other end of the consciousness-raising continuum, explicit rule articulation, has been investigated by Fotos and Ellis (1991), who have designed consciousness-raising tasks for this purpose. In these tasks, learners worked interactively in small groups to solve grammar problems in the target language. Fotos (1993) showed that learners are more likely to notice target structures in consciousness-raising tasks than when not directed in any way toward the target (i.e., in purely communicative tasks) and that learning outcomes in consciousness-raising tasks where students figure out the rules are as least as effective as students' being given the rules.

Here is an example adapted from Fotos and Ellis (1991: 626) of a consciousness-raising task:

> Put students in groups of four. Hand each group a set of cards.
> For example:
>
> 1. *Correct*   The teacher pronounced the difficult word for the class.
> 2. *Incorrect*   The teacher pronounced the class the difficult word.
> 3. *Correct*   I bought many presents for my family.
> 4. *Correct*   I bought my family many presents.
>
> Students are told that different verbs may have their objects in different orders. In groups they are to study the correct and incorrect English sentences, then work together to decide where the direct and indirect objects can be located for the verbs in their sentences.

Thus these consciousness-raising tasks work to make students aware of specific features of the target language by figuring out for themselves the properties of these features.

Perhaps the experienced teacher of EFL in Malta in Borg's (1998) study put it most cogently when he said:

> I find that when I learn languages I like finding out about rules myself. It helps me if I can perceive patterns, it really helps me. And I think that's true for many students, and I think it's part of their expectations too. And I see it as part of my role to help them to become aware of language rules...whenever possible, yes. And lying behind that is the rationale that if they can be guided towards a reformulation of a rule through largely their own endeavours, it is more likely to be internalised than if it was explained to them.

Input Processing

VanPatten's (1996) theory of input processing holds that processing instruction is key to development of learners' IL systems. In input processing, learners are guided to pay particular attention to a feature in the target language input that is likely to cause a processing problem, thereby increasing the chances of the feature's becoming *intake*, "that subset of filtered input that the learner actually processes and holds in working memory during on-line comprehension." (Van Patten, 2002: 761). Since humans are limited in their processing capacity, and since, according to VanPatten, learners cannot attend to the content and the form of a message simultaneously, they need assistance in attending to a selective subset of the input. Input-processing tasks seek to alter the way in which learners perceive and process the input by pushing learners to attend to form differently than they would with their L1.

Here is an example of an input-processing task designed by Cadierno (1992) and discussed in Doughty and Williams (1998).

For this task, students are shown a picture and are asked to imagine that they are one of the characters in the picture. They have to listen to a sentence in the target language and to select the picture that best matches.

For example, the target language is Spanish and the students hear:

Te busca el señor. ("The man is looking for you.")

Later when viewing two more pictures, the students hear:

Tú buscas al señor. ("You are looking for the man.")

English speakers use word order to determine subjects and objects. Presumably, however, with information about differences in Spanish and with enough of this input-processing practice, students will learn to discern the difference in meaning, and that distinguishing subjects from objects requires paying attention to the ends of words and to small differences in the function words themselves (e.g., *te* vs. *tú* and *el* vs. *al*).

Collaborative Dialogues

Thus far I have discussed noticing, consciousness-raising, and input processing, but have made no mention of output practicing. We will later see that the value of output practice is rather controversial. However, a role for speaking, which relates to consciousness-raising, has been proposed by Swain (1985; 1995). Swain has argued that learners need to produce the language in order to notice the gap between what they want to say and what they are able to say. Production forces learners to pay attention to the form of intended messages. By doing so they will recognize the areas where they have problems and will seek out relevant input in a more focused way.

In keeping with sociocultural theory is the use of *collaborative dialogues* for promoting learners' attention to form. As learners work together, they are able to use the language and reasoning of others both to expand their knowledge of the language and to regulate their own cognitive functioning.

In the following excerpt from Swain and Lapkin (1998: 332), two learners of French, Rick and Kim, discuss the verb *sortir*, which does not take the reflexive form in French. Rick begins, hesitates, and then seeks guidance from Kim as to the form of the verb.

Rick: Un bras...wait...mécanique...sort?

Rick: An arm...wait...a mechanical [arm] comes out?

Kim: Sort, yeah.

Kim: Comes out, yeah.

Rick: Se sort?

Rick: Comes out [itself]? [incorrect reflexive form]

Kim: No, sort.

Kim: No, comes out. [correct nonreflexive form]

Having to produce the French sentence causes Rick to discover what he does not know and to seek Kim's focused feedback in order to co-construct the sentence. In this way, as Swain and Lapkin note, their dialogue serves as a tool both for L2 learning and for communicating with each other. In Kim and Rick's language use, the processes of language learning and communication are simultaneous.

Instructional Conversations or Prolepsis

Another name for a scaffolding-teaching process is *instructional conversation* (Tharp and Gallimore, 1988) or *prolepsis*. I like the concept of proleptic teaching because I now have a name for what I have done as a teacher for many years. I used to think that my teaching approach was inductive. I used a discovery process—some might call it a constructivist approach—to encourage students to come to their own understanding of a particular linguistic point. However, I now believe that prolepsis is a more apt description than either of these for what I do. Prolepsis requires teacher and students to achieve a degree of intersubjectivity, which makes it possible for the teacher to guide the student and for the student to be guided through the process of completing a task. In other words, both teacher and student try to come to an understanding of how each of them views the task and its solution, with the goal of helping the student reshape and extend his or her use of language.

Here is an example of proleptic instruction being used in a French lesson (data from Donato and Adair-Hauck, 1992):

T: *You have chosen number 10 then? It's on the outside of the car.*

(S1 writes "de l'essuie" [pauses] "de" [pauses])

Ss: *Oh no, no…*

T (to S1): *Write what you think it is.*

(S1 hesitates. He begins to erase "essuie.")

T: *That's it. You have it, "essuie."*

(S1 writes "essuie de glace.")

T: *That would make sense, but it's shorter. What would it be?*

S1: *Hyphen.*

T: *Hypen.*

(Student writes "essuie-glace.")

T: *Yes, "essuie-glace."*

We see that the teacher uses several ways to engage the student in the task of writing the French for *windshield wiper*. First, the teacher encourages the student to stay involved, to ignore what the other students say and to go with his own sense of what is right. She marks the critical features of the problem for him. She does not give him the answer or solve the linguistic form problem for him, but coaches him to do so. Thus, through proleptic instruction, formal instruction can take on an evolving and dynamic relationship embodied in the discourse.

Community Language Learning Dialogues

See a discussion of this method and others in Larsen-Freeman, 2000a.

Based on principles from Carl Rogers' humanistic psychology, Charles Curran developed a language teaching method called Community Language Learning. One of the tenets of this approach to language teaching is to provide for learner security. One way to do this is to have students choose for themselves what they wish to learn to say in the target language. The students first speak in their native language, what they say is translated, and then they are recorded speaking the translations. Next, a transcript of the recording is made and the native language equivalents are added. Then students are invited to reflect on the transcribed dialogue. They can ask questions about what they observe.

I have found this to be a particularly good way in which to raise consciousness because, since learners generated the dialogue, they are invested in it. Furthermore, they know the meaning of what they have said in the L2. What is left for them to focus on is how the target language forms are mapped onto the meaning in an appropriate manner.

A related pedagogical approach that has been used to teach literacy is the Language Experience Approach (LEA). In the LEA, students dictate to the teacher something that they want to express accurately in the target language. As the teacher writes down what the student is saying, the teacher modifies it so that it adheres to the grammatical conventions of the target language. Students can then compare what they said with what the teacher has written in order to raise their consciousness about target language features.

9. SHOULD I GIVE MY STUDENTS EXPLICIT RULES?

I argued in Chapter 2 that it was a mistake to equate the teaching of grammar with giving students grammatical rules. However, I did not, and would not, deny that there might be merit to explicit rule-giving as one means of teaching grammar. Although the results of research conducted to date are somewhat mixed, the trend does favor giving students explicit rules if the rules are relatively straightforward. If the rules are complex, students may be better off being exposed to examples rather than to an explicit rule, or to a combination of an explicit rule and carefully considered examples. Nevertheless, research by Carroll and Swain (1993) suggests that even complex rules may be helpful if they are given to students after they commit errors that knowledge of the rule might have averted.

Researchers have also speculated that acquisition of certain aspects of an L2 may require more conscious explicit instruction. This may be true, for instance, of particular L1 and L2 differences where an L2 feature is more marked than the L1. It may also be true with pragmatic differences, or what I have been calling differences of use, which are not as salient as more formal grammar phenomena. Another category that explicit knowledge may help with is particular patterned sequences, that is, lexicogrammatical units and collocations.

Rejecting polarized views of explicit provision versus implicit inferencing of rules, Adair-Hauck, Donato, and Cumo-Johanssen (2000) carve out a middle ground. Rather than the teacher providing the learner with explanations, or the learners being left to analyze the grammar explanation implicitly for themselves, Adair-Hauck, Donato, and Cumo-Johanssen recommend that teachers and learners collaborate on and co-construct the grammar explanation. From the vantage point of a Vygotskyan approach to instruction, they suggest that a guided participatory approach to rule formulation is the best procedure.

Of course, verbal rules are not the only way to capture generalizations about the language and to make important relationships salient, and, in fact, verbal rules have the distinct disadvantage that students have to be able to process language in order to understand the rule. Other, perhaps more direct approaches that make generalizations explicit include the use of charts, formulas (S+V+O), or iconic devices, such as scales (e.g., showing the degree of probability that certain modal verbs convey), or even pictures to show such things as the relationship among spatial prepositions.

With this caveat, I will leave MacWhinney to sum up my position on the giving of explicit instruction:

> Students who receive explicit instruction as well as implicit exposure to forms, would seem to have the best of both worlds. They can use explicit instruction to allocate attention to specific types of input…, narrow their hypothesis space…, tune the weights in their neural networks,…or consolidate their memory traces. …From the viewpoint of psycholinguistic theory, providing learners with explicit instruction along with standard implicit exposure would seem to be a no-lose proposition (MacWhinney, 1997: 278).

10. SHOULD I USE LINGUISTIC TERMINOLOGY (METALANGUAGE) WITH MY STUDENTS?

When verbal rules are employed, a corollary issue of fundamental concern to teachers is raised: whether or not—and if so, to what degree—to use explicit metalinguistic terminology with students. I know of no SLA study that has resolved the matter with regard to the efficacy of language acquisition, and as Sharwood Smith (1993) has noted, its use is still an empirical question. As Alison d'Anglejan pointed out long ago (Lightbown, personal communication), some languages (e.g., French) would be almost impossible to write correctly without a knowledge of some explicit grammar terms. For example, the masculine and feminine forms often sound the same (*bleu*, masculine for *blue*, and *bleue*, feminine), so that the concept of masculine and feminine gender and the associated grammatical markers would be needed to disambiguate them.

As far as teachers are concerned, there appears to be a range of views, with some teachers feeling that the use of metalanguage provides a useful shortcut to refer to grammatical phenomena, while others feel that the proliferation of grammatical terminology only adds to students' learning burden. Here is what some teachers from Borg's (1999) study have to say about the matter of using linguistic terms with students.

Hannah, a 27-year-old native speaker of English who has taught EFL for four years, answers the question of whether she ever labels grammar structures in her approach to teaching grammar in this way:

Teachers' Voices

Hannah, Martha, Tina

> My God, no. Why is it necessary? I don't do it because I don't really think that it's necessary. I could write it up on the board and I could label them all but it doesn't help, after they've done that they know the labels of each part, but it doesn't help them to be able to go out and use that. That's the reason I think.

Martha, a 24-year-old female native speaker of English who has been teaching EFL for three years, was teaching an intermediate level class when she offered this:

> A lot of people get worried about what a name is, when the most important thing is to understand why we're using it and when we're using it…. So if they know it, fine, they give you the name; if they don't know it, I'll give them the name. I'll say "Usually in a grammar book this is what it's called, so if you come across it again, you'll recognize it." Often they know the names and don't even know what it's for. So I'd rather they know what it's for rather than its name. But I know they like to have labels and I'll give them the name if they haven't got it.

And this is what Tina, a woman in her late 30s, also a native speaker of English, who has been involved in TEFL for over 10 years, said about the issue:

> If they can name the pattern it's easier to remember… when you give them the different parts and name them you're sort of explaining what they're doing, "This is the 'if' clause plus 'would' plus the past participle." Well, obviously if you can generalize it, I suppose it could be a generalization.

It is interesting to note that Tina teaches advanced-level students. So perhaps, in addition to the teachers' beliefs and degree of comfort in using metalanguage, we might add that teachers' decisions about whether or not to use grammatical terminology are often informed by their assessment of their students' metalinguistic sophistication. Eric, a 40-year-old TEFL teacher, also takes into account his students' learning styles. His sensitivity to these has meant for him that "some students like and feel comfortable with grammatical labels. This needs to be respected" (Borg, 1999: 109). Like Martha, though, Eric cautions that teaching the terminology is no substitute for what he calls the "crux of the matter—what is this language and how is it being used?"

It should be clear by now that much of the SLA research on the learning of grammar has been directed at consciousness-raising, in the broad sense of the term, rather than output practice. There is considerable agreement that learner awareness is required in order for grammatical acquisition to be accelerated beyond what ordinarily takes place in naturalistic acquisition. Pure implicit learning may work, but it is very slow. Researchers remain divided on whether or not learners' attention has to be conscious and focal, and even more so on whether there has to be accompanying output practice. This is because the traditional rationale for practice derived from habit formation—the idea that grammar patterns should be repeated and repeated, in fact overlearned, in order to overcome the habits of the native language and to establish firm new habits in the target language. It is understandable why SLA researchers are reluctant to endorse any practice that risks a return to pure behaviorism.

However, I have often seen the futility of teachers' attempts to move directly from raising students' awareness about a grammar point to expecting them to use it in communication. Students' understanding is necessary for expedient learning, but by itself is insufficient. Grammaring is a skill, and as a skill, requires practice. Meaningful practice of a particular type not only helps learners consolidate their understanding or their memory traces or achieve fluency, it also helps them to advance in their grammatical development. This train of thought led me to literature in psychology, to which I will turn in the next chapter.

Suggested Readings

Research on second language acquisition has been compiled and discussed in Larsen-Freeman and Long (1991), R. Ellis (1994), and Gass and Selinker (2001). As I have indicated several times in this book, very interesting work on multi-word lexical strings or formulaic language is being done at this time. Nattinger and DeCarrico (1992) and Wray (2002) are worth reading. N. Ellis's (1994) anthology on implicit and explicit learning of language deals with some of the issues discussed in this chapter. The case for a connectionist account of language acquisition is cogently put forth in *Rethinking Innateness* by Elman et al. (1998).

9

OUTPUT PRACTICE AND PRODUCTION

DIFFERENT PERCEPTIONS OF THE VALUE OF OUTPUT PRACTICE

I had originally intended to entitle this chapter simply "Practice." Recently, however, the term *practice* has been applied to both input processing and output activities. Having dealt with input processing in the previous chapter, it is the latter that I want to discuss here. Output practice entails using the productive skills of writing and speaking, although unless qualified in some way, *output practice* or *productive practice* is usually reserved for speaking. For me, output practice to learn grammar means using the target patterns or structures in a meaningful, hopefully engaging, focused way.

Practice has long been a mainstay in grammar teaching. After all, teachers who follow the commonplace *Present–Practice–Produce* (PPP) sequence in grammar teaching have felt that some sort of practice is obligatory. Here is what Ed (a name I have given a subject in a study by Borg, 1998), a teacher in a language institute in Malta, has to say about the matter of output practice:

> The underlying principle of everything is that if you're going to have a language focus, and there's going to be conscious language learning in the classroom, then I think I would do practice activities as well. So they've reached awareness, they've come to a conclusion about a rule, then they need some kind of practice of that rule. That's the underlying principle there...as a general principle I give learners controlled (if possible, communicative) practice when it comes to accuracy work (cited in Borg, 1998: 24–25).

Ed is a highly experienced teacher of EFL and probably speaks for many teachers in acknowledging the value of practice, albeit in a qualified manner. However, Ed may not speak for you. Take a moment, therefore, to think about your position on the issue of practice.

9.1

What do you think about output practice in grammar teaching? Define for yourself what output practice is and what benefits or drawbacks it holds.

While I have already speculated that there are many teachers who think as Ed does, Pica (1994) reminds us that, at least at the level of approach, the place of practice in language teaching has diminished over the past two decades.

> Under the influence of the Natural Approach (Krashen and Terrell, 1983) and indeed the broader spectrum of communicative approaches to language teaching, the engagement of learners in drill and practice has been on the decrease in many classrooms...
> (Pica, 1994: 58).

Communicative approaches to language teaching have had a major impact on language teaching. However, to my mind, they have not eliminated the need for practice, though not necessarily the practice associated with drills. It seems to me that the great contribution of communicative approaches is that they turn the Present–Practice–Produce sequence upside down (Willis, 1996; Skehan, 1998). Students first work on comprehension and production through engagement with meaningful content or tasks. This initial phase should be followed by teacher-supported input and output practice, still meaningful and engaging. Later a consciousness-raising phase may take place in which teachers guide learners to induce particular grammatical explanations. In short, the "P" for practice should still occupy a central position.

My support for practice in grammar teaching stems from both my own experience of teaching and learning languages over the years and my role as a teacher educator. For instance, I have been an observer in classrooms where I have been told that communicative language teaching is the methodology being used. As opposed to the "inverted PPP" scenario I have just depicted, I have seen novice teachers introduce a grammar point or function and then ask students to role play, problem solve, or use the teaching point in some other rather open-ended way. And I have witnessed these attempts fail. Students do not speak, or if they do, they do not use the function or structure that has just been presented. While there could be many explanations for the students' reluctance to speak, one highly plausible explanation for why students do not use the target structure is that they have not had practice in doing so.

It has long been held in the language teaching field—and most learners would attest to this—that comprehension most often precedes production, but I believe that comprehension does not guarantee production. Of course, this is not to say that there is no overlap between the two; however, there is evidence that input processing and speech production require distinct types of processing mechanisms (White, 1991). Other research suggests that comprehension skills and production skills are to some extent learned separately (DeKeyser and Sokalski, 2001). My own experience as a learner of Spanish bolsters this claim. Having earlier been a student of Spanish for several years, I am able to understand a great deal of spoken and written Spanish. However, when it comes to speaking Spanish, which I have had very little practice doing, my production is not only halting, but also inaccurate. I find that I cannot worry much about the endings on verbs, for example, when I am preoccupied with just getting something out that is meaningful, relevant, and timely.

Before going on to discuss what sort of output practice would be helpful, it is worth considering what arguments have been made for and against practice in the language classroom. Some may be content to use practice because "it works." Although I respect this position, I myself have never found such pragmatism very satisfying. Given the attitude of inquiry I bring to bear on professional issues, I want to know more. I want to know why "it works," and conversely, why some people feel that practice is not necessary, is even counter-productive. At the 1999 TESOL Convention I made a presentation in which I stated that in contrast to the recent theoretical justification for promoting noticing, consciousness-raising, input processing, and so forth, and the earlier the-oretical justification for practice in the ALM, the role of output/productive practice in modern grammar teaching had been neglected and that post-ALM empirical investigation and clarification were needed in this area as well. Following my presentation, a colleague critiqued what I had said, implying that there was no justification whatsoever for output practice. In the spirit of inquiry, I ask, "What can I learn from this colleague and others who do not believe as I do?"

Further, if practice "works," I want to know what function it serves. I certainly do not dismiss intuitions and experience, but whenever possible, I want to dig deeper. I want to understand why things are the way they are or work/do not work as they do in order to understand and be able to offer a rationale for my experience and/or to know how to change what I do when it does not appear to work with a particular group of students.

Having raised the expectation that I will offer a definitive rationale for the value of practice, I now risk failing to deliver. The truth is that there are hypothe-ses about why practice does or does not "work" in language teaching, but as with so many other issues, there is no accord on the value of practice, and little empirical evidence to support one position over another. Nevertheless, in the spirit of inquiry, I would like to examine the various positions held with regard to practice, beginning with why some researchers question the value of practice.

SLA Research on the Value of Output Practice

It is certainly the case that SLA researchers have not chosen to investigate out-put practice as much as form-focused activities of the consciousness-raising or input-processing sort, which were reviewed in the previous chapter, and there are some researchers who consider such research a waste of time. However, given that practice occupies an important place in most teachers' grammar ped-agogy, and in most language teaching materials, researchers' disinterest, skepti-cism, or even outright rejection may be difficult to comprehend. It may be more understandable, though, when we realize that their attitude can be traced to the long-term association between grammar practice and meaningless drills (Lightbown, 2000). Many an ALM veteran will attest to the soporific effects of an unremitting series of form-based repetition, slot and filler, and transforma-tion drills designed to establish and reinforce speech habits.

Then, too, as always, there is the inert knowledge problem, which I have con-sidered several times already in this book. The fact is that it is all too common for students to practice a grammar point in the classroom only to find that dur-ing another part of the lesson, or outside the classroom, what has been practiced is not transferred. A *strong interface* position, which is implicit in traditional grammar teaching, assumes that learners will acquire what they are taught and that, with practice, they will be able to use the structure in communicative situ-ations—in other words, that there is a direct, proximate connection or interface between practice and use. Clearly this is not the case. We know that learners require time to integrate new grammatical structures into their interlanguage systems. However, it is not only that the transfer is delayed. For instance, learners often produce forms that bear no resemblance to what has been presented to them or practiced. From such observations, R. Ellis (1998) concludes: "It is uncertain, then, whether production practice directed at...structures in the course of a lesson, or even a series of lessons, can enable learners to construct the kind of knowledge needed for communication." In order to accommodate such observations, R. Ellis (1993b) has proposed a *weak interface* position, suggesting that instruction draws learners' attention to language features and permits them to develop knowledge of those features, but that learners will not incorporate such features into their interlanguage until they reach the requisite developmental stage.

Not only are structures that have been taught not always available for transfer, even material that appears to "stick" during and after practice does not endure. Teachers can certainly vouch for the fact that students appear to have mastered a particular form at the end of the week, only to return the next week with no evidence of anything having been retained. In terms of SLA research, one explanation for this observation would be that students may not be developmentally ready to assimilate the structure, and therefore the practice is in vain. Corder (1967) hypothesizes that learners have a built-in syllabus according to which they acquire some structures before others. Motivated to search for an explanation for observed stages of development in the acquisition of German, Pienemann (1998) proposed Processability Theory, which accounts for the stages by pointing to their differences in syntactic processing requirements. "If the production practice is directed at a structure the learners are not yet ready to acquire, it is likely to fail (Pienemann, 1984) or [worse] to result in some misrepresentation of the rule (Eubank, 1987)" (R. Ellis, 1998: 51).

It was problems such as these that led Krashen to adopt a *non-interface* position, postulating that there would be no crossover from explicit form-focused practice to language acquisition. "Practice does not make perfect," Krashen (1982: 60) has written. "For him [Krashen], speaking skills are improved more from getting comprehensible input when reading a book than from practice in speaking" (DeKeyser, 1998: 51), although he notes that speaking does present the possibility that learners will then be in a position to elicit more input from their interlocutors. Krashen weighs in more recently (Krashen, 1998: 177): "There are numerous studies that confirm that we can develop extremely high levels of language and literacy competence without any language production at all (Krashen, 1994)." Further, "there is no direct evidence that CO [comprehensible output] leads to language acquisition" (1998: 180), opportunities for producing comprehensible output are scarce in language classrooms, and increasing these by pushing students to speak before they are ready can have negative consequences.

The *comprehensible output* hypothesis (Swain, 1985) emerged from the observation that, despite Canadian French immersion students' having received comprehensible input for years, their French interlanguage, though fluent, was grammatically inaccurate. In other words, even massive quantities of comprehensible input were insufficient for immersion students to develop an interlanguage that conformed to the target grammar. The students could understand the meaning of what was said to them through understanding some vocabulary and making use of extralinguistic cues; similarly, they could get their message across, even with grammatically incorrect forms. What they were missing, according to Swain and Lapkin (1995: 375), were opportunities to produce comprehensible output, which might force the learner to move from semantic processing prevalent in comprehension to the syntactic processing needed in production. It might be that producing language forces learners to recognize what they do not know or know only partially. This may trigger an analysis of incoming data—that is, a syntactic analysis of input—or it may trigger an analysis of existing internal linguistic resources in order to fill the knowledge gap.

Earlier Schachter (1984) had suggested that producing output affords learners an opportunity to test their hypotheses about the target language—to see if they work. Others see output production as desirable because it is through interaction with others that learners get the opportunity to negotiate meaning, which leads to interactional modifications that make the input easier to process. In other words, when meaning is not clear, steps have to be taken to clarify what is intended. These steps, such as in the use of a confirmation check by a native speaker of English (NS) ("You're a worker") while engaged in conversation with a nonnative speaker of English (NNS), are exemplified in the following (data from Larsen-Freeman and Long, 1991):

NS: *Good. Are you a student in Japan?*

NNS: *No I am not... I am worker.*

NS: *You're a worker. What kind of work do you do?*

Cues such as this that occur naturally in interaction might help learners notice linguistic forms in the input (here, perhaps, the use of an article before *worker*); when these forms lie within the learner's processing capacity, they can become intake (Long, 1996). Notice that the important thing about negotiation is that it enables learners to receive **positive evidence** (what is grammatical in the target language) and **negative evidence** (indirect or direct evidence to the learner that something is ungrammatical).

Some proponents of a Universal Grammar perspective on SLA see correction or negative evidence following learner output as necessary for SLA, but they do not see speech production itself as contributing to grammar building. "In other words, speech processing relates more to language use than the building of grammatical competence" (White, 1991 in Braidi, 1999: 135). Long (1996: 448) also sees spoken production as "useful...because it elicits negative input and encourages analysis and grammaticization; it is facilitative but not necessary" (in R. Ellis, 1999: 13).

Notice that, while these are modest endorsements for encouraging learner output, they are not arguments for output practice; rather, the benefits that are hypothesized to accrue for producing output have to do with its potential for facilitating noticing, its role in testing hypotheses, encouraging analysis, and its elicitation of more input. Others who do address the value of output practice directly hold a correspondingly circumscribed view of such practice, saying that it may have a role in the development of explicit conscious linguistic knowledge or in increasing learners' access to the implicit acquired system, but not in the development of the acquired system itself (Schwartz, 1993; VanPatten and Cardierno, 1993; however, see Salaberry, 1997).

9.2

The following is a compilation of the views on output production that have just been reviewed. Is there one or more that seems plausible based on your experience? Why or why not?

Figure 9.1: Benefits and Drawbacks of Output Production/Practice

+	−
Moves learners from semantic to syntactic processing; encourages syntactic analysis	Is not needed for language acquisition, or at best is out of sync with the natural development of grammatical competence
Promotes noticing, especially of what learners do not know	Is scarce in the classroom
Learners can test hypotheses and gain negative feedback through which to modify their hypotheses	Pushes learners to speak before they are ready, which might lead to negative affect and misrepresentation of the grammatical rule
May help learners gain more comprehensible input or better access to the developing system	Does not directly affect the system itself

As can be seen from the table in Investigation 9.2, even the benefits of output production/practice are indirect, affecting the developing systems only after some sort of cognitive processing by the learners, such as analyzing or noticing features in the input. Most SLA researchers would say that output production has little direct influence on the development of the underlying grammatical system itself. Further, the feeling is that output practice may help with fluency or facilitating access to grammatical competence, but not with construction of new grammatical knowledge, with Swain's (1985) *semantic to syntactic processing* hypothesis being a possible exception. This is presumably why SLA researchers, who are primarily concerned with the acquisition of learners' mental grammars (Long, 1997), have not paid much attention to output practice. Nothing is directly hypothesized to occur as a result of production itself. Such positions are a very far cry from the ALM days when practice was deemed essential in order to establish and reinforce speech habits.

I am certainly not about to advocate a return to the ALM, with its limited role for learners and its view that language teaching involves modifying verbal behavior. Nevertheless, despite the retrospective criticisms of the ALM, let me run the risk once again of saying that while the ALM may have been short on teaching students to communicate in the target language, no matter what the context was or who the interlocutors were, one thing that the ALM was long on was a theoretical rationale for practice. The target goal was clear: to overcome old habits and establish new ones, and these goals were thought unlikely to be accomplished without abundant practice. Furthermore, the rationale was accompanied by a theoretical framework for categorizing and sequencing drills—from completely manipulative, to predominantly manipulative, to predominantly communicative, to completely communicative (Prator, 1965) or from mechanical, to meaningful, to communicative, M–M–C, as Paulston (1970) framed it. Since the decline from dominance of the ALM, no coherent framework for practice activities has taken its place.

Having reviewed the SLA research literature, I now understand why output practice has been ignored in comparison to consciousness-raising. Many researchers associate output practice with mechanical drills that seek to alter verbal behavior. There is no regard for human cognition in such a view. With the metamorphosis of research focus from the shaping of human behavior to the acquisition of mental grammar, output production was seen to be possibly useful, but output practice was considered, at best, unnecessary.

However, based on my combined experience as a language learner, teacher, and teacher educator, I believe that output practice has an important role to play in language learning. Furthermore, I believe that its role is not only in enhancing fluency; I believe it can also impact the underlying grammatical system. This requires a certain type of practice, however. Two questions will therefore occupy me for the remainder of this chapter. First, is there any theoretical basis or empirical evidence to support my belief in the value of practice? Second, if so, is there a theoretical framework that I can adopt (besides a truncated version of the M–M–C) or create in designing suitable practice activities?

SUPPORT FROM PSYCHOLOGY FOR OUTPUT PRACTICE: AN INFORMATION-PROCESSING PERSPECTIVE

Automaticity

To look for a theoretical position, I have to leave SLA and linguistics and make a foray into the psychological literature, that branch of cognitive psychology known as information processing. A prominent position on practice in cognitive psychology is represented in the work of John Anderson (e.g., 1985), who has distinguished declarative knowledge from procedural knowledge. Anderson has proposed a three-stage model of skill learning. In the first stage, learners acquire declarative knowledge, or "knowledge about." For example, in the case of grammar, DeKeyser (1998) equates declarative knowledge with knowing a grammar rule such as that English requires an *s* at the end of a third person singular verb in the present tense. In the second stage, the declarative knowledge is proceduralized, which means that "a method for performing the skill is worked out" (Anderson, 1985), that is, learners develop procedural knowledge, "knowledge of how to." The third stage is when the procedural knowledge is automatized, that is, when one uses the rule without having to think about it. Thus, according to an information-processing approach to skill acquisition, learners move from controlled-information processing, which requires a great deal of attention on the part of learners, to automaticity in information processing, in which the procedure is executed with little attention, leaving more capacity for further action planning.

This model represents the experience many of us have in learning some skill, such as how to drive a car. Then, too, most teachers will find this theoretical model compatible with a traditional approach to grammar teaching, and many researchers would not object to this portrayal of skill learning if incorporation of the target form into learners' interlanguages was not expected to be immediate and the purpose of the practice was to develop fluency. One limitation of the third person singular example used, however, is that it is clearly not the case that all grammatical knowledge is rule-governed.

Especially if one broadens one's view of grammar to embrace patterned sequences, which are so important for fluency, then one would have to include knowledge of such patterns in declarative knowledge. Indeed, this is just what Gatbonton and Segalowitz (1988) do, proposing that productive practice should be directed at formulaic patterns, not grammatical rules. They believe this is the type of practice that can lead to automaticity of certain aspects of performance, which in turn frees up students' attentional resources to be allocated elsewhere. It can also contribute to a degree of fluency that may make users of the target language more willing to engage in conversation with the learners, thereby gaining the learners' affective support as well as increased access to input.

9.3

Arevart and Nation (1991) conducted a simple study. Students were asked to deliver a four-minute talk on a familiar topic to a partner. They then changed partners and delivered the same talk to a different partner, but with a three-minute time limit. Finally, they changed partners again and delivered the same talk in two minutes to their new partner. The mere repetition of the talk under increasingly severe time constraints was effective not only in enhancing fluency but also, somewhat unexpectedly, in improving grammatical accuracy.

Can you account for their finding from a cognitive psychological point of view?

Restructuring

An important additional awareness concerning practice also comes to us from an information-processing approach in cognitive psychology. Practice does not merely automatize procedures; it also involves "the establishment of new procedures which reorganize a body of facts and rules previously acquired" (Hulstijn, 1990). As cognitive psychologist/SLA researcher McLaughlin (1987:

136) has written:

> But there is more to learning a complex cognitive skill than automatizing subskills. The learner needs to impose organization and to structure the information that has been acquired. As more learning [in 1990, he says "practice"] occurs, internalized, cognitive representations change and are restructured. This restructuring process involves operations that are different from, but complementary to, those involved in gaining automaticity.

While no one knows exactly what operations are involved in restructuring, the development of organizational *schemata* might provide an example. For instance, research on chess masters has demonstrated that, given only five seconds to view a midgame chessboard, chess masters can remember with 90 percent accuracy where all the pieces are placed—something that eludes chess novices. Experts are able to do this because the practice in which experts have engaged enables them to recall clusters that form attack or defense configurations—schemata—whereas beginners lack the skill to form such higher-order abstract representations. Thus experts replace complex sub-elements with schemata that allow more abstract processing.

See Chapter 2.

Analogous to this in grammar might be rules and *constructions*, or higher-level systematicities that emerge from the interactions of lower-level forms. For example, in construction grammar, the meaning of a clause or sentence is dependent on the pattern of elements at the subclausal level. Thus sentences such as *Pat mailed Bill a letter, Pat faxed Bill a letter, Pat left Bill a message*, and so forth have the clausal meaning of Bill's receiving something, whereas sentences such as *Pat ran Bill ragged, Pat made Bill happy, Pat knocked Bill silly*, and so forth have the clausal meaning of Bill's becoming something. With enough examples of these two patterns, learners could presumably abstract the clausal meaning of these constructions. They could then call upon these clausal meanings to facilitate their processing of subsequent tokens of the constructions.

See Prototype Theory (Rosch, 1978).

Prototypes are another example of abstract patterns that might result from the organizing and structuring of information. For example, a learner of English may hear and use the preposition *on* a number of times. At some point the learner may be able to abstract from all these encounters with *on* its prototypical meaning of *to come into contact with a flat surface*. Doing so will presumably not only help learners use *on* prototypically but may also facilitate their acquisition of the preposition's extended meanings, such as *on time* and *on task* (see Celce-Murcia and Larsen-Freeman, 1999).

Instance-based theories (see Truscott, 1998) offer a fourth example of how information that has been processed might subsequently be organized. Again, the learner encounters a number of instances of a given grammar structure. Each instance is analyzed into a number of basic features. It is then categorized based on the similarity of its features to other members of a given category. This differs from the creation of rules and prototypes in that when a new instance of a particular grammar structure is encountered, it is not categorized in terms of necessary conditions for clausal meaning or by its resemblance to a prototype, "...but on the basis of comparisons with the features of one or more (usually more) of those instances already stored…. As the store of instances becomes large, instances appropriate to the current task are more quickly and efficiently retrieved from memory, and are therefore more easily and effectively applied to the task" (Truscott, 1998: 259–260). Truscott notes that such an explanation is more in keeping with the attested gradual, incremental character of language learning than is a notion such as resetting a UG parameter, which would register an abrupt shift in a learner's grammar.

Unlike schemata, rules, and prototypes, instance-based theories de-emphasize abstraction and instead treat knowledge as a collection of discrete, experienced items. It is important, however, to recognize that even practices that involve abstraction are not solely unidirectional from the bottom up of specific tokens to their abstractions in the form of schemata, rules, constructions, or prototypes. For instance, practice might lead to the formation of a schema, which might direct what we pay attention to as we continue to practice, but then, in turn, the schema might be modified by additional practice. The process is therefore a cyclical one, with bottom-up and top-down processes in continual interaction.

Whether or not these particular implicit abstraction processes have a role in SLA restructuring remains to be seen. The important point, not to be missed in this discussion of restructuring operations, is the underlying assumption that "learning involves a constant modification of organizational structures…[or] internal representations" (McLaughlin, 1987: 138–139). It is also important to realize that practice can sometimes lead to decrements in performance as the system is reorganized. In McLaughlin's words (1987: 152):

> It seems that the effects of practice do not accrue directly or automatically to a skilled action, but rather accumulate as learners develop more efficient procedures…. Performance may follow a U-shaped curve, declining as more complex internal representations replace less complex ones, and increasing again as skill becomes expertise.

I am now in a position to add possible benefits of output practice to the list of hypothesized benefits of output production described in Investigation 9.2. Output practice potentially:

- helps learners develop fluency through the control of formulaic speech;

- increases automaticity, which in turn frees up attentional resources; and

- leads to restructuring, which modifies and reorganizes underlying representations.

This last benefit of output practice is quite different from the function normally ascribed to practice. Notice that most teachers and researchers assume that students achieve fluency or automaticity by practicing preexisting knowledge; practice is not seen as a means of modifying, and thereby altering, such knowledge (Gass, 1997).

However, if the practice is meaningful and engaging, and if McLaughlin is right, I can see no reason why output practice cannot contribute to both automaticity and restructuring. In sum, an information-processing perspective accounts for how a learner might somehow "know" the grammar explicitly, but not be able to produce it consistently, due to the limited attentional resources available. It suggests that the automaticity, which can be achieved with increasing control of rule-governed or formulaic utterances, frees up attentional resources to be directed elsewhere, such as to the necessary syntactic processing. It also shows how understanding the message is not immediately transferable to output production. Output practice is necessary for this to happen. Finally, restructuring explains that information that has been stored needs reorganizing at some point, and that when this occurs, performance regresses. For a while, at least, learners are no longer able to correctly produce target structures that they once were able to produce.

See Chapter 8.

SUPPORT FOR PRACTICE: CONNECTIONISM

As insightful as an information-processing perspective seems to be with regard to the value of practice and its role in SLA, there is a newer modeling approach from psychology, *connectionism*, which also deserves consideration. Connectionists attribute implicit learning to unconscious associative learning. As the language data are taken in to connectionist neural network models, certain connections in the networks are strengthened, others weakened. In this way, language is seen to be a "statistical ensemble" of interacting elements (Cooper, 1999: ix). Nothing is static. A connectionist model of language is therefore constantly changing, best depicted by the dynamic relationships among the network connections. Learning is thus a consequence of repeated neural network activation that results in stronger, and therefore more easily activated, connections.

However, connectionist models have also demonstrated that repeated activation can result in temporary degradation of performance, modeling the now-familiar U-shaped learning curve. Notice that whereas information-processing theory necessitates a separate process—restructuring—to account for declines in performance, connectionism accounts for incremental and decremental learning with a single process, the continual adjustment of patterns of connectivity in response to the continual processing of examples. Thus connectionist models have certain advantages over information-processing theory. They account for the same phenomena—the incremental learning with periodic and unpredictable decrements in performance—but they do so utilizing a single process (Mellow and Stanley, 2001). In the case of N. Ellis (1996), that one associative process is sequence learning, the gradual strengthening of memory for language sequences or chunks. They also combine a way to represent language and a way to model its development, obviating the need for two different theories (Hulstijn, 2002). Also a commendable quality is that connectionist models offer a neurologically plausible account of brain processing. They are constructed based on what is known about the brain and its functioning, and thus conceivably provide a good model of how the brain works (but, see Gregg, forthcoming).

Of course, there are limitations to connectionist accounts, as well. For one thing, connectionists model implicit learning, perhaps more relied on in first than in second language acquisition. After all, not all second language acquisition is successful. For another, computer models are disembodied from the world, and they are asocial (Elman, undated manuscript); they purport to model brain processes but they ignore the social dimension to human behavior, the very reason for the existence of language.

SUPPORT FOR PRACTICE:
CHAOS/COMPLEXITY THEORY

It may be too much to expect everything in one theory or model. They are, after all, only partial models of reality. Nevertheless, before concluding this part of Chapter 9, I would like to briefly explore a somewhat related theory, *Chaos/Complexity Theory* (C/CT). C/CT deals with the study of complex, dynamic, nonlinear systems, usually naturally occurring systems such as those studied by meteorologists and population biologists. However, I can think of few phenomena more complex, dynamic, and nonlinear than language, and so I have justified appropriating its perspective to matters concerning language and language acquisition (Larsen-Freeman, 1997).

There is much to be said about C/CT and its close cousin, dynamical systems theory, but that is the stuff of another book, one I have been writing in my head for a few years now. For my purposes here, I would like to point out that both information-processing and connectionist perspectives stop short of a more radical position, a position that I have been drawn to for almost a decade. From a C/CT perspective, one might argue that the language system is not only restructured or reweighted as a result of use; it is created. For in a dynamical system it is not just the state of a system that changes over time; the nature of the relations among the elements that constitute it also change, as with a developing embryo. And, after all, language is not a closed, entropic system. It does not settle down to a point of equilibrium. Instead, as with other naturally occurring systems, language is dynamic, constantly evolving, self-organizing. As Harris pointed out "We do not communicate through reference to prior fixed abstract forms, but rather '...we create language as we go, both as individuals and as communities...'" (Bybee and Hopper, 2001: 19).

And although I may be criticized for collapsing time scales, (which should not matter if there is a self-similarity at different levels of scale, see also MacWhinney, 1999) what is true of evolution of language in general may be no less true of the interlanguage development of individuals. In other words, every use of language changes its resources, and the changed resources are then used in the next learning event (Cameron, n.d.). I am not merely speaking of the creation of novel forms, such as the well-known case of overgeneralization of the past tense morpheme to irregular verbs, whereby first and second language learners produced *eated* and *goed*. Rather, I am speaking of the generation of novel forms by learners that are more complex than the input language.

One objection to analogizing language evolution to language acquisition might be that evolution is a slow process, one in which change occurs over generations, not within the life span of a language learner. However, these days, a great deal of research by evolutionary biologists is pointing to the nonlinear nature of evolution—to the rapid unleashing of novel forms in response to changes in the environment, often triggering changes from one generation to the next. For instance, scientists have recently learned that Galapagos Island finches, once studied by Charles Darwin, respond quickly to changes in food supply by evolving new beaks and body sizes, all within a very short span of time—a few generations at most. (See, for example, the June 22, 2002 issue of *Science News*). Such observations corroborate Stephen Jay Gould's theory of *punctuated equilibrium* (Gould, 1977), wherein evolution is punctuated by bursts, (Could these be like the attested rapid "vocabulary bursts" of first language acquisition?) not always marked by gradual development.

Morphogenesis

In any case, if the same type of evolutionary process is operable at the level of the individual, the nonlinear rate of language development would occur much faster anyway. And so, as with other dynamic systems, language development may be characterized by *morphogenesis,* or the generation of new patterns. After all, human brains are fundamentally pattern detectors (Harris, 1993) and creators. As Mohanan (1992: 653–654) puts it, "Suppose we free ourselves from the idea that [first] language development is the deduction of the adult grammar from the input data, and think of it as the formation of patterns triggered by the data." In other words, rather than viewing grammar development solely as a process of conforming to the grammar of the community, which is governed by deductive and inductive operations, it is suggested in addition that language development involves the spontaneous creation of grammatical patterns, which then, as speakers communicate with each other, adapt themselves to the overt patterns of the grammars of other individuals in the community.

Besides the attractive (to me) idea of allowing for the creativity of new patterns in language, which are triggered by the input data but which are not pure imitations of it, this point of view has the added advantage of including a social dimension. After all, interacting with others provides the stimulus as well as the check, which keeps individuals' idiolects mutually intelligible. Of course, since the language development process is nonlinear, interaction may be followed by more interaction with little obvious lasting change in learners' interlanguage. Then, one day, for any given learner, the penny will drop. All we can say for sure is that it is a very lucky teacher who is there to witness its happening.

Emergentism

Emergentism refers to the fact that dynamical systems exhibit complexity that is not due to any specific innate capacity and is not a priori predictable or obvious from any input. Nor is the complexity the creation of some central executive who oversees the system. Instead, the complexity emerges at the global level from the repetition of fairly simple processes or the actions and interactions of agents at the local level. Simulations of bird flocks, for instance, have been achieved by observing how each bird interacts with its neighbors. The macro level flock emerges from the actions of the individual birds acting at a micro level within their own "neighborhood."

Also, honeycombs take the shape they do, because each of its cell is hexagonal in shape. Cells of that shape are structurally strong and represent the emergent solution to the problem of packing relatively uniformly sized balls of honey together. The shape of a honeycomb does not derive from properties of the wax or of the honey, or from the packing behavior of bees (Bates and Goodman, 1999: 32). Because it is assumed in C/CT that dynamic processes such as emergentism can apply to all forms of systems, animate as well as inanimate, a similar argument has been made to explain the emergence of grammars in human beings: they represent the class of possible solutions to the problem of how to map a rich set of meanings onto a limited speech channel, heavily constrained by the limits of memory, perception, and motor planning (Bates and MacWhinney, 1989 cited in Bates and Goodman, 1999).

9.4

Those who subscribe to an emergentist view of language acquisition might say that "the complexity of a solution emerges from the interaction of problem and solver." Explain why the fact that the number of people queued up in checkout lines at a supermarket stays roughly the same is an example of an emergent solution (MacWhinney, 1999: ix).

In sum, thought and behavior emerge as dynamic patterns of activity. They arise in response to the intended task at hand, shaped by the organism's architecture and previous history of activity. Along with the assumption that patterns emerge in the process, C/CT erases the traditional boundaries of mental life. There can be no description of a purely "inner life." Every mental and behavioral act is always emergent in a social context (Thelen, 1995).

Thus, both morphogenesis and emergentism present us with intriguing alternatives to the way that practice/production has been recently construed. These alternatives allow output production and practice to contribute to the creation of new language forms; they are not limited to imitation and rehearsal of previously learned material. They also account for the acquisition of grammar as different from the acquisition and application of rules and, finally, they unite the cognitive with the social.

ON THE UNITY OF LANGUAGE ACQUISITION AND LANGUAGE USE

Earlier, in conjunction with my proposal that language use and language change were synchronous, I quoted Gleick's remark about complex, dynamic, nonlinear systems (1987: 24): "The act of playing the game has a way of changing the rules." It seems to me that, in light of the discussion on emergentism, I can analogize this same dynamic to language acquisition. Complexity can emerge out of the iteration of relatively simple processes. In this way, connectionist/emergentist models can be said to straddle the performance/competence distinction (Broeder and Plunkett, 1994). In other words, real-time performance or practice is simultaneous with changes in underlying competence. From this perspective, through language use, language changes; through language use, language is acquired. Use, change, and acquisition are all instances of the same underlying dynamic process and are mutually constitutive. As MacWhinney (1999) observes, all three are examples of emergentism (use or real-time emergence, change or diachronic emergence, and acquisition or developmental emergence) operating in different time frames—and, I would add, at different levels of scale.

See Chapter 3.

See also Dickerson (1976) concerning the psycholinguistic unity of language learning and language change.

Although sociocultural theory is not the source of my thinking about these ideas, it is similar to what I have just claimed about the unity of language acquisition and language use. According to Lantolf and Pavlenko (1995: 116), sociocultural theory "...erases the boundary between language learning and language using." Newman and Holzman (1993: 39), discussing Vygotsky's notion of linguistic tool(s), state, "... their function is inseparable from the activity of their development." Output practice, then, does not simply serve to increase access to previously acquired knowledge. Doing and learning are synchronous. On this point, there appears to be convergence between newer psychological and social perspectives (Larsen-Freeman, 2002b).

Just to be clear, from my point of view, although acquisition and use are synchronous, this does not mean that they are indistinguishable. Because someone is able to use a new structure in a scaffolded practice activity does not mean that the structure is necessarily available for later use during a nonmediated activity. Since acquisition and use are operating at different time scales, mediated practice can go on for some time before someone is able to use a structure independently.

I am aware that this is still a radical departure from the given view. In other words, it is different from other intuitively appealing accounts that distinguish between competence and control (Bialystok and Sharwood Smith, 1985)—that is, the learner may have acquired a given grammar structure but may not have the requisite processing control to produce the structure. It is also different from accounts that attribute only enhanced fluency or automaticity to practice activities. I am also aware that I have overlooked the incredibly complex issues of language processing, such as those captured in Levelt's (1989) model. Also, while Chaos/Complexity Theory's morphogenesis and emergentism offer us interesting and potentially profitable ways to think about and model language acquisition, I do not want to be guilty of reductionism. At the very least, I need to further consider the relationship among accuracy, fluency, and complexity in learners' developing grammars (Wolfe-Quintero et al., 1998; Larsen-Freeman, 2002c). I also do not want to be guilty of the same perspective that I criticized earlier—ignoring the learners' autonomy. Clearly, the emergentist process as I have just described it is highly simplified and completely overlooks the important issue of human agency.

Furthermore, there is a great deal of imprecision in the account I have just given. I could be persuaded that I have just replaced the black box of the input–output model with one labeled *connectionism, morphogenesis, and emergentism*. Nevertheless, the second black box has the desirable qualities of being neurologically plausible (although see Gregg, forthcoming); having a biological corollary; taking into account both individual creativity and social interaction and adaptation; treating language and humans as open, not closed, systems (not entropic systems); and unifying change at all levels of scale—that is, that the language system is created by output practice and production within the individual, the classroom community, and the wider community of users of the language is a very intriguing idea. For all these reasons, I will continue to think and explore such matters.

A Lesson in Humility

Having acknowledged that there remain issues to be addressed, but having found theoretical support for the value of output practice and perhaps even more profound insight into the dynamics of acquisition/use, it is time now to take up the other question I posed earlier: What theoretical support or empirical evidence can I draw on in designing appropriate post-ALM practice activities? But before I attempt to answer this question, for the sake of humility, it is important to consider teacher Elsa Del Valle's voice.

Elsa Del Valle

As a teacher and a former language learner, I have always thought that grammar practice was critical. My thoughts about grammar practice come from my own language learning and language teaching experiences. I am a heritage speaker of Spanish and learned English as a child. In college (late 70s and early 80s), I studied Portuguese through the ALM for two semesters and a summer and later lived in Brazil for a year. After about a month in Brazil, the drills really paid off. I really feel that what came out of my mouth then had already been learned even though I had never actually used Portuguese before going to Brazil. The regular forms, the irregular subjunctives, the word order, etc. seemed to just "be there" when I needed it. My grammar and pronunciation were native by the time I left.

By the time I started studying my third language (Hebrew) in 1986, the communicative method was in full swing. I took two semesters of Hebrew at the University of Texas before moving to Israel. The Hebrew course at UT was not ALM but grammar-based, and I liked it, but I would prepare my own practice drills. I had not studied nearly as much Hebrew as I had Portuguese before going to Israel, and I was looking forward to the intensive language study that I would do there. But, as I said, the no-explicit-grammar variety of the communicative method was in style. I felt cheated in the intensive Hebrew language program (ULPAN). Little or no grammar explanations were given and we did mostly pair work. (I have no problem with pair work or with using communicative activities in class, but I felt that it was inefficient since I lived in the country and had ample opportunities to use Hebrew with native speakers, who by the way, could never explain their language to me. I hoped that my class would do that and also serve as a laboratory for the practice I couldn't do in the real world.)

The difference between these two experiences for me as a learner was in the practice and the presentation of the grammatical syllabus. I would have liked more grammatical explanation in Portuguese, but since I knew Spanish, the drills were enough. I figured out the grammar by analogy. For Hebrew, I always felt that I never got a complete foundation in the basics and that the grammar practice in those communicative activities was a waste of time. It all felt so incomplete and sporadic, and I spent a lot of time learning on my own.... I understand the goals of my ULPAN teacher, but I didn't agree that hers was the best or most efficient way to get there. Furthermore, it was no less boring than the ALM drills, which weren't all that boring for me. Learning the skill aspects of language has never been boring or meaningless to me. I suppose one could argue that I was so motivated to learn Portuguese, that the meaningfulness was in my personal goal, and so the repetitive drills didn't bother me. In fact, I rather liked them. It may also be that one can't learn everything one needs in a language class meaningfully. I do remember making the drills more interesting by changing the names of the people in the drills to names of people I knew. When it did get tedious, I'd play around with the meaning. Another reason I liked the ALM aspect of the practice was that it was so controlled [that] I was able to focus on one thing at a time and master it (form and pronunciation) before I had to use it. In a sense, the ALM practice was the pedagogical equivalent of the sub-vocalized rehearsing learners often do—it was non-threatening and necessary. I do have to admit that I learned Hebrew very well, and although I was always frustrated with the instruction I got, I probably learned it as well as I did Portuguese. Still, I think it could have been even better if I had learned it as systematically as I did Portuguese.

One thought Elsa's voice prompts in me is the need to bear in mind individual learner differences. When someone says that "ALM didn't work," the experience of such learners as Elsa is disregarded. Unqualified criticisms or endorsements will never apply to all learners and learning contexts. In fact, contrary to the case I have been working so hard to make in this chapter, I admit that there is anecdotal evidence of learners who never or rarely engage in output practice, but when they do speak, they do so perfectly. In addition, Elsa's voice is a reminder of the importance of learner agency. Elsa created drills to compensate for the practice she felt that she needed, but was not getting, in her study of Hebrew. I sometimes feel that we teachers do not get accurate feedback on our teaching because humans, being such versatile and gifted learners, compensate for our inadvertent oversights. Then, too, building on the idea of learner agency, we must always remember that all we teachers can create, together with our students, is learning opportunities. We cannot say a priori whether learning will take place or even that our students will undertake a particular task in the way that we anticipate (see, for example, Coughlan and Duff, 1994). Whether and to what extent our students see the tasks we set for them as opportunities for learning and utilize them accordingly is beyond our control. As I have written elsewhere (Larsen-Freeman, 2000a), we know that teaching does not cause learning, but we must act as if it does.

Having had my sense of humility renewed, let me be clear: My purpose here is to share my explorations in thinking about questions I have had. Indeed, some of the research and theoretical positions I have reviewed are nascent. The dust has hardly settled. It is not my purpose to declare with finality here or anywhere that I have found answers that will work for or satisfy everyone. Nevertheless, I am satisfied that I have found theoretical justification for the value of practice: From an information-processing perspective, practice activities are essential in language teaching because they encourage automaticity, which frees learners' attention to be directed elsewhere, and they may contribute to restructuring learners' grammars. From the perspective of connectionism, practice strengthens the connections among the nodes in a neural network, accelerating future access. From the perspective of C/CT, practice may even lead to the creation of new language forms. And from a C/CT and sociocultural perspective, practice (of the right sort) and learning are synchronous.

ESSENTIAL CRITERIA FOR DESIGNING OUTPUT PRACTICE ACTIVITIES

From my readings in applied linguistics and in educational psychology, and from my experience, I would say that two essential criteria must be met when designing practice activities of the right sort. First, the activities should be meaningful and engaging. Second, they should be focused. More specifically, practice activities should be designed in such a way that the learning challenge is in focus. I will address each of these criteria in turn.

Be Meaningful and Engaging

Grammar practice activities are designed to facilitate students' acquisition of the target grammar by systematically focusing on grammatical structures or patterns. However, students will best acquire the structures or patterns when they are put into situations that require them to use structures and patterns for some meaningful purpose other than decontextualized or mechanistic practice. Indeed, a neurological perspective suggests that the kind of language practiced in meaningless drills is unavailable for use beyond the classroom (Lamendella, 1979). Thus, the conjunction of grammar and meaningfulness will, to some measure, help overcome the inert knowledge problem (See discussion of psychological authenticity on page 122). If done well, grammar capacity will be built up at the same time that students will come to know grammar as a resource for meaning-making.

Meaningful practice activities also serve to engage learners. As I have said, I do not think that my function as a teacher is to entertain my students, but it is crucial to engage them. If they are not engaged, then they are probably not attending, and their attention is important. Thus, any practice activities have to be independently motivating, seen by learners as worth doing.

Focus on the Learning Challenge, Be It Form, Meaning, or Use

Again, we have little or no control over what learners choose to focus on, but at least for planning purposes it is important to recognize that different types of activities address different dimensions of grammar.

Activities that address grammatical **form** (morphology and syntax) need to provide frequent opportunities to use a target structure/pattern. As we have already seen, frequency is important in learning form, whether one is a behaviorist (repetition conditions and reinforces verbal habits), a cognitivist (frequent exposure provides more opportunities to figure out the rules and then contributes to automaticity in applying them), a connectionist (frequent tokens strengthen nodes in a neural network), or a socioculturalist (repetition improves the chances of alignment between the student's internal objective and the external objective of the activity, without which learning would not take place) (Donato, 2000; Talyzina, 1981).

On the multiplicity of interpretations regarding frequency, see my discussion (Larsen-Freeman, 2002b) of N. Ellis (2002).

Also, of course, repetition in the classroom serves social purposes. (See Johnstone, 1994; Cook, 1994; Duff, 2000; Tarone, 2002).

In any event, in keeping with the first essential criterion of grammar practice activities, the frequent use of a structure will not be mechanical repetition. Instead, students should engage in a meaningful activity that requires the frequent use of a form. An example of an oft-used activity that does this quite naturally is the game "twenty questions," where players attempt to guess what someone else has in mind by asking up to twenty yes–no questions. If this is done as a whole-class activity the teacher, or other more proficient students, can scaffold the grammar and vocabulary for all students, enabling them to pose the questions that they wish to pose.

Gatbonton and Segalowitz (1988), who also call for repeated use of forms in their *creative automatization* approach, point out that an additional advantage to a whole-class activity is that students get many exposures to the target pattern. Another way that they recommend for making an activity inherently repetitive is to have students carry out a series of related activities. For example, one could establish conditions for the repetition of the pattern "X is (not) working" by setting up a situation where one student tries to get a photocopier repaired and has to report and elaborate on the problem, first to an office secretary (a second student), who in turn explains it to the person who answers the phone at the repair shop (a third student), who has to inform the repair person (a fourth student), and so forth. Then, after the repair is made, the message that the photocopier is working again can be passed along the chain in reverse order.

While frequent use is important for activities that are designed to work on the form of a grammar structure, it is not so much of an issue when the challenge is for students to learn the *meaning* of a grammar structure. This is because, when the challenge is a structure's meaning, students need to make an association between a grammar form and its essential meaning. Output production in the form of frequent use may facilitate the bonding, but it may not be altogether necessary. As I mentioned in the previous chapter, there are attested cases of instantaneous learning, especially when it comes to meaning. The fact that learning meaning can be accomplished by association is the reason Krashen (1994) can make the claim that a lot of language can be learned without output production. He is speaking of vocabulary in particular when he says *language*.

A typical meaning-focused activity that allows for form and meaning of several different forms to be connected is the use of Total Physical Response (TPR). For instance, students can first be directed to, and later direct others to, place an object *under* their chairs, *on* their desks, *next to* their books, and so forth. In this way, rather than focusing on a single pattern or structure, the contrasting meaning of three to six prepositions (the ideal number of new forms, according to TPR originator and psychologist James Asher) can be associated with their meanings at one point in time.

When working on the use dimension, neither frequent use nor association is the operating mode. Instead, students must learn to make the appropriate choice according to given contextual constraints. Rea, Dickins, and Woods (1988) speak of this as *the* challenge in learning grammar—and it is an important one to my mind—but choosing appropriately is the challenge in working on use, not so much when working on form or meaning. In practice activities that work on use, students must be put into a situation where, given two or more different forms, they have to choose the most appropriate form for that context. They must then receive feedback on the appropriateness of the choice they have made.

A classic example of an activity where use is in focus is when students are asked to role play an interview. The interviewer and interviewee must choose between using the present perfect and the past tense to refer to past events. For example:

Student A: *Have you had any experience with computer programming?*

Student B: *Yes, I have. I worked as a computer programmer for two years.*

In the discussion above, I used three common activities (a game, an activity sequence, a role play) to illustrate the features (frequent use, association, choice) that apply to practice activities that focus on the different dimensions of grammar. These same three features can also be applied to the design of more creative activities.

WORKING WITH TEXTBOOKS

An important point, not to be missed in this discussion of designing activities, is that the criteria also apply to selecting activities. Textbook exercises and activities should be inspected carefully to see which dimension of language is being addressed. Just because a student is having trouble with the present perfect in English does not mean that any exercise labeled "present perfect" will do. The precise source of the problem will have to be diagnosed (this will be discussed in the next chapter) and the correct kind of exercise selected.

Investigations

9.5

Here are four practice activities drawn from the textbook series Grammar Dimensions: Form, Meaning and Use, *for which I am Series Director. Decide which dimension of grammar each one addresses.*

1. **Conditionals:** Consider some of the family or school rules that you had to follow when you were younger. Create a list of rules that could be expressed with *if, unless,* or *only if* conditions. Use the categories below for ideas. If possible, form groups that include different cultural backgrounds and discuss some of the cultural similarities and differences revealed by your lists.

   - eating snacks
   - watching television
   - dating
   - visits with friends
   - classroom rules

   Examples: In Taiwan, we could speak in class only if we raised our hand. I couldn't visit with my friends unless one of my parents was home. (Adapted from Frodesen and Eyring, 2000: 281)

2. **Indirect Objects:** Work with a partner. Write sentences about North American customs using the words below. Then write sentences about customs in the country you come from.

   Birth: When a baby is born:

   1. mother / flowers / the / to /give / friends.
   2. cigars / gives / friends / father / his / the / to
   3. send / and / parents / friends / family / to / birth / announcements / their / the

   (Adapted from Badalamenti and Henner Stanchina, 2000: 207)

3. **Passive Voice:** Decide whether active or passive forms should be used in sentences, and write the correct form in the blank.

   The age of pyramid-building in Egypt (1) _____ (begin) about 2900 B.C. The great pyramids (2) _____ (intend) to serve as burial places for the pharaohs, as the kings of Egypt (3) _____ (call). (Adapted from Thewlis, 2000: 59)

4. **The phrase "Would you like...?":** Work with a partner on each of the following situations. The first person should make a polite offer using *"Would you like...?* and the other person should politely accept or refuse the offer.

   Take turns making and replying to the offers.

   1. The English teacher is ready to show a video. The switch to turn on the video player is next to Stefan.
   2. The dinner at Mrs. Zimunga's house is almost finished. Mrs. Zimunga sees that some of the guests ate their dessert—cherry pie—very quickly, and she thinks they might want another piece.
   3. Alfredo has a seat at the front of the city bus. He sees that an elderly woman has just gotten on, but there are no more seats left. (Adapted from Riggenbach and Samuda, 2000: 243–44)

What the features of frequent use (activities 2 and 4), association (activity 1), and choice (activity 3) offer is a principled means for practicing grammar. They should help teachers be clear about the reasons behind the decisions they make when teaching grammar. They should help teachers design effective activities, or choose from those in a textbook, without making the assumption that just because a textbook activity deals with the target structure, it necessarily addresses the particular learning challenge that their students are experiencing.

GRADING (OVERCOMING THE INERT KNOWLEDGE PROBLEM)

From my reading of the psychological literature I have gathered that, when the conditions of learning match the conditions of use/recall, the inert knowledge problem can be overcome. In other words, in order for transfer to occur, the practice activity has to be "psychologically authentic: The activity should be designed to allow learners to experience some of the normal psychological pressures felt by people engaged in real communication" (Gatbonton and Segalowitz, 1988: 486).

According to Johnson (1994), it was the remoteness of the cognitive demands during productive practice as compared with the cognitive demands of production in communication that caused the ALM to fail.

Indeed, extrapolating from the psychological research on *procedural reinstatement* (Healy and Bourne, 1995) or *transfer-appropriate processing* (Blaxton, 1989; Roediger, 1990) leads one to conclude that practice activities should meet the minimal conditions present in target performance. In the case of language learning, when fluent and accurate spoken communication is the end goal, this would mean that practice activities should be communicative, where learners perform independently, with little or no planning time, at a certain rate of speed, using the same modality as is expected in the performance, conveying messages with the same information density, (un)predictability, linguistic complexity, and so on. However, these are clearly conditions that students have to learn strategies to deal with. I am reminded of Widdowson's apt warning: "The central question is not what learners have to do to use language naturally, but what they have to do to *learn* to use language naturally" (1990: 46–47). Therefore, rather than manipulative to communicative and mechanical to communicative frameworks, I propose a new framework that would grade activities, starting from at least minimally meaningful practice activities and stretching to psychologically authentic communication.

Although we want to ensure transfer from what has been practiced in the classroom to use for other purposes, it is clear that learning to cope with the conditions of psychological authenticity needs to operate along a gradient. The following parameters for output production of informal speaking, then, would be adjusted, depending on the grammatical proficiency of the students:

- **Social scaffolding to independent production**—From a greater to lesser degree of reliance on the teacher or classmates for assistance in producing the target form accurately, meaningfully, appropriately.

- **Planning time**—From more time for planning and rehearsal to less time. Informal speaking, of course, unlike planned speech or writing, entails an immediacy of response that permits little time for reflecting, planning, or monitoring.

- **Modality match**—From writing to speaking. Sometimes students are asked to practice grammar points by completing written grammar exercises. Written grammar exercises have their place in language teaching, but we should not be too surprised to find that students are not able to use the grammar correctly in speech if they have only practiced it in written form. The shift of modality leads to a change in cognitive demands, and transfer will be unsuccessful.

- **Speed of output production**—From slower to faster, increasingly approximating the speed at which ordinary communication takes place (see the earlier investigation based on Arevart and Nation for one way that this may be accomplished). As Johnson (1994) notes, this may be a good use of computer-assisted instruction, where the time learners take to produce a form can be attenuated.

- **Information density**—From shorter utterances to longer utterances, lengthening the information students have to remember as they engage in output practice. Length would be a crude measure, at least, of information density.

- **Predictability of language use**—From greater to lesser predictability, where students have to rely less on formulaic language and more on syntactically processed output.

- **Complexity of language use**—From shorter texts to longer texts.

- **Self-generated language use**—From lesser to greater generation of what one says.

Stevick (1996) cites psychological research in support of the *generation effect*—that is, that students remember best what they themselves construct. However, he also astutely points out that there are tasks—such as being able to identify a word quickly and accurately—where subjects are aided more by reading practice than by self-generating associations. In other words, the advantage for constructing or generating what one says may simply be another manifestation of transfer-appropriate processing. When the demands of output practice match the demands of subsequent use, students' performance is maximized.

Of course, none of these parameters is precisely calibrated. Teaching is a contingent activity. Teachers must continually adjust the parameters of a given activity as they learn what the appropriate level of challenge is for a given group of students or, as is commonly the case, for the heterogeneous challenges present in a given class. It is worth underscoring the idea that psychological authenticity is the goal but that "…inauthentic language-using behavior might well be effective language-learning behavior…" (Widdowson, 1990: 46-47). Thus, practice activities will not always be authentically communicative, but will work toward authenticity.

I have yet to discuss the circumstances of practice. I have in mind such factors as the spacing of practice, whether or not students receive feedback on their performance during practice activities, and the "power law of practice," which states that the effects of practice are often greatest at early stages of learning. However, these are matters that will be taken up in the next two chapters, which look specifically at feedback and at syllabus design/pedagogy, respectively.

Suggested Readings

Doughty and Williams (1998), R. Ellis (2001), and Hinkel and Fotos (2002) contain chapters/articles of interest in terms of designing form-focused and innovative activities to teach grammar. Platt and Brooks (2002) contrast interactionist and sociocultural approaches to the study of task engagement. So much has recently been written concerning connectionism and emergentism that it is difficult to know what to mention. I should at least include Clark's (1997) *Being There*, Elman et. al.'s (1998) *Rethinking Innateness*, MacWhinney's (1999) anthology, *The Emergence of Language*, and Bybee and Hopper's (2001) *Frequency and the Emergence of Linguistic Structure*. Larsen-Freeman (1997), N. Ellis (1998; 2002), Meara (1997;

1999), and Cameron (n.d.) discuss modeling of second language acquisition processes in terms of connectionism, emergentism, and chaos/complexity or dynamical systems theory.

10

FEEDBACK

FEEDBACK VERSUS CORRECTION

I will use the term *feedback* to mean evaluative information available to learners concerning their linguistic performance. It can be positive ("That's correct") or negative ("That's not the right verb tense"). It can be explicit and direct, as in the two examples I have just given, or explicit and indirect, such as someone saying to a language learner "I don't understand," or giving a learner a bewildered look in response to the learner's saying something perceived to be incomprehensible. It can also be implicit, as when a learner's interlocutor, in the next turn of a conversation, correctly recasts or reformulates what the learner has just produced incorrectly. Feedback can be initiated by others, as in the examples given so far, or it can be self-generated, as when learners notice a match or mismatch between what they wanted to say and what they actually said. Compared to the traditional term *error correction*, (negative) feedback is broader in scope. It also has a less punitive connotation. And while error is by definition an externally norm-referenced notion, feedback, as we will see later, is not necessarily so.

Zoe Morosini

> I tell my students that they don't need to be accurate to communicate. They do need to be accurate to be respected.

Which norm to use in determining whether some learner production is an error is not, of course, purely a linguistic question, but also a sociopolitical one, as Zoe, a teacher of elementary-level ESL high school students in the U.S., rightly implies in her comment above. A student of Zoe's who said "No want read" could well be understood, but Zoe would probably respond to the form of this student's utterance because of its pronounced deviation from native speaker norms.

The question arises, though, as to whether learners, particularly where a language is taught as a foreign language, should be expected to conform to native speaker norms. Even if the answer to this question is affirmative, which native speaker norms are appropriate? For instance, in the English-speaking world, there are many "Englishes." Should learners of English be held to the same norms as native BANA (British, Australian/New Zealand, North American) English speakers, or should they adopt a regional English—Nigerian, Singaporean, South Asian—as their standard? Regardless of the answer to this question, another question remains: whether second language learners should be assessed in light of what native speakers do, no matter what the norm. Cook asks, "Should acquisition of a second language be measured against monolingual standards, or should second language learners be viewed as language users who can use more than one language, and not as 'failed monolinguals'?" (Cook, 1999: 46). These contextually embedded and value-laden questions are important ones that teachers and their students should answer for themselves.

For now, let me note that a final reason that I prefer the term *negative feedback* to *error correction* is that the former is neutral with regard to expectation. This is why I wrote that feedback is information "available to learners." As we know, written or oral input does not necessarily become intake, let alone *uptake*—the term used to mean that learners have not only perceived the feedback, they have altered their performance as a consequence. The neutrality of feedback also respects the agency of the learner. Learners who receive negative feedback may be left to do with it what they will and are able to do. Elimination of errors will not necessarily be an immediate or even a remote consequence.

A MOST CONTROVERSIAL AREA

Since, for many teachers, providing feedback is an important function in their teaching, it may be surprising to learn that treatment of learner errors is one of the most controversial areas in language pedagogy (Larsen-Freeman, 1991). One end of a continuum of theoretical positions is represented by those who say that negative feedback or error correction is unnecessary, counterproductive, and even harmful. (See, for example, Truscott, 1996; 1999.) Such thinking has been partly shaped by Chomsky's claim (Chomsky, 1981: 9) that negative feedback is unnecessary in L1 acquisition: "There is good reason to believe that direct negative evidence is not necessary for language acquisition..." Children can learn from *positive evidence* (evidence of what is permissible in the language). Of course, L1 learners also have access to *indirect negative evidence* in the language itself, in that they may notice what is *not* said. In addition to Chomsky's observation concerning L1 acquisition, opponents of correcting errors or giving negative feedback in SLA contend that negative teacher evaluations of student performance provokes anxiety in students, which adversely affects their learning. Besides, opponents argue, under propitious conditions, learners will eventually self-correct—provided that they continue to be open to input and, therefore, positive evidence.

At the other end of the continuum is the behaviorist view of language acquisition, one with no tolerance for errors. According to behaviorists, errors are to be prevented if possible, in order to avoid learners' establishing bad habits. Learners are exposed to tightly controlled input, carefully calibrated in terms of differences between the L1 and L2, so as to anticipate where errors would be likely to occur, and thus prevent them. If prevention fails, as it always does, errors should be corrected immediately.

In between these two poles on the continuum are less extreme views. One such view comes from a cognitive perspective. According to this view, learners are bound to commit errors. This is inevitable, not regrettable. Errors arise when learners test hypotheses about the target language. For instance, a learner of English who is aware that *sick* can be used both predicatively and prenominally, as in:

John is sick. He is a sick man.

might incorrectly infer that the same is true for the adjective *ill*:

John is ill. *He is an ill man.

How, Bley-Vroman (1986) asks, are learners to know that *ill* is not used prenominally? No matter how many times learners receive positive evidence that *ill* is used predicatively and *sick* used predicatively and prenominally, they will not necessarily conclude that *ill* cannot be used in the same positions as *sick*. Indirect negative evidence, such as never hearing *ill* used prenominally, may easily escape learners' attention. In such cases learners may need to be told about the limitations of *ill* and/or they may need to make an error and receive negative feedback on their performance in order to learn its restricted syntactic distribution.

Errors do not merely present opportunities for feedback. They can also provide helpful windows on learners' minds, showing teachers and researchers what learners are thinking, their stage of development, and what strategies they are adopting.

10.1

Here are some actual errors made by young ESL students. Can you imagine what they are thinking? In other words, what hypotheses about English might they be entertaining?

1. *He is a seven-years-old boy.

2. Do you like ice cream? *Yes. I like.

3. *We discuss about that.

Of course, analyzing errors is only the first step in a teacher's knowing how to respond. A teacher must also consider whether any feedback should be given at all and, if it should, which feedback strategy is likely to be most effective.

10.2

For many teachers, introduction of communicative language teaching, and the accompanying shift of focus from the form of the target language to its use, encouraged a more tolerant attitude toward learner errors.

This would be a good time to clarify your own position with regard to feedback and error correction. What do you think about the use of feedback in the language classroom? Do you use it or support its use? Why or why not?

PROVIDING FEEDBACK IS ESSENTIAL

Here are my answers to these questions. Providing feedback is an essential function of teaching. In fact, research has shown that students want to be corrected more than teachers generally feel is necessary (Cathcart and Olsen, 1976; Chenoweth et al., 1983). One of the subjects in Cohen and Robbins' study (1976) offers an explanation. The subject, Ue-Lin, reported that being corrected contributed to her feeling that she was learning something. As Lyster Lightbown and Spada (1999) assert, just because it is difficult to know when, how, and what to correct does not mean that "error correction" should be abandoned. Indeed, Francisco Gomes de Mateo (2002), in drafting a declaration of learners' grammatical rights, asserts that learners have the right to receive "constructive, humanizing feedback on their grammatical errors." All the same, it is important to be mindful of many people's fear of failure, fear of making mistakes. Thus, in my opinion, affectively supportive, nonjudgmental, judicious, focused feedback that helps students say what they wish to say is vital to successful teaching.

One way to remain affectively supportive when it comes to giving feedback is to see oneself less as the guardian of the norms and more as a nurturer of students' language development. Some years ago, Bley-Vroman (1983) pointed out that we language teachers and researchers operate under the *comparative fallacy*. We see learner errors as failures to achieve target language norms rather than as evidence of what learners have achieved in terms of their own evolving interlanguage. For instance, if a learner of English were to say *I goed yesterday* or *I go yesterday*, both utterances could be said to contain errors—that is, non-targetlike productions. However, the first one shows that the learner has some knowledge about the need to mark past tense in English. Thus, on the face of it at least, *goed* could be evidence of interlanguage development. In other words, learners' errors can be interpreted as showing development rather than deficiency. Bearing this in mind may lead to a more respectful treatment of learners' efforts.

See Chapter 2.

The other fallacy that is relevant here is the *reflex fallacy*, of which I have written earlier in this book. Teaching is not a mere reflex of natural language acquisition. Our job as teachers is to accelerate, not to emulate, the natural language acquisition process. It is doubtful that naturalistic learners have much access to negative feedback. Conversational analysts, for instance, tell us that there is decided dispreference for other-initiated repair. This means that it is unlikely that learners will receive direct explicit feedback from their conversational partners. Even when indirect feedback does present itself in naturalistic situations, it is questionable how much feedback the learner can notice and process when there are competing demands for the learner's time and attention. Conversely, feedback on learners' performance in an instructional environment presents an opportunity for learning to take place. An error potentially represents a teachable moment. As Chaudron (1988) asserts, "for most learners, the use of feedback may constitute the most potent source of improvement in target language development."

Before proceeding to an exploration of ways of working with errors, it is, as is my custom, important for me to try to understand views that differ from my own. I need, therefore, first to consider the arguments against providing explicit negative feedback.

What are the criticisms of error correction?

As we have seen, in light of assertions (although some maintain that they are unfounded) that children acquire their native language in the absence of negative feedback, it has been argued that negative feedback is unnecessary for native language acquisition. Some SLA researchers have followed suit, arguing that feedback on the part of the teacher can be futile, even harmful, ambiguous, and inconsistent. I would like to discuss each of these criticisms in turn.

Futile

Many teachers have questioned whether their efforts are well spent. Do learners even pay attention to the circled errors on a composition, for instance, and do they actually learn from them if they do? Quite honestly, the answers to these questions derived from research studies are very mixed. Some studies suggest that students benefit from focused attention to their errors; other studies show no enduring gain from such attention.

If there is a question about whether or not learners pay attention to marks on a paper when they have ample time to do so, their doing so during some communicative activity would seem even less likely. Further, it has been suggested that the alleged futility of teachers' efforts might stem from failure to respect developmental sequences. In other words, it may be in vain to correct students on grammatical items that they are not yet ready to acquire.

The perception of futility can also be attributed to the existence of seemingly intractable errors that appear to be very resistant to correction. Sometimes it happens that, despite continued exposure to the target language, motivation to learn it, and opportunity to practice it, learning ceases. When such is the case, a learner's interlanguage is said to have *fossilized*, to have reached a terminal learning plateau. While no one knows for sure what causes fossilization, its existence is said to distinguish L1 from L2 acquisition.

Harmful

Truscott worries that error correction will lead students to limit the complexity of their writing as an avoidance strategy. Students who are frequently corrected may become inhibited. It is not only negative feedback that some feel is potentially harmful. Gattegno (1976) cautions against the use of positive feedback. If a teacher praises students often, then students will get the impression that learning a language is something out of the ordinary—something supposed to be difficult. Such an impression may make learning a language more difficult than it is.

Ambiguous

In an attempt to draw a student's attention to an error, it is quite common for a teacher to repeat what a student has just said. However, as Lyster and Ranta (1997) point out, repetition can be ambiguous because it can be used for different functions. While one function of repetition may be to provide students with an opportunity to self-correct, at other times a teacher's repetition of a student's utterance may simply be a request for confirmation of the sort that any two proficient speakers of a language may engage in. Such is the case with the following French example taken from Lyster (1998).

> *Student:* Il faut qu'ils fassent plein de travail. (*They have to do a lot of work.*)
>
> *Teacher:* Il faut qu'ils fassent plein de travail? (said with rising intonation)

There is nothing wrong with what the student has said in French. However, the teacher's confirmation request might be misinterpreted as suggesting that a problem exists.

Inconsistent

A long time ago, Allwright (1975) pointed out that teachers were inconsistent in correcting students' errors. Of course, teachers may have very good reasons for varying how they respond to students' errors. Teachers may know that certain learners benefit from encouragement while others gain more from direct, explicit negative feedback. A teacher may be inconsistent in that a particular error may sometimes be corrected while at other times, when an activity is aimed more at developing fluency, it may be ignored. Or a teacher may use one type of feedback with a particular error at one time and, seeing it fail, may resort to a different type another time. A teacher's "inconsistency" can derive from legitimate, nuanced, and rational pedagogical decisions.

By the same token, one can understand Truscott's alarm at the inconsistency in the way errors are treated. As Truscott (1998) notes, a teacher who ignores one student's error and corrects another is sending a mixed and confusing message to the class as a whole that may compound the learning difficulty.

Responding to the Criticisms

While these criticisms of error correction may have merit, notice that they deal with error correction in general. To appreciate the importance of supplying negative feedback, it may be useful to adopt a particularistic stance, that is, to look more narrowly at error types. For example, Pica (1983) reports the interesting finding that tutored and untutored learners make different types of errors. Tutored learners tend to make *errors of commission*; they overuse forms, presumably because the forms have received attention during instruction. Untutored learners, on the other hand, tend to make *errors of omission;* they tend not to use certain structures. Significantly, Long (1988) notes that errors of omission are more likely to persist in a learner's interlanguage. It is easier to notice that something is superfluous than to notice that one is not doing something. In this way, feedback may reduce the likelihood of inflexibility and fossilization in language development.

Another type of error that may be persistent unless students receive feedback is L1-induced errors in conspiracy with violations of natural principles in UG (White, 1987). Margaret Rogers (1994), in discussing the learning of German word order, makes much the same point. Where there is an L1–L2 contrast, the learner may need direct explicit negative feedback from the teacher to notice that the input only provides evidence about the non-application of a rule.

For example, there is a contrast between English and German with regard to adverbial fronting. In German, one can front an adverbial, but must adhere to the word order of Adv + V + Sub + Obj when doing so:

Gestern sah ich den Film.

Yesterday saw I the film.

When learning German, an English speaker's original hypothesis might be that the order Adv + Sub + V + Obj is possible, as it is in English. Without negative feedback, learners may never receive evidence that the English word order is impossible in German. In other words, they would receive positive evidence about the German word order, but without feedback, they might never notice the negative evidence that would show that the English word order does not occur in German. Thus, the logic goes, if the learner has positive evidence about the application of a rule in natural input, then that is sufficient to accelerate learning. But if the natural input only provides negative evidence about the non-application of a rule, then explicit negative feedback from the teacher is required.

We also need to ask what the critics mean when they say that error correction does not work. Learners' performance may not immediately be altered after learners receive negative feedback; however, that does not mean that nothing has been registered. For instance, *priming* may be occurring, from which future benefits will be derived. Moreover, Schachter (1991) observes that even telling a learner "No, it's not that way" may be of tremendous help by reducing the learner's hypothesis space, thereby narrowing the set of possible hypotheses to be tested. While it is true that there have been long-term studies that showed no evidence of beneficial effects for negative feedback (Robb et al., 1986), there is also research that reaches the opposite conclusion. For example, in a recent longitudinal study of Thai–Norwegian interlanguage, Han and Selinker (1999) documented that fine-tuned corrective feedback provides a cure for persistent errors that result from multiple factors working in tandem.

As for fossilization, it seems to me that teachers still have the responsibility to provide learners feedback on even the most persistent of errors. If they abdicate this responsibility, fossilization becomes inevitable. While our expectations about feedback must be realistic, we should never abandon the quest for a way to help students when it is their goal to use a standard form for what they wish to convey. As is well known, the acquisition of grammar is a gradual process; what teachers tell students and what students learn are not always directly and proximally linked.

THE ROLE OF FEEDBACK

What I conclude from the research literature, then, is that the issue of feedback is a complex one. Blanket proscriptions and prescriptions are unlikely to be reliable. This is an area where local, particularistic research—research that takes into account the contingent nature of teaching, characteristics of the context, the nature of the native language and the target language, and the goals of both teachers and students—is more likely to shed light.

I do not mean to overlook the powerful lessons of my own experience, and the experience of others, as learner, teacher, and teacher educator. For example, Schulz (2001) surveyed Colombian and U.S. foreign language teachers and their students and found that there was considerable agreement concerning the value of error correction. Such experience alone might be reason enough to endorse the use of feedback. But there is more. Another reason for my belief in the value of feedback stems from my interest in looking at problems and issues in second language acquisition and second language teaching from a Chaos/Complexity or dynamical systems perspective. One prominent characteristic of such systems is that they are responsive to feedback. In nature this means that such systems can "learn," that is, they can change and develop in ways that are novel. When an innovation occurs within a species, positive feedback will cause it to endure, even amplify; negative feedback will contribute to its eradication. As Joseph Ford put it, "Evolution is chaos with feedback" (in Gleick, 1987: 314). Moreover, with newer models of evolution, such as the late biologist's Stephen Jay Gould's *punctuated equilibrium*, evolutionary changes do not always take place in a linear fashion, at a fairly constant rate. When confronted by environmental stresses (negative feedback), genetic diversity that is normally concealed can emerge and generate diverse physical forms in surprisingly short order. Thus, change can occur rather rapidly within a single generation, overnight from an evolutionary sense of time.

See Larsen-Freeman (1997) and Cooper (1999).

From a dynamical systems perspective, then, I take all this to mean that feedback is not merely useful in corralling the linguistic performance of learners. Feedback can also be very helpful in stimulating the growth of a linguistic system (except when it has fossilized) while keeping it within limits that are neither completely flexible nor rigidly inflexible in nature. In other words, from a dynamical systems perspective, feedback is not simply about maintaining equilibrium. This would be true if the system were simple and closed; however, in complex, open systems, feedback is not about closing the loop between input and output. Feedback helps a system develop beyond the set point of the norms, stimulating the creative pattern-formation process that results in linguistic novelty or morphogenesis. And, finally, the consequences of feedback may be nonlinear; sometimes nothing will seem to occur, while at other times change will be sudden.

Now, of course, language acquisition does not exist independently of the language learner. It is embodied in the language learner. Nevertheless, if the neural networks of the brain are forged by the same processes that are responsible for evolution—morphogenesis, emergentism, self-organization, nonlinear dynamics—then it may not be too much of a stretch to claim that, since the same underlying processes characterize both evolution and the creation of neural networks, the outcomes of both processes are altered by feedback. After all, even the most elementary connectionist models of neural networks have feedback loops built in, whereby the output is compared to the input and adjustments in the connection weights are made through a process called *backpropagation*.

CHARACTERISTICS OF EFFECTIVE FEEDBACK

Whether this turns out to be the case or not, for the time being, in this chapter, I will take a stance that argues for the value of feedback when done judiciously, using appropriate techniques, appropriately focused, in an affectively supportive, nonjudgmental manner. I will elaborate on each of these characteristics in the text that follows.

Judicious

Even if correcting students' every error were pedagogically feasible, socially acceptable, not demoralizing to learners, and did not lead to their undue dependence on the teacher, it would still not be a psychologically sound practice. Pervasive correction ignores such important psychological limitations as memory capacity and attention span. Negative feedback, therefore, has to be judicious to be effective. However, selectivity is not sufficient in and of itself.

One of the criticisms of traditional error correction is that it is often directed at isolated points "without reference either to the processes by which the linguistic system develops or the learner's current developmental stage" (Truscott, 1996: 347). While it seems to me that this is a valid criticism from a psycholinguistic perspective, it presents a tall order for any teacher to fulfill. How are teachers to decide which learner errors impede the development of the learner's systemic knowledge?

There are no absolute answers to this question, of course, because it will depend as much on the learner as it will on any linguistic system; however, the following guidelines, extrapolated from the literature and the experience of practitioners, including my own experience, may be of use in helping teachers attend judiciously to certain errors.

1. Attend to errors that show that a student is ready to learn.

Errors in structures that learners appear to be newly producing with some frequency are likely candidates. Research has shown that such structures, called *emergent forms*, are much more likely to be influenced by feedback than are structures that are rarely attempted. For instance, research by Williams and Evans (1998) has demonstrated that students' acquisition of an emergent form, participial adjectives, was facilitated by an input flood, and even more so by contextualized explanations, whereas the same learners did not benefit from similar explanations directed at the passive voice, presumably because the learners were not ready to sort out the complex form, meaning, use relationship involved in the passive. Participial adjectives were already being used by these students, though often inaccurately, and when students received consistent corrective feedback concerning them, greater accuracy resulted.

Chaos/Complexity theorists have a colorful way of putting it. They claim that complex, adaptive, dynamical systems evolve "at the edge of chaos" (Kauffman, 1995), a zone between order and disorder. Identifying emergent forms in students' interlanguage requires a close monitoring of students' performance. Significantly, it also suggests a somewhat unusual dynamic in that, rather than teachers leading learners, teaching is learning to follow the students' lead. In other words, the students' errors will tell us where to teach. I will return to this theme in the next chapter.

2. Work on errors, not mistakes.

Another judgment on the part of the teacher is whether a non-target form is a mistake or an error, a distinction proposed by Corder (1967). Whereas an error results from lack of knowledge about the correct form, a mistake is merely a performance slip. Errors, being systematic, would be natural candidates for feedback, while mistakes might better be ignored. Further discernment by teachers is called for, with the suggestion that error gravity should be a criterion and that only those errors that most egregiously interfere with communication should be marked for feedback.

Here is what a teacher in the ELI (English Language Institute) at Malta has to say about exercising judgment when providing feedback.

> Occasionally when I'm writing down errors they're making during speaking fluency, well first of all I'm discarding a lot of slips and a lot of errors which I don't think are especially important... and I occasionally slip in something which they may not have made that day but is often made by students at that level, and I know instinctively and from experience that that is something which they need to come to grips with or they want to come to grips with (Borg, 1998: 16).

Thus, this EFL teacher is not only selecting errors to focus on, the teacher is also anticipating students' needs even before an error has been made. Such a practice would seem to draw support from Lightbown's (1991: 193) observation that focusing on form is most effective when "learners *know* what they want to say, indeed are trying to say something, and the means to say it more correctly are offered to them." The next characteristic follows from this.

3. Work with errors where students show that they know what they want to say, recognize that they do not know how to do so, and try anyway.

Realizing that such is the case requires that teacher and students achieve a certain level of intersubjectivity so that the teacher is aware of what the student is trying to say and can supply an acceptable linguistic formulation. Although there is no guarantee that one's feedback will be heeded, of course, knowing one's students well enough to infer their intentions would seem to increase the chance of this happening. This is why blanket proscriptions and prescriptions fail. While linguistic and psycholinguistic considerations are important, they are not the whole story. If a teacher fails to achieve intersubjectivity with her students, her efforts may be fruitless.

10.3

Identifying the source of an error can be very helpful in determining what sort of feedback to offer in response. To put it in the vernacular, it helps to know where one's students "are coming from." Consider the following error in English. Can you figure out what the student was trying to say and why he or she was misled?

*I hope I could go.

4. Deal with errors that are committed during accuracy activities.

Unlike my other suggestions, this one has less to do with learners' development and more to do with the nature of the activity they are engaged in and the social dynamics of the classroom. It is an old pedagogical adage that there are times when students should have opportunities to develop fluency without worrying much about accuracy. Of course, during fluency activities, students' errors can still be discreetly noted by the teacher, but providing feedback on them can be put off for another time. As the EFL teacher from Malta in Borg's study puts it:

Teachers'
Voices

> We do a lot of fluency work, and sometimes learners' expectations of the language classroom differ from this reality. Giving them opportunities to focus on accuracy in language work that springs from (or is related to) these fluency activities helps these types of learners to accept more enthusiastically the fluency activities.

Even during fluency activities, however, there may be times when unobtrusive feedback may be warranted. Such might be the case, for example, when a student describes an event using verb forms that create confusion about time. The point is that during a fluency-based activity, the goal should simply be to achieve successful unself-conscious communication, not to make everything a student says accurate.

A final consideration concerning judicious feedback is based on the language system itself.

5. Give feedback on errors where learners need negative evidence in order to eliminate a hypothesis.

Not all hypotheses are of the type that may benefit from negative evidence. Some incorrect hypotheses are compatible with a certain subset of the available data. For example, in English, the following are all acceptable:

John was fearful.

John was frightened.

John was afraid.

An English learner might make note of such sentences. Later, when the learner hears that *John is a fearful person* or *John is a frightened person*, the learner might incorrectly infer that it is also possible to say *John is an afraid person.*

Overgeneralization errors such as this may benefit more than others from error correction. In fact, Tomasello and Herron (1988) have demonstrated that, when learners are in the process of generalizing and make an overgeneralization, an effective technique is to point out the error at the moment the overgeneralization is made. Tomasello and Herron call this the *"garden path" technique.* It receives its name from the fact that learners may be "led down the garden path." In other words, learners may not know or may not be told that there are problems with a particular structure. For example, English learners may believe that all English past tense verbs are regular. Initially, they may be given the rule for forming regular past tense verbs without being told of the existence of irregular verbs. It would be quite natural for such learners to produce overgeneralization errors, saying *eated* for *ate*, for example. Once they do, and only after they do, learners would receive feedback concerning their errors. Tomasello and Herron found the "garden path" technique to be more effective than telling learners in advance about exceptions to a rule.

Appropriate techniques appropriately focused

By bringing up the "garden path" technique I have moved from discussing which errors to correct to which techniques to use. In actual fact, a great variety of feedback techniques exists. For instance, Aljaafreh and Lantolf (1994) offer a thirteen-point scale of feedback practices, from more implicit techniques to more explicit ones. At the implicit end of the scale, students are asked to find their errors in an essay they have written and to correct the errors on their own. Toward the middle of the scale, the nature of the error is identified for the student using explicit direct negative feedback of a metalinguistic nature (e.g., "There is something wrong with the tense marking here") but it is left up to the student to identify the precise error and to correct it. At the explicit end of the scale, when other forms of help fail to produce an appropriate action, the learner is given an explanation for the use of the correct form and, if needed, examples of the correct form.

It is often assumed that self-correction is best because, when learners do their own correcting, they are more likely to remember it. Then, too, simply telling students what is wrong or giving them the correct answer does not teach students to correct themselves. In general, many teachers and teaching methodologists suggest abiding by conversational maxims that favor self-repair over other-repair.

A variety of techniques have been proposed to help learners identify the problem in what they have said and to self-correct, such as various forms of repetition and elicitation (echoaic, echoaic with rising intonation, echoaic stressing the trouble spot, etc.). Schachter (1986) suggests that even such indirect means of negative feedback as signaling a failure to understand can be helpful to learners. However, favoring self-correction does not mean that teachers should always be so indirect.

> I think there is a place ... for leading students to a situation where they perceive that they need this knowledge and want this knowledge, and trying to lead them to an awareness of it themselves, and providing the knowledge if they can't get to it themselves (A teacher in Borg, 1998: 22–23).

When it is necessary for a teacher to provide explicit feedback, it is important to let students know that the corrections are offered as help, not criticism. To this end, it is sometimes pointed out that teachers should highlight not only what is wrong, but what is right in what their students say or write as well.

10.4

Here is a short piece of writing produced by a male intermediate ESL student, a native speaker of Arabic. What would you tell a student to correct here? What would you tell the student is right?

I saw a movie about a man in a city (big city). I want to tell you what I saw and what is my opinion. The movie began with a man about forty years old, in his apartment in a big city. He was disturbed by many things like Alarm O'Clock, T.V., Radio and noisy outside. He want a fresh air, but he could not because the city is not a good place for fresh air. There are many factories which fill the air with smoke. The movie showed the daily life of a man in the city. He is very busy day and night. He had to go to his work early by any means of transportation, car, bus, bicycle. The streets are crowded, everything in the city is crowded with people, the houses, streets, factories, institutions, even the seashores...

(Data from Selinker and Gass, 1984)

Of course, the teacher is not the only purveyor of feedback. Students can learn a great deal from their peers. Here is an example of peer correction given to French learner S1 by learner S2 (Swain, 1998: 78):

S1: La nuit dernière je marchais dans un long passage étroit.

(Last night I was walking in a long narrow passage.)

S2: Non, étroite.

(No, narrow [feminine form].)

S1: Avec un "e"?

(With an "e"?)

S2: Oui.

(Yes.)

A lot of attention in the second language acquisition literature has been given to a feedback strategy known as a *recast*. Perhaps the most widespread of all teacher responses to learner errors, recasting involves teachers reformulating all or part of what a student has just said so that it is correct. For example:

Teacher: *What did you do this weekend?*

Student: *I have gone to the movies.*

Teacher: *Oh. You went to the movies last night. What did you see?*

Han (in press) suggests that the most successful recasts are ones where students receive individual attention, where recasts deal with a consistent focus—for example, for a period of time, all recasts might deal with verb tense usage—where it appears that learners are developmentally ready to benefit from the evidence provided by recasts, and when there is a certain level of intensity to the recasts, thereby heightening their frequency and saliency. However, the "success" of a recast cannot be determined by an immediate change in learner performance alone. For one thing, the learning process is nonlinear, and so a shift in performance may not immediately follow the recast. For another, the learner may find the recast useful for his or her own purposes, such as its use in private speech rehearsal, again with no immediate concomitant change in performance (Ohta, 2000).

Of course no technique—even giving the student the correct form, as the teacher in the example did with the past tense of *go*—is effective unless the student can perceive the difference between the recast and what he or she has just said. It would seem necessary, therefore, that students *notice the gap* between what they are producing and what the target language demands at that point. The same could be said for the teacher's efforts at correction. Indeed, Nicholas, Lightbown, and Spada (2001), in their review of the research literature on recasts, concluded that recasts are most effective when they are not ambiguous, that is, when learners perceive that the recast is in reaction to the form, not the content, of what they have just said. Otherwise, there could be a mismatch between the teacher's intent and the learner's perception of it. Han (2002: 24–25) recognizes the need for fine-tuning, for achieving

> 1) congruence between a teacher's intention and a student's interpretation, and 2) between a teacher's correction and a student's readiness for it.... In tuning feedback to learning problems, it seems important that a teacher has a range of strategies readily available so as to be able to adopt one that is most fitting to the targeted problem as well as to the ongoing dynamics of the communicative activities.

In other words, it is unlikely that there is one feedback strategy that is better than others for all occasions. Instead, teachers need to develop a repertoire of techniques that can be deployed as appropriate. Effective use of strategies results when teachers adapt their practice to their students' learning. Thus, error correction ultimately comes down to adjusting feedback to the individual learner. Adjustments cannot be determined a priori; rather, they must be collaboratively negotiated on-line with the learner. As Aljaafreh and Lantolf (1994) explain, from a sociocultural or Vygotskyan perspective, learning takes place when there is a bridge between the dialogic activity, collaboratively constructed by the teacher and the student, and the student's internal mental functioning. Here is an example from their study (page 477) illustrating this point. The student (S) is going over an essay she has written with her teacher (T):

T: *We can see a grey big layers in the sky with a dense smog. What is...do you see anything wrong here?*

S: Dense smog with ah heavy or...

T: *That's fine, yeah this is good*

S: This is good?

T: *But what do you see wrong in these sentences...*

S: Ah just a moment. "We can...see we can...we can...see

T: *Uhum*

S: It...grey

T: Okay

S: Big

T: Okay, grey big

S: Layers

T: Layers

S: Layers in the sky

T: Uhum

S: Because is no one only, is all…

T: Layers, it is not singular. Right, that's good.

S: Grey big layers…yes (laughs)

T: In the sky

S: With dense

T: Okay

S: (laughs)

T: Dense, that's good

S: Dense smoke

T: With dense smog

S: Produced by carbon monoxide of the vehicle.

Aljaafreh and Lantolf note that:

> the learner is immediately able to correct her misuse of the indefinite article with the mass noun "smog" in line 1. Of even more interest is what we observe in lines 6 and 7, where the learner overtly interrupts the tutor's utterance and subsequently inhibits his attempt to offer assistance. In so doing, she assumes fuller responsibility for finding and correcting the error in "a grey big layers." (1994: 477)

Much of what has been written in this section conforms to the traditional view that learning grammar means learning formal accuracy. In this book, though, I have challenged this notion and explained that, for me, learning grammar is also learning to use grammar structures meaningfully and appropriately. As such, any feedback techniques that are used not only have to be appropriate, they have to be appropriately focused.

10.5

To drive this point home, consider the following English learner statements. Each contains an error (although you undoubtedly will find some more obvious than others). Can you sort them into the categories of form, meaning, and use?

1. *A:* I like math.
   B: Really? I am boring in math class.
2. Please explain me the answer.
3. Our company has a lot of people.
4. Please extinguish your cigarette here. This is a non-smoking area.
5. The cocoa tasted good. It was too hot.
6. Give the person sitting at the end of the table the salt.

Affectively supportive and nonjudgmental

Teachers try to be affectively supportive of their students. As teachers learn that some of their students have a greater fear of rejection than others, they may provide feedback selectively. Then, too, learners differ in the degree to which they commit errors. Some learners are cautious; they do not speak until they are quite sure that what they say will be right. Others are more impulsive, and they actively participate in class whether or not what they say is in acceptable form. "Igor," a language learner given this pseudonym and studied by Allwright (1980), was such a learner. Igor was extroverted and unafraid to say things that were not targetlike. Allwright speculates that all students might benefit from having an "Igor" as a classmate, someone who asks questions that other students may be reluctant to ask and who receives feedback from the teacher from which everyone can learn.

So far I have said little about positive feedback. Of course, positive feedback was considered very important from a behaviorist standpoint. Giving students positive comments about their successful performance was considered crucial in reinforcing target language habits. Many teachers who do not see themselves as behaviorists nonetheless quite naturally praise students when they are successful in their language learning efforts, or give them positive feedback for their efforts even when their performance does not conform to target language norms.

However, being affectively supportive does not necessarily mean giving positive feedback. For one thing, giving students positive feedback on their linguistic performance may send the implicit message that students are succeeding at something extraordinary, whereas perhaps we should be suggesting instead that language learning is quite natural and not that difficult (Gattegno, 1976). Another concern about providing students with positive feedback is that it may be confusing to students if they are not sure what they are being praised for. A number of years ago, Vigil and Oller (1976) made a useful distinction between *cognitive feedback* and *affective feedback*. Both types of feedback can be negative or positive. These researchers reported that a combination of negative cognitive feedback and positive affective feedback was most likely to stimulate development in learners' interlanguage. Thus, giving students evaluative information on their linguistic performance in a nonjudgmental manner, while being affectively supportive of them and their efforts, may be the best combination to strive for.

In this chapter I have taken up the matter of feedback, what I have called one of "the big three" (consciousness-raising and output practice being the other two). Although noting that the need for feedback is controversial, I have staked out a position in favor of providing students with feedback. Further, I believe that feedback provision is most effective when it is judicious, appropriate, and nonjudgmental. If this seems like a tall order to fill, it is. If it seems unrealistic, it may well be. But if we abandon the quest, we give up an essential function of teaching, for how else are students to efficiently learn where they are on target and where they are off? Thus, "feedback" is one answer to a question I often ask myself: "What is it that I can give my students that they can't (easily) get on their own?"

Suggested Readings

A great deal has been written over the years on error correction, and more recently on feedback. A classic treatment of the former is H. V. George (1972). Of course, Selinker (1972) coined both the terms *interlanguage* and *fossilization*. Han (2002; in press) is a researcher who has recently written a great deal about feedback. Recent reviews of the literature concerning the role of recasts can be found in Nicholas, Lightbown, and Spada (2001) and Braidi (2002).

11
TEACHING GRAMMARING

I do not intend to be prescriptive in this chapter. Grammar teaching (any teaching!) is a complex process, which cannot be treated by repeating the same set of procedures while expecting the same results.

To briefly connect with the complexity, consider the following excerpt from Lampert's (2001) *Teaching Problems and the Problems of Teaching*. In this excerpt Lampert reports her thinking as she conducts a fifth-grade mathematics lesson. Earlier, one of the students, Richard, gave the incorrect answer "eighteen" to one of the problems that Maggie had posed.

Teachers' Voices

Maggie Lampert

> Still puzzled about where "eighteen" came from, I ask the class if "anybody" can "explain what Richard was thinking." This was something I had by now done several times this year in response to a student's answer, and I had done it in every lesson. It often gives me an insight about how to proceed when I cannot explain the student's answer to myself. And it draws more students into practicing how to talk about mathematics.
>
> Several hands go up. I look around and take note of who wants to say something, checking on who seems to be paying attention to the discussion at this point. It is a few minutes from the end of class, and we are working on the most complex part of today's work. I wonder if we should just hold off until the next day to continue the discussion. I call on Catherine. My experience with her contributions to class discussions so far leads me to expect that she will be polite and articulate, whatever she says, possibly helping me out of the impasse with Richard. But instead of trying to explain Richard's thinking, she says, hesitatingly, "Ummmm, I disagree with that." She pauses for a moment, looks at me, and begins again, "Ummmm…" indicating that she is getting ready to tell us why she disagrees. Do I let her continue? (Lambert, 2001: 15–16)

In this brief reflection, we see the tremendous complexity of the situation that Maggie is trying to manage. If such complexity were not enough to discourage me from offering pedagogic recipes, I know from personal experience the stultifying effects of mechanical teaching for both teachers and students. Such teaching is frequently a consequence of teaching being divorced from the perceptions and conceptions of teachers. I therefore do not wish to use this chapter to discuss applications of the ideas of this book for others. Neither is it is my intent here to review the research literature on grammar pedagogy, looking for implications, although others have ably done so.

See, for example, Doughty and Williams (1998) and Mitchell (2000).

What I will do instead is play out the ideas I have been discussing in this book in order to make pedagogic sense of them for me. However, I should first warn readers that not all that I discuss here—perhaps precious little—will differ dramatically from past practice. On my bad days, I worry about this. I am impatient with my inability to "think outside the [pedagogical] box." On my good days, I imagine that fresh pedagogical ideas may yet occur to me or to others and that it is an act of hubris to think that I can solve the inert knowledge problem. I am also consoled by the fact that people have found a way to learn second languages for centuries without the benefit of modern theories. Besides, I have been able to interpret research findings, make sense of my own experience, and come to an understanding that has some coherence and some ideas that are likely to keep me engaged for some time to come.

I also intend in this chapter to deliver on promises that I have made throughout this book. The first was made in the Introduction, where I promised to define language and grammar by completing an open-ended sentence. Before I fulfill that promise, you may wish to try it for yourself.

11.1

Look over the definitions of language that you wrote for Investigations 1.1 and 1.2. Do you want to change them in any way? How would you complete the following?

Language is...

Next, do so for grammar.

Grammar is...

DEFINING LANGUAGE AND GRAMMAR AGAIN

For my answer, I am tempted to go back to the ten definitions of language I culled from the literature and listed in Chapter 1 and say "My definition of language is all of the above." As Cook and Seidlhofer note, language can indeed be viewed as

> a genetic inheritance, a mathematical system, a social fact, the expression of individual identity, the expression of cultural identity, the outcome of dialogic interaction, a social semiotic, the intuitions of native speakers, the sum of attested data, a collection of memorized chunks, a rule-governed discrete combinatory system, or electric activation in a distributed network....We do not have to choose. Language can be all of these things at once (Cook and Seidlhofer, 1995: 4).

I believe this to be true enough because perceptions differ depending on the eyes of the beholder. Besides, I believe that language is a fractal, composed of many different interacting levels of scale; thus, depending on which level of scale one is observing, a different perspective of the same phenomenon is entirely possible. Nevertheless, an all-embracing definition is rather unwieldy if one's intention is to use the definition to inform one's practice. So, instead, I will answer simply. Here is my definition of language:

Language is a dynamic process of pattern formation by which humans use linguistic forms to make meaning in context-appropriate ways.

Although my definition features patterns, language is not seen as a set of patterns (as in definition 3 in Chapter 1) but rather as a process of pattern formation. It is not the only such pattern-formation process available to humans, but it is certainly a potent one, for it allows people to draw on the systemic nature of language to build and interpret texts. As such, it facilitates communication with others. Communication with others, though, is a primary, but not exclusive, function of language. Language also facilitates thinking and allows self-expression and creativity. Then, too, appropriateness does not necessarily mean conformity to norms, and context does not only mean the physical context. A context is also created by the relationship between and among people. (See Chapter 6.)

Following from this definition, I can then say that *grammar(ing) is **one** of the dynamic linguistic processes of pattern formation in language, which can be used by humans for making meaning in context-appropriate ways.*

In order to elaborate on this second definition, the remainder of this chapter is organized into sections around the Wh-questions: *what,* in which grammaring will be further defined; *when,* the all-important question of the timing of grammaring; *why* and *how* to teach grammaring; and *to whom* to teach it.

WHAT?

Grammar

One of my goals in writing this book was to deconstruct the conception of grammar as a static product that consists of forms that are rule-governed, sentence-level, absolute, and constitute a closed system. I have suggested that, by viewing it solely this way, we have overlooked important qualities of grammar, such as that it is a dynamic process in which forms have meanings and uses in a rational, discursive, flexible, interconnected, and open system. I do not wish to perpetuate the dichotomous thinking that I have sought to overcome in this book. Nevertheless, I have found myself arguing against the "left-column" characterizations of grammar in Figure 1 in Chapter 1 as a counterpoint to what I feel is a misconception about grammar. This misconception contributes to confusion about the role of grammar, sometimes generates negative affect, and even makes the matter of whether grammar should be taught at all subject to the caprice of methodological fashion.

I have also tended to favor a dynamic view of grammar because the traditional view of grammar is biased in the other direction. Grammar is much more about our humanness than some static list of rules and exceptions suggests. Grammar allows us to choose how we present ourselves to the world, sometimes conforming to social norms yet all the while establishing our individual identities. Further, we can marshal the grammatical resources at our disposal to guide our readers' or listeners' interpretations of what we are saying or writing. Thus, rather than promoting the association in students' minds between grammatical failure and punitive repercussions (the red ink), we should seek to promote the positive association between grammar and empowerment.

And I have argued that a better way to think of grammar, which may help learners overcome the inert knowledge problem, is to think of grammar as something we do, rather than only something we know. But doing implies an ongoing process, so the question naturally arises as to how to help students participate in the process. Or another way to ask the question, if I may be permitted a linear metaphor, is "How do we help our students get on a train that is moving and has already left the station?" And my answer, at this moment in time, is "by grammaring."

Grammaring

At various times in this book I have discussed grammaring in the context of language change over time, language use in real time, an organic process connecting the two, learning and participating. Perhaps it is a mistake to imbue grammaring with such polysemy. However, I have done so to underscore the dynamism connecting these processes. At the risk of compounding the mistake, let me restate an additional, but here most relevant, definition of grammaring.

Grammaring is the ability to use grammar structures accurately, meaningfully, and appropriately. To help our students cultivate this ability requires a shift in the way grammar is traditionally viewed. It requires acknowledging that grammar can be productively regarded as a fifth skill, not only as an area of knowledge. It may be that the fifth skill is intimately interconnected with the other skills; nevertheless, mindful practicing with grammatical structures, and using them for one's own purpose(s), will hone the grammaring skill. Innovation, as opposed to imitation, will also be facilitated if our students are grammatically aware—aware not only of rules, but also, importantly, of reasons. The rules and reasons may not need to be stated in metalinguistic terms, but they should always inform the nature of the pedagogical activity. As the specific nature of the learning challenge will shift among the three dimensions of form, meaning, and use, due to the inherent complexity of the target structure and the characteristics of the students—for example, their native language and target language proficiency—the learning challenge will always have to be determined anew.

11.2

Imagine that you are a teacher of beginning-level English students. Arrange the following structures in the order in which you would teach them.

- the verb *to be* (present tense)
- possessive determiners (*my, her*, etc.)
- subject pronouns (*I, you*, etc.)
- articles (*a* and *the*)
- basic statement word order
- *yes–no* questions with the verb *to be*
- negative statements with the verb *to be*
- the present progressive
- singular and plural nouns

In doing this Investigation, many of you probably sequenced the structures according to tried-and-true pedagogic sequencing principles. For example, appealing to the principle of sequencing from linguistic simplicity to linguistic complexity may have led you to place the articles toward the end of the sequence. Others of you may have resorted to the principle that certain structures would be needed to form complete sentences—for example, subject pronouns and the verb *to be*, along with basic word order—and therefore should be taught together. Perhaps you took into account the communicative utility of the structures and determined, for example, that the possessive determiners, or at least a few of them, and the verb *to be* and basic word order should be taught early on to allow students to be able to introduce themselves and others, saying "*My/his/her name is ...*". Knowing that the present progressive requires the verb *to be* may have persuaded you to teach the simple present with *to be* prior to presenting the present progressive. Or, because of frequency of occurrence, you may have decided to do just the reverse— that is, to teach the prevalent present progressive before the simple present. Maybe you took into account discourse organization, realizing that learning how to ask *yes–no* questions should arguably precede being able to make negative statements, so that one's students can truthfully answer questions that they are asked.

Now, one or more of these principles, and perhaps others that you may have invoked, have at one time or other been offered as a rationale for sequencing grammatical structures in a syllabus or in a grammar textbook. They do address the real issues of selection and grading—how to segment and sequence the subject matter. After all, the grammar of a language cannot all be taught on the first day of a course. However, there are several drawbacks to applying one or more of these principles in order to construct a pedagogical sequence. For one thing, even the most carefully considered sequence will always be decontextualized, and unless it is created with a particular group of students in mind, it will not necessarily take into account particular learners' needs or learning readiness. Then, too, such a sequence overlooks the fact that a pedagogical grammar is probably not the same as a learner's internal mental grammars. Moreover, pedagogical sequences are linear; the learning of grammar is not.

Not Aggregation but Morphogenesis

Selecting and sequencing grammar structures also runs contrary to the holistic view of language and grammar that I have been extolling in this book. There may be developmental sequences for individual structures such as negatives, interrogatives, and relative clauses. But overall, learners use a whole linguistic system from the beginning in however a simple or incomplete a form. This imperfect system is then revised and elaborated successively as a system. The development of grammar in the learner is thus seen to be more organic and holistic than linear and atomistic.

Building grammar in students bit by bit makes sense if what we are building is a grammar machine. But if we are instead trying to promote growth, albeit of the grammatical system, then we must think differently. And borrowing a term from biology, I have proposed that we think not in terms of our students aggregating grammar structures, but rather that they are involved in a process of morphogenesis, generating new patterns that are not pure imitations of parts of the grammar of a language. As Van Lier (2002) notes, by mentally taking apart a butterfly, we can identify a leg, an antenna, and a wing, but we would miss the stages of a butterfly's growth, never discovering its life as an egg, a pupa, and a caterpillar.

By the same reasoning, looking at the target language and dividing it up into bits and pieces to be acquired gives us an inventory of the target language but overlooks the process of its morphogenetic development in which "not every phase and transformation looks unambiguously like a step closer to the goal of proficient language use" (Van Lier, 2002: 159). While I think teachers should seek to improve upon, not to emulate, the natural process of language acquisition, I do think that good teaching harmonizes rather than conflicts with the natural process, so recognizing that it is a morphogenetic process rather than an aggregative one is important. And this is no less true of a foreign language teaching/learning environment than it is of a second language environment.

WHEN?
A Responsive Approach

No matter how skillful the syllabus developer, it is impossible to create a syllabus that will work for all learners in all situations. I acknowledge that we cannot teach everything at once, but what we can do is to use the natural learning process as a guide as to when to teach certain aspects of grammar. So during the course of normal classroom activity, teachers need to be alert to "teachable moments" when they can focus learners' attention on emergent forms in learners' interlanguage, the forms around which learners are beginning to create new, albeit non-targetlike, patterns (Long and Robinson, 1998). In such a responsive approach, the grammaring lesson may not take place immediately, but the need for it will be triggered by something in the learners' performance that tells a teacher that the learner is open to its learning. As I proposed in the previous chapter, it is thus students' learning that guides the teaching rather than vice versa.

A Proactive Approach

At other times it may be necessary for teachers to be more proactive in creating activities where grammar structures and patterns are needed, ones that do not arise during the course of normal classroom activity, a teaching function that has been called *filling the gap in the input* (Spada and Lightbown, 1993; Lightbown, 1998). For instance, it is known that linguistically unplanned teacher talk uses mainly imperatives and present tense verbs, providing little exposure to other tenses (Harley, 1993). Activities that are designed to elicit specific structures and patterns are important because of the issue of **avoidance**. In certain open-ended communicative activities, students may well use only those structures to which they have already been introduced or with which they feel somewhat comfortable, avoiding those with which they do not feel comfortable. However, teachers must look as much at what students are not using as what they are using. Whether students are unaware of the existence of certain grammatical structures or are consciously avoiding ones that they find difficult, students need to have practice with all grammar structures and patterns in order to truly be free to express the meanings they want in the ways that are appropriate to them. Of course, if the grammar structures are not ones that students are ready to learn, perhaps all that can be accomplished is priming for subsequent use. Perhaps Vygotskyans would describe this as *trailblazing*. As Dunn and Lantolf put it, teaching activities "do not ride the tail of development but instead blaze the trail for development to follow" (Dunn and Lantolf, 1998: 419).

Allison Petro, a teacher in my TESOL Summer Institute course in 1995, summarized the issues nicely in a note to me after class one day.

Allison Petro

> Dear Diane,
>
> I was talking with fellow students after class, and then thinking some more on my own, and I had a revelation about why the process of teaching beginners and teaching high intermediate/advanced students is so different for me.
>
> With beginners, the process is that of *building up* form, meaning and use. The teacher should control and choose input carefully. It should be meaningful, useful, and challenging. Meaningful drills and grammar lessons have their place as long as there is also a place for communication. With high intermediate or advanced learners, the process is that of *breaking down* their fossilized systems and trying to rebuild by focusing on careful noticing of form, meaning, and use. In this case, teachers should be building sensitivity and working on students' noticing skills.
>
> Allison

I am not sure that I would agree entirely with Allison's characterization, and I think the two processes are rather more braided than sequential; however, I do find her distinction between building up and breaking down illuminating—and I think that her distinction does overlap somewhat with my discussions of proactive, trailblazing (building up) approaches and organic, responsive (breaking down) approaches. Allison has also contributed the point that one type may be more at play than the other depending on the students' level of proficiency.

A Checklist, Not a Sequence

It is frequently the case that a particular grammatical syllabus or a particular grammar text has been adopted, and it is the teacher's responsibility to "cover" certain grammatical structures. In such common circumstances it may be helpful to think of transforming the syllabus into a checklist rather than a sequence. This means that teachers are freed from teaching the grammar structures in a strict linear order. As new material is introduced—say, a reading passage—the teacher looks to see which grammar structures it contains that correspond to items on the checklist. These could then be taught as advanced organizers to help students process the reading passage and enhance their ability to monitor their subsequent performance (Terrell, 1991). Along these same lines, Willis (2002) discusses the importance of the reporting phase after a task has been completed for giving students the necessary opportunity to work on the grammar the task naturally elicits. In this way, some grammar structures and patterns can be taught as they arise in the context of skills-based, task-based, or content-based work, as long as their immediate mastery is not expected.

See Breen's (1984) process syllabus.

Selective Focus

Another common situation is that the book being used has an underlying grammatical sequence in which later chapters build on earlier ones. In such a case teachers may feel that they have no choice but to follow the order set down in the book. In order to avoid such a situation, when I directed a student grammar series, *Grammar Dimensions*, it was decided to make each unit freestanding; thus teachers could cycle back and forth in the book, working with only part of a unit at one time, skipping parts, or returning to activities in earlier units, constructing a responsive syllabus based on the learning readiness and needs of their students. However, in some cases, the texts that are being used follow a sequence in which work done later in the book depends on the groundwork laid earlier in the book. When this is the case, teachers may need to follow the sequence in the book. Even here, though, selectivity of focus is important. Just because a particular structure appears as a unit in a textbook does not mean that students know nothing about it. So whether or not a linear sequence is prescribed, a good place to begin is to find out just what the students already know and are able to do. This is an essential step in responsive teaching.

11.3

Investigations

This was the rationale for having diagnostic tasks open each unit of Grammar Dimensions. *To cite one example of an opening task from Book 1 of the series, students are asked to look at a picture of a room that might be a studio apartment. There is a desk with books and a computer, a small kitchenette, a closet, a bed, a dresser, and so forth. Students are then asked to figure out the identity of the occupant. For instance, they are asked in turn if they think that the occupant of the room is a man or a woman, an athlete, someone who likes animals, and so on. After each answer, students are asked why they have answered as they did.*

Proficient users of English do not always answer in the same way, but they do frequently answer using the same form. They give answers such as the following:

I think it is a man because there are dishes in the sink.

Or

I think that it is a woman because there is a jewelry box on the dresser.

Since the tasks are meant to be diagnostic, what would be your diagnosis of the following ESL student's answer to the question, "Is it a man or a woman?"

ESL student: "A woman. Because it has a jewelry box."

I would say that in the absence of other evidence, nothing definitive could be inferred, but if this pattern persisted in all the answers to the questions, a plausible hypothesis would be that the student does not know that an answer with the existential *there* is appropriate, that is, that a better answer would be "A woman...because there is a jewelry box (there)." Whether or not the student knows how to form sentences with the existential *there* cannot be determined by such an answer, but this should and could be ascertained. "Teaching" something to students that they already know is hardly teaching, and the time saved by avoiding this unnecessary step can more appropriately be spent addressing genuine learning challenges.

Of course, students can learn something that they have not been taught, either because they were able to learn it on their own or because they were able to generalize from something for which they had received instruction. Gass (1982), for instance, showed how teaching students a particular type of relative clause allowed them to generalize to other types of relative clauses that they had not yet been taught. On a closely related note, one of the more attractive, though as yet unfulfilled, promises of the principles-and-parameters model of UG is the claim that the setting of one parameter could determine a whole range of syntactic options. For example, the pro-drop parameter not only sets up empty pronoun slots when they are easily supplied from the context, it also licenses subject–verb inversion. It may be the case therefore that teaching one syntactic option of a parameter would facilitate the learning of other options such that the learning return could exceed the teaching time investment.

See Chapter 8.

Horizontal Planning

Another factor in considering the "when" of grammaring has to do with the timing of practice. Research has suggested that spacing practice is more effective than concentrating it all into a single point in time. Therefore, in order to achieve more synchronization between the rhythms of teaching and those of learning, I have suggested to teacher interns with whom I have worked that they plan "horizontally." By this I mean not planning to teach a different structure each class and therefore moving "vertically" through the various phases of the lesson in one class, but planning to string these phases out "horizontally"—over the course of several class sessions. It may seem that I am advocating a spiral or cyclical syllabus, but I think of horizontal planning as a bit different. I don't mean merely returning to a structure or pattern from time to time, but rather spreading the various phases of a lesson—be it presentation, practice, production or its more modern, inverted counterpart—across a period of time. For example, for several sessions, a teacher might spend five minutes or less promoting the noticing of a particular grammatical structure or pattern. At some later point in time the teacher might provide appropriate tasks or content in which the structures are contained with greater frequency (along with other naturally occurring structures or patterns). Next some consciousness-raising activity might take place. Still later the teacher might create an additional activity or series of activities that would require meaningful use of the structure or pattern.

Such a horizontal or elongated treatment of the target structure takes into account the nonlinearity of the learning process, spacing practice sessions optimally, allowing for recycling, allowing the necessary learning time, and conceivably allowing the teaching to be better synchronized with the learning process in that learners may learn the system sketchily at first, but through the process of morphogenesis or pattern formation, the imperfect system can be subsequently fleshed out and elaborated as a system over time.

Fractals and Nucleation

Because the teaching of a single structure occurs over time, as a corollary, horizontal planning permits several structures/patterns to be worked on simultaneously. Since language is a fractal, its nested levels of scale compress a significant amount of information into a small space. In each of its parts there is an image of the whole (Briggs and Peat, 1989). Therefore, working on structures/patterns that naturally cluster together in texts can give students a great deal of information about the whole system. To make this point, I once boasted to a group of teachers that I could teach an entire grammar course to second language learners using a single paragraph. Of course, no student would want to take such a course, and I would not get very far ignoring the interaction of grammar and the lexicon. I exaggerated to underscore the fact that even a restricted sample of language can be exploited to reveal much about the underlying grammatical system. Thus the syllabus units that would follow from my definition of language and grammar would be short written and oral texts—cohesive and coherent stretches of meaningful language.

A powerful learning experience can be created by giving students a lot of practice creating meaningful patterns with a limited set of co-occurring structures. Having students talk about topics or related topics again and again over time is one way to make this happen. In my experience, having them do so by playing with patterns in the target language, probing the system in order to learn what can be put together and what cannot, can make for powerful learning opportunities. As one teacher of Italian in Rome put it:

> To offer a rule to a student puts him or her in a false position because it makes the student believe that it is enough to learn the rules in order to use a language, while we know that to acquire a language is quite a different process. Learning a language involves experimenting until one discovers how it functions.

Teachers' Voices

Filippo Graziani

I believe that experimenting with language, as Filippo puts it, works because it enlists learners in active pattern formation and contributes to *nucleation*. Kenneth Pike wrote about nucleation in 1960. Just as I have drawn ideas from the physical sciences, specifically Chaos/Complexity Theory, Pike (1960) applied the concept of nucleation from physics to language learning. Nucleation occurs "...when a droplet is condensed out of a gas, or when a crystalline solid is precipitated out of a liquid.... [It] is involved in the first small clustering of molecules...into a structural pattern, which will then be extensively duplicated in a repetitive fashion to form a crystal" (Pike, 1960: 291). Initially, it is difficult for these molecules to clump together, but once they do, growth is rapid. According to Pike, language nucleation occurs within the social context. He writes that "Language is more than organized verbal sound. It is a structural part of a larger whole—part of life's total behavioral action and structure, intimately linked to social interaction" (1960: 292).

Although I was Pike's student, I do not recall reading the nucleation article at the time, or his ever mentioning it. Perhaps I was influenced in ways I am unaware of. In any case, the notion of working on a small set of co-occurring structures or patterns in a social context seems to me to be a means of overcoming the dichotomy between Sfard's acquisition and participation metaphors. It is through partic-

See Chapter 3.

ipation/use of language in a social context that the system grows, which in turns allows for greater or more satisfying participation in social contexts. As Atkinson (2002) has recently put it, it is not just that the cognitive and social interact, it is that they are mutually constituted. Then, too, Hall and Verplaetse (2000: 8), discussing the work of A. A. Leontiev (1981), note, "The fundamental core of what gets learned and the shape it takes are defined by the environment, constituted by the myriad activities available to us and our particular ways of participating in them. These dynamic environments shape at the same time both the conditions for and the consequences of our individual development."

Ultimately, of course, there is a diminishing rate of return from the practice of a small set of forms, and it becomes time to work on new structures in another context. If the new structures can be linked to the first set in some way, the system will continue to grow in a radiating network, like the fractal that it is.

WHY (AND HOW)?

Explicit Teaching of Form, Meaning, and Use

I have written several times in this book of the value of harmonizing teaching with the natural process of learning. However, no matter how hard I work to set up conditions that enhance the implicit learning of language, I feel that I would be doing my students a disservice if I did not also try to tap their potential to learn from explicit teaching of form, meaning, and use. In most cases, students do not need to know about the language—they need to be able to use the language. However, there is no doubt that some analytically-inclined students are aided by explicit attention and explanations of form, meaning, and use, be they reasons or rules of thumb, especially when the reasons/rules are abstract or complex. While these are but means to an end, they can be effective means, at least for some students. Attending to features that differ in unexpected ways from the L1, are irregular, infrequent, or non-salient, differences in the L2 that are likely to create confusion or invoke negative attitudes among speakers (Harley, 1993) are good candidates for form, meaning, use focused L2 teaching. Explicit teaching can speed up the learning of these features/patterns by making them more salient, encouraging students to allocate attention to them and by narrowing learners' hypothesis space concerning their behavior.

Thus, in addition to the consciousness-raising activities (Chapter 8), output production practice (Chapter 9), and feedback strategies (Chapter 10) that I have already discussed, what follows are some additional explicit grammaring teaching practices. To illustrate them I will appeal to another metaphor, that of four different types of camera or camera lens: slow motion, zoom, wide-angle, and camcorder. I use these metaphors because I believe that an important function of teaching lies in helping students "learn to look" (Larsen-Freeman, 2000d). I once heard a radio interview of an entomologist. The entomologist said that there was more insect diversity among beetles in Glacier National Park than in the tropics. The interviewer expressed disbelief and asked why, then, we don't see all the beetles around us, why are we oblivious to beetles? The entomologist replied, "Ah. But you have to learn to see." I was very taken by this reply because I do believe that an important function of explicit teaching is helping students learn to look.

By using slow motion, a teacher can slow the language action down, perhaps even freeze it. In this way the teacher can call students' attention to a particular structure or pattern and its meaning or discourse function. For instance, if I had decided that students were having problems with particular structures, I might provide an explanation and then highlight one or more of them in reading passages for a while. Or I might tell students the same story several times over time in a way that highlights critical grammar structures (Adair-Hauck, Donato, and Cumo-Johansen, 2000). In this way I would transform the language movie into a series of frames, slowing down the discourse in order to promote the noticing of the target structure.

There is an output production counterpart. In discussing my concept of grammaring, Thornbury (2001: 25) writes about computer-mediated communication as offering a "rich site for grammaring." Live chats "allow people to communicate across distances by sending and receiving short written messages to each other in real time. Because the communication is both informal and immediate, but slightly delayed by the demands of writing, it has been called a 'conversation in slow motion.'" By asking my students to have a written live chat with another person in the class either on-line that night for homework, or right there in a triad in the classroom (so that everyone is always responding to someone), the interaction can be slowed down. This should enable students to focus a bit more on the problematic target structures, assuming that the chat topic I assign elicits their use. A final example of the effectiveness of slowing language down in order to promote attention to forms comes from Arabic teaching materials prepared by Mahmoud Al-Batal at Emory University. Arabic language radio broadcasts are recorded. Then, they are slowed down to 75% speed. This rate is fast enough to keep the speech from becoming distorted, but slow enough to be able to promote students' noticing of particular features of the language code.

In addition to using slow motion, I might use a zoom or telescopic lens. Here, I would give students another text with the difficult structure(s). Depending on the nature of the learning challenge, I would invite students to examine the passage differently, in order to encourage their abductive reasoning. For a form challenge, I would suggest that they look at the form of the structure itself, what precedes and what follows it, and "the company the structure keeps"—what sort of collocations frequently accompany it. For meaning, I would ask them to see if they could determine the meaning being expressed by the form. And for use, I would ask them why they thought that a particular form was being used as opposed to another form that would convey more or less the same meaning. I might suggest an alternative way of conveying the same meaning and ask students what constituted the difference between the two in order to encourage them to become sensitive to the contextual differences in the use of target structures.

If I were working top-down on a reason instead of a particular linguistic structure, I might again work with contrasts. For example, if I were working on the principle that given information occurs in initial position in a sentence, followed by new information, I might describe a scene like the following, or construct one with Cuisenaire rods, and ask students why *there* is used in the first two sentences in my description and not in the second two sentences:

There is a town common or plaza in the heart of town. On the common there are trees, park benches, and a war memorial. Running south from the common is Main Street. The library is on one side, the town hall on the other.

Together we would become co-observers of this bit of language, with me guiding their looking so that they learn to see that *there* introduces new information in the first two sentences, but is not needed in the second two sentences because the existence of Main Street, a library, and a town hall has been presupposed. On another day I might ask them to describe a place that is especially meaningful to them, using manipulables such as the Cuisenaire rods to make the abstract concrete and to give them something to associate with the need to mark given and new information for their listeners.

At another time I might use a wide-angle lens approach, or what I earlier called an aerial view. I would want my students to understand that structures are part of a system, and that they are defined not only by their inherent meaning but also by their relationship to other members of the system. For example, just as it is difficult to say where one vowel leaves off and another begins, it is impossible, in my opinion, to understand what distinguishes the present perfect from the past tense—a persistent learning challenge for many students of English—if students do not understand how they relate in the overall system (Larsen-Freeman, Kuehn, and Haccius, 2002).

Finally, I would want to restore the flow by using a camcorder approach. I would want my students to encounter target structures once again in the normal flow of discourse, as they are used in texts. Having students retell a story or an anecdote that I have told them or using a dictogloss might be a perfect activity for this step. In the dictogloss, texts are created that contain structures with which students are having difficulty. The teacher reads the text to students. Then, either alone or with another student, using a collaborative dictogloss (Todeva, 1998), the students try to reconstruct the original text. This process could be iterative in the sense that the teacher at some point might want to read the text again so students can check their work and fill in what they are missing. Requiring students to aim for an exact replication means that students have to negotiate grammar structures that are difficult for them to produce on their own.

Students have to be helped to go beyond what they know already—it is not just a process of mapping forms on existing meaning. And for this, they will need feedback from others. In fact, it is this feedback from teachers and students that keeps their developing system intelligible, just as the greater speech community keeps its users' idiolects from evolving along completely different trajectories. While the process of morphogenesis may be aided by interaction and negotiation of meaning with peers, to prevent the creation of a classroom dialect, there should also be opportunity for interaction with, and feedback from, more proficient users of the language.

Engagement

No matter what type of activity is designed, student engagement is essential. Earlier I stated that I did not think it was important for students to be entertained, but I did think it was important for them to be engaged. Unmotivated learners will learn despite themselves when they are engaged, and the learning of motivated and unmotivated students alike will be enhanced when they are able to interact in a way that is meaningful to them. Engaged learners are the ones who are most likely to continue with their language study, thereby achieving higher levels of proficiency. As McIntyre and Clement (2002) put it, language learners' willingness to communicate should be a fundamental goal of language instruction. Engagement does not merely increase the quantity of language or the time spent on task, it increases the quality of the production as well (Dörnyei, 2002).

These days, engaging activities often take the form of tasks. Some advocates of task-based approaches to language pedagogy have proposed the creation of tasks that by their nature require that particular structures be used (Nunan, 1989). Others find this unnecessary. However, one potential advantage of creating tasks that require the use of certain structures is that task-essential use can provide practice of structures that are rarely found in other communicative activities. As we found out with *Grammar Dimensions*, though, and as Loschky and Bley-Vroman (1993) acknowledge, creating tasks where certain structures must be used not for comprehension, but for production, is very difficult. Indeed, Widdowson pointed out some years ago the difficulty of reconciling the exactness of linguistic analysis with the open-endedness of communication (Widdowson, 1979: 243 cited in Rutherford, 1987: 32).

It is also difficult to set up strict criteria for engagement, as what is boring for the teacher is not necessarily so for students (and vice versa). And since engagement presumably differs from one group of students to the next, what works with certain students one term might not work with a different group at another time. Thus there are no absolute criteria I can offer in this regard, although I have long promoted Stevick's concept of *technemes* to my teacher interns. Stevick (1959) wrote about technemes and the rhythm of class activity in 1959. Although some of the examples are out of date, the underlying principle remains sound. Stevick maintains—correctly, I think—that a teacher need not always turn to a completely new activity to restore student engagement. Instead, altering a technique a little bit sometimes re-engages students in the practice that they need. For example, if their attention appears to be waning, changing the activity from whole class to pair work, or from writing to speaking, or adjusting any one of the grading parameters that I listed at the end of Chapter 9, may be enough to restore engagement. Of course, this means that once again teachers need to be responsive to students, reading and responding to their energy.

Tools of Inquiry

Even if grammar were a set of finite, static rules, we simply do not have enough time to teach it all. We must help students learn how to learn—to become our partners in the teaching/learning process. Now, the usual response to such observations is to discuss learning strategies. While I have nothing against learning strategies, their use is not what I wish to discuss here. Instead, my message should be obvious, given the stance that I have adopted in this book. In order to help students learn how to learn grammar, I believe that we must work to change what students think grammar is. This, in turn, requires that they be given tools of inquiry. Here is what I have done.

1. I've given students the pie chart with the three wedges corresponding to the three dimensions of grammar and with the wh-questions in each wedge. I've helped them learn to use the questions to analyze target structures.

2. I've introduced students to the linguistic principle that no two forms will have the same meaning and the same use. I have co-constructed with students reasons for why things are the way they are.

3. I've taught students to learn to look. I've given them time in class to report what they have observed about language use from that day's activities. At times, I've presented them with data and asked them what they see. In a second language context, I've given them assignments to bring to class some observation that they have made concerning language use outside the class.

4. I've encouraged them to formulate hypotheses and think of ways that they might be able to test them; encouraged them to experiment and to play with language patterns.

5. I've encouraged them to see that mistakes they make are "gifts" to them and to class members (S. Gattegno, personal communication). The teacher's attitude toward mistakes frees students to make bolder and more systematic explorations of how the new language functions.

6. I've been mindful of the need for learner security. Students often ask for rules—rules are their security blanket. However, as much as possible, I have avoided the "one-right-answer" syndrome.

7. I have shown students that grammar can be fun, that it can be a puzzle to figure out. Teachers' attitudes make a big difference. I have cultivated an attitude of inquiry and have become a co-learner along with my students. Of course, this is not feigned. I am genuinely interested in language and can learn much from my students' observations.

To Whom?

I have earlier made the point that we are not teaching language, rather, we are teaching students. From age-related language learner research it is clear that postpubescent learners need, or at least benefit from, instruction in order to attain levels that younger learners come to naturally. But even young learners gain from grammar instruction of the right sort (Cameron, 2001). Giving young learners appropriate instruction accelerates learning in children as it does in adults. Of course, the type of grammar instruction needs to take into account age differences, but many of the activities that I have discussed here, including games and role plays, tasks and communicative activities, stories and dictoglosses would serve children's learning equally well.

I once observed a very skillful first grade teacher in a bilingual school in Mexico. Every day she would bring the children to the front of the class where they would read a letter she had written to them on the blackboard. The letter told them what they would be doing that day. It also contained errors that she had observed the students making. Their job was to find the "teacher's mistakes" and to correct them. The children loved doing this; they may or may not have known that what they were actually doing was working on aspects of the target language that were causing them difficulty.

It is also clear from language learner research, and from any teacher's observations, that there are individual differences among students that will also have to be taken into account. Perhaps the most oft-discussed individual difference trait that has relevance for grammaring is the contrast between data gatherers and rule formers, although clearly there are other individual differences that are germane.

See Breen's (2001) book for more information on these.

Then, of course, every teacher, as we were reminded most graphically by Maggie Lambert at the beginning of this chapter, needs to be mindful of students' affect. Since some students have a grammar phobia, such sensitivity may be all the more necessary.

A RELATIONSHIP, NOT A RECORD

With all this talk of being mindful of students' affect and my earlier metaphor of viewing and lenses (slow it down, zoom in on it, use a wide-angle lens, use a camcorder to speed it up), I would like to make one final point by way of conclusion. On one occasion several years ago I had the good fortune of watching local puppeteer Eric Bass perform a series of vignettes. At the conclusion of the performance, in the intimate setting of a small theater, Eric Bass invited questions from the audience. One of the questions from an admirer was actually a suggestion. The audience member asked if the puppeteer had ever considered videotaping his performances. In that way, more people would be able to enjoy his artistry. I will never forget Bass' reply. He said that while he was not against videotaping the performance, such a tape would be only a record, not a relationship, and it was a relationship that he strove to create with us, his audience.

As with performances, good teaching depends on a teacher's ability to create a positive, trusting relationship with his or her students. No matter how well versed in grammaring teachers are, absent a relationship with their students, they will fail. By writing in the personal genre of this series, I hope that I have begun something of a relationship with you, the reader. What I have tried to offer here is not a prescription for institutional or individual actions, but rather some ideas that have fascinated me. I have offered them with the hope that you may find them useful to interact with and perhaps be influenced by in pursuit of your own professional growth and in your commitment to your students' learning. Happy Grammaring!

References

Adair-Hauck, B., R. Donato, and P. Cumo-Johanssen. 2000. Using a story-based approach to teach grammar. In J. Shrum and E. Glisan (eds.), *Teacher's handbook: Contextualized language instruction*. Second edition. Boston: Heinle & Heinle.

Aljaafreh, A., and J. Lantolf. 1994. Negative feedback as regulation and second language learning in the zone of proximal development. *Modern Language Journal* 78 (4): 465–483.

Allwright, D. 1975. Problems in the study of the language teacher's treatment of learner error. In M. Burt and H. Dulay (eds.), *New directions in second language learning, teaching and bilingual education: On TESOL '75*. Washington, DC: TESOL. 96–109.

Allwright, D. 1980. Turns, topics and tasks: Patterns of participation in language teaching and learning. In D. Larsen-Freeman (ed.), *Discourse analysis in second language research*. Rowley, MA: Newbury House. 165–187.

Anderson, J. 1983. *The architecture of cognition*. Cambridge: Cambridge University Press.

Anderson, J. 1985. *Cognitive psychology and its implications*. Second edition. New York: W. H. Freeman and Company.

Arevart, S., and P. Nation. 1991. Fluency improvement in a second language. *RELC Journal* 22 (2): 84–94.

Atkinson, D. 2002. Toward a sociocognitive approach to second language acquisition. *Modern Language Journal* 86 (iv): 525–545.

Badalamenti, V., and C. Henner Stanchina. 2000. *Grammar dimensions: Form, meaning, and use*. Book 1. Platinum edition. Boston: Heinle & Heinle.

Bates, E., and J. Goodman. 1999. On the emergence of grammar from the lexicon. In B. MacWhinney (ed.), *The emergence of language*. Mahwah, NJ: Lawrence Erlbaum Associates, Publishers. 29–79.

Batstone, R. 1995. Grammar in discourse: Attitude and deniability. In G. Cook and B. Seidlhofer (eds.), *Principles and practice in applied linguistics*. Oxford: Oxford University Press. 197–213.

Becker, A. L. 1983. Toward a post-structuralist view of language learning: A short essay. *Language Learning* 33 (5): 217–220.

Beebe, L. 1980. Sociolinguistic variation and style shifting in second language acquisition. *Language Learning* 30 (2): 433–447.

Beebe, L. 1995. Polite fictions: Instrumental rudeness as pragmatic competence. In J. Alatis, C. Straehle, B. Gallenberger, and M. Ronkin (eds.), *Georgetown University round table on languages and linguistics 1995*. Washington, DC: Georgetown University Press. 154–168.

Bialystok, E., and M. Sharwood Smith. 1985. Interlanguage is not a state of mind: An evaluation of the construct for second language acquisition. *Applied Linguistics* 6 (1): 101–117.

Biber, D., S. Conrad, and R. Reppen. 1998. *Corpus linguistics: Investigating language structure and use.* Cambridge: Cambridge University Press.

Blaxton, T. 1989. Investigating dissociations among memory measures: Support for a transfer-appropriate processing framework. *Journal of Experimental Psychology: Learning, Memory, and Cognition* 15 (4): 657–668.

Bley-Vroman, R. 1983. The comparative fallacy in interlanguage studies: The case of systematicity. *Language Learning* 33 (1): 1–17.

Bley-Vroman, R. 1986. Hypothesis testing in second-language acquisition theory. *Language Learning* 36 (3): 353–376.

Bley-Vroman, R. 1988. The fundamental character of foreign language learning. In W. Rutherford and M. Sharwood Smith (eds.), *Grammar and second language teaching.* Rowley, MA: Newbury House. 19–29.

Bolinger, D. 1968. Entailment and the meaning of structures. *Glossa* 2 (2): 119–127.

Bolinger, D. 1975. Meaning and memory. *Forum Linguisticum* 1: 2–14.

Borg, S. 1998. Teachers' pedagogical systems and grammar teaching: A qualitative study. *TESOL Quarterly* 32 (1): 9–38.

Borg, S. 1999. The use of grammatical terminology in the second language classroom: A qualitative study of teachers' practices and cognitions. *Applied Linguistics* 20 (1): 95–126.

Borkin, A., and S. Reinhart. 1978. "Excuse me" and "I'm sorry." *TESOL Quarterly* 12 (1): 57–69.

Bourdieu, P. 1991. *Language and symbolic power.* Cambridge, MA: Harvard University Press.

Braidi, S. 1999. *The acquisition of second-language syntax.* London: Arnold.

Braidi, S. 2002. Reexamining the role of recasts in native speaker/non-native-speaker interactions. *Language Learning* 52 (1): 1–42.

Brazil, D. 1995. *A grammar of speech.* Oxford: Oxford University Press.

Breen, M. 1984. Process syllabuses for the language classroom. In C. Brumfit (ed.), General English syllabus design: curriculum and syllabus design for the general English classroom, *ELT Documents 118.* Oxford: Pergamon Press. 47–60.

Breen, M., ed. 2001. *Learner contributions to language learning.* Harlow, England: Longman.

Briggs, J., and F. Peat. 1989. *Turbulent mirror: An illustrated guide to chaos theory and the science of wholeness.* New York: Harper & Row.

Broeder, P., and K. Plunkett. 1994. Connectionism and second language acquisition. In N. Ellis (ed.), *Implicit and explicit learning of languages.* London: Academic Press. 421–453.

Bybee, J., and P. Hopper, eds. 2001. *Frequency and the emergence of linguistic structure.* Amsterdam/Philadelphia: John Benjamins Publishing Company.

Cadierno, T. 1992. Explicit instruction in grammar: A comparison of input-based and output-based instruction in second language acquisition. Ph. D. dissertation, University of Illinois.

Cameron, L. 2001. *Teaching languages to young learners.* Cambridge: Cambridge University Press.

Carroll, S., and M. Swain. 1993. Explicit and implicit negative feedback: An empirical study of the learning of linguistic generalizations. *Studies in Second Language Acquisition* 15 (3): 357–386.

Carter, R., and M. McCarthy. 1995. Grammar and the spoken language. *Applied Linguistics* 16 (2): 141–158.

Cathcart, R., and J. Winn Bell Olsen. 1976. Teachers' and students' preferences for correction of classroom conversation errors. In J. Fanselow and R. Crymes (eds.), *On TESOL '76: Selections based on teaching done at the 10th annual TESOL Convention.* Washington, DC: TESOL. 41–53.

Cazden, C. 1981. Performance before competence: Assistance to child discourse in the zone of proximal development. *The Quarterly Newsletter of the Laboratory of Comparative Human Cognition* 3 (1): 5–8.

Celce-Murcia, M. 1980. Contextual analysis in English: Application in TESL. In D. Larsen-Freeman (ed.), *Discourse analysis in second language research.* Rowley, MA: Newbury House. 41–55.

Celce-Murcia, M. 1991. Discourse analysis and grammar instruction. *Annual Review of Applied Linguistics* 11: 135–151. Cambridge: Cambridge University Press.

Celce-Murcia, M. 1992. A nonhierarchical relationship between grammar and communication. Part 2. In J. Alatis (ed.), *Georgetown University round table on languages and linguistics 1992.* Washington, DC: Georgetown University Press. 166–173.

Celce-Murcia, M., and D. Larsen-Freeman. 1999. *The grammar book: An ESL/EFL teacher's course.* Second edition. Boston: Heinle & Heinle.

Chafe, W. 1987. Cognitive constraints on information flow. In R. S. Tomlin (ed.), *Coherence and grounding in discourse.* Amsterdam/Philadelphia: John Benjamins Publishing Company. 21–51.

Chaudron, C. 1988. *Second language classrooms; Research on teaching and learning.* Cambridge: Cambridge University Press.

Chenoweth, A., R. Day, A. Chun, and S. Luppescu. 1983. Attitudes and preferences of ESL students to error correction. *Studies in Second Language Acquisition* 6 (1): 79–87.

Chomsky, N. 1965. *Aspects of a theory of syntax.* Cambridge, MA: MIT Press.

Chomsky, N. 1981. *Lectures on government and binding.* Dordrecht: Foris.

Chomsky, N. 1986. *Knowledge of language: its nature, origin, and use.* New York: Praeger.

Chomsky, N. 1995. *The minimalist program.* Cambridge, MA: MIT Press.

Clark, A. 1997. *Being there: Putting brain, body, and world together again.* Cambridge, MA: MIT Press.

Clift, R. 2001. Meaning in interaction: The case of "actually." *Language* 77 (2): 245–291.

Close, R. 1992. *A teacher's grammar: The central problems of English.* Hove, England: Language Teaching Publications.

Cohen, A., and M. Robbins. 1976. Toward assessing interlanguage performance: The relationship between selected errors, learners' characteristics, and learners' explanations. *Language Learning* 26 (1): 45–66.

Cook, G. 1994. Repetition and learning by heart: An aspect of intimate discourse, and its implications. *ELT Journal* 48: 133–141.

Cook, G., and B. Seidlhofer. 1995. An applied linguist in principle and practice. In G. Cook and B. Seidlhofer (eds.), *Principle and practice in applied linguistics.* Oxford: Oxford University Press. 1–23.

Cook, V. 1999. Going beyond the native speaker in language teaching. *TESOL Quarterly* 33: 185–209.

Cooper, D. 1999. *Linguistic attractors: The cognitive dynamics of language acquisition and change.* Amsterdam/Philadelphia: John Benjamins Publishing Company.

Corder, S. P. 1967. The significance of learners' errors. *International Review of Applied Linguistics* 5: 161–170.

Coughlan, P., and P. Duff. 1994. Same task, different activities: Analysis of SLA task from an activity theory perspective. In J. Lantolf and G. Appel (eds.), *Vygotskyan approaches to second language research*. Norwood, NJ: Ablex Publishing Corporation. 173–193.

Culler, J. 1976. *Ferdinand de Saussure*. New York: Penguin.

DeKeyser, R. 1998. Beyond focus on form: Cognitive perspectives on learning and practicing second language grammar. In C. Doughty and J. Williams (eds.), *Focus on form in classroom second language acquisition*. Cambridge: Cambridge University Press. 42–63.

DeKeyser, R., and K. Sokalski. 2001. The differential role of comprehension and production practice. *Language Learning* 51, Supplement 1: 81–112.

de Saussure, F. 1916. *Cours de linguiste générale*. Translated 1959 as *Course in general linguistics* by W. Baskin. New York: Philosophical Library.

Dickerson, W. 1976. The psycholinguistic unity of language learning and language change. *Language Learning* 26 (2): 215–231.

Diller, K. 1995. Language teaching at the millennium: The perfect methods vs. the garden of variety. Unpublished manuscript.

Donato, R. 1994. Collective scaffolding in second language learning. In J. Lantolf and G. Appel (eds.), *Vygotskyan approaches to second language research*. Norwood, NJ: Ablex Publishing Corporation. 33–56.

Donato, R. 2000. Contextualizing repetition in practice(s): Perspectives from sociocultural theory and a dynamical systems approach. Paper written for the course Dynamical Systems Approach to Language and Language Acquisition, Carnegie Mellon University.

Donato, R., and B. Adair-Hauck. 1992. Discourse perspectives on formal instruction. *Language Awareness* 1: 73–89.

Dörnyei, Z. 2002. The integration of research on L2 motivation and SLA: Past failure and future potential. Paper presented at the Second Language Research Forum, October 4, University of Toronto.

Doughty, C., and J. Williams, eds. 1998. *Focus on form in classroom second language acquisition*. Cambridge: Cambridge University Press.

Duff, P. 2000. Repetition in foreign language classroom interaction. In J. Kelly Hall and L. Stoops Verplaetse (eds.), *Second and foreign language learning through classroom interaction*. Mahwah, NJ: Lawrence Erlbaum Associates, Publishers. 109–138.

Dunn, W., and J. Lantolf. 1998. Vygotsky's zone of proximal development and Krashen's i+1: Incommensurable constructs; incommensurable theories. *Language Learning* 48 (3): 411–442.

Eisenstein Ebsworth, M., and C. W. Schweers. 1997. What researchers say and practitioners do: Perspectives on conscious grammar instruction in the ESL classroom. *Applied Language Learning* 8 (2): 237–259.

Ellis, N., ed. 1994. *Implicit and explicit learning of languages*. London: Academic Press.

Ellis, N. 1996. Sequencing in SLA: Phonological memory, chunking, and points of order. *Studies in Second Language Acquisition* 18 (1): 91–126.

Ellis, N. 1998. Emergentism, connectionism and language learning. *Language Learning* 48 (4): 631–664.

Ellis, N. 2002. Frequency effects in language processing: A review with implications for theories of implicit and explicit language acquisition. *Studies in Second Language Acquisition* 24 (2): 143–188.

Ellis, N., and R. Schmidt. 1998. Rules or associations in the acquisition of morphology? The frequency by regularity interaction in human and PDP learning of morphosyntax. *Language and Cognitive Processes* 13 (2/3): 307–336.

Ellis, R. 1989. Are classroom and naturalistic acquisition the same? A study of the classroom acquisition of German word order rules. *Studies in Second Language Acquisition* 11 (3): 305–328.

Ellis, R. 1993a. Interpretation-based grammar teaching. *System* 21 (1): 69–78.

Ellis, R. 1993b. Second language acquisition and the structural syllabus. *TESOL Quarterly* 27 (1): 91–113.

Ellis, R. 1994. *The study of second language acquisition.* Oxford: Oxford University Press.

Ellis, R. 1998. Teaching and research: Options in grammar teaching. *TESOL Quarterly* 32 (1): 39–60.

Ellis, R. 1999. Theoretical perspectives on interaction and language learning. In R. Ellis (ed.), *Learning a second language through interaction.* Amsterdam/Philadelphia: John Benjamins Publishing Company. 3–31.

Ellis, R., ed. 2001. Form-focused instruction and second language learning. *Language Learning* 51: Supplement 1.

Elman, J., E. Bates, M. Johnson, A. Karmiloff-Smith, D. Parisi, and K. Plunkett. 1998. *Rethinking innateness: A connectionist perspective on development.* Cambridge, MA: MIT Press.

Fotos, S. 1993. Consciousness-raising and noticing through focus on form: Grammar task performance versus formal instruction. *Applied Linguistics* 14 (4): 385–407.

Fotos, S., and R. Ellis. 1991. Communication about grammar: A task-based approach. *TESOL Quarterly* 25 (4): 605–628.

Fries, P. 1997. Theme and new in written English. In T. Miller (ed.), *Functional approaches to written text: Classroom applications.* Washington, DC: United States Information Agency. 230–243.

Frodesen, J., and J. Eyring. 2000. *Grammar dimensions: Form, meaning, and use.* Book 4. Platinum edition. Boston: Heinle & Heinle.

Futuyama, D. 1986. *Evolutionary biology.* Second edition. Sunderland, MA: Sinauer.

Gass, S. 1982. From theory to practice. In M. Hines and W. Rutherford (eds.), *On TESOL '81.* Washington, DC: TESOL. 129–139.

Gass, S. 1997. *Input, interaction, and the second language learner.* Mahwah, NJ: Lawrence Erlbaum Associates, Publishers.

Gass, S., and L. Selinker. 2001. *Second language acquisition: An introductory course.* Second edition. Mahwah, NJ: Lawrence Erlbaum Associates, Publishers.

Gasser, M. 1990. Connectionism and the universals of second language acquisition. *Studies in Second Language Acquisition* 12 (2): 179–199.

Gatbonton, E., and N. Segalowitz. 1988. Creative automatization: Principles for promoting fluency within a communicative framework. *TESOL Quarterly* 22 (3): 473–492.

Gattegno, C. 1976. *The commonsense of teaching foreign languages.* New York: Educational Solutions.

Gell-Mann, M. 1994. *The quark and the jaguar: Adventures in the simple and the complex.* London: Abacus.

George, H. V. 1972. *Common errors in language learning.* Rowley, MA: Newbury House.

Givón, T. 1993. *English grammar: A function-based introduction.* Amsterdam/Philadelphia: John Benjamins Publishing Company.

Givón, T. 1999. Generativity and variation: The notion "rule of grammar" revisited. In B. MacWhinney (ed.), *The emergence of language.* Mahwah, NJ: Lawrence Erlbaum Associates, Publishers. 81–114.

Gleick, J. 1987. *Chaos: Making a new science.* New York: Penguin Books.

Goldberg, A. 1995. *Constructions: A construction grammar approach to argument structure*. Chicago: University of Chicago Press.

Goldberg, A. 1999. The emergence of the semantics of argument structure constructions. In B. MacWhinney (ed.), *The emergence of language*. Mahwah. NJ: Lawrence Erlbaum Associates, Publishers. 197–212.

Gomes de Mateo, F. 2002. Learners' grammatical rights: A checklist. In V. Cook (ed.), *Portraits of L2 users*. Clevedon, England: Multilingual Matters. 315.

Gould, S. J. 1977. Punctuated equilibria: The tempo and mode of evolution reconsidered. *Paleobiology* 3: 115–151.

Granger, S. 1998. *Learner English on computer*. London & New York: Addison-Wesley Longman.

Granger, S., J. Hung, and S. Petch-Tyson, eds. 2002. *Computer learner corpora, second language acquisition and foreign language*. Language Learning and Language Teaching 6. Amsterdam/Philadelphia: John Benjamins Publishing Company.

Graves, K. 2000. *Designing language courses*. Boston: Heinle & Heinle.

Gregg, K. Forthcoming. The state of emergentism in SLA. *Second Language Research*. Revision of paper presented at the PacSLRF Meeting, October 6, 2001. University of Hawaii.

Gunn, C. 1997. Defining the challenge of teaching phrasal verbs. *Thai TESOL Bulletin* 10 (2): 52–61.

Haiman, J. 1985. *Natural syntax. Iconicity and erosion*. Cambridge and New York: Cambridge University Press.

Hall, J. Kelly, and L. Stoops Verplaetse, eds. 2000. *Second and foreign language learning through classroom interaction*. Mahwah, NJ: Lawrence Erlbaum Associates, Publishers.

Halliday, M. A. K. 1994. *An introduction to functional grammar*. Second edition. London: Edward Arnold.

Halliday, M. A. K., and R. Hasan. 1976. *Cohesion in English*. London: Longman.

Halliday, M. A. K., and R. Hasan. 1989. *Language, context, and text*. Oxford: Oxford University Press.

Han, Z-H. 2002. Rethinking the role of corrective feedback in communicative language teaching. *RELC Journal* 33 (1): 1–33.

Han, Z-H. In press. A study of the impact of recasts on tense consistency in L2 output. *TESOL Quarterly*.

Han, Z-H., and L. Selinker. 1999. Error resistance: Towards an empirical pedagogy. *Language Teaching Research* 3 (3): 248–275.

Harley, B. 1993. Instructional strategies and SLA in early French immersion. *Studies in Second Language Acquisition* 15 (2): 245–259.

Harnett, I. 1995. Lost worlds: Saussure, Wittgenstein, Chomsky. *Nagoya Seirei Junior Bulletin* 15: 105-135.

Harris, R. 1993. *The linguistics wars*. New York: Oxford University Press.

Hatch, E. 1974. Second language learning—universals? *Working Papers on Bilingualism* 3: 1–17.

Hatch, E. 1978. *Second language acquisition: A book of readings*. Rowley, MA: Newbury House.

Hawkins, R. 2001. *Second language syntax: A generative introduction*. Oxford: Blackwell.

Healy, A., and L. Bourne. 1995. *Learning and memory of knowledge and skills*. Thousand Oaks, CA: Sage Publications.

Herdina, P., and U. Jessner 2002. *A dynamic model of multilingualism*. Clevedon, England: Multilingual Matters.

Heubner, T. 1979. Order-of-acquisition vs. dynamic paradigm: A comparison of methods in interlanguage research. *TESOL Quarterly* 13 (1): 21–28.

Higgs, T., and R. Clifford. 1982. The push toward communication. In T. Higgs (ed.), *Curriculum, competence and the foreign language teacher.* Skokie, IL: National Textbook Co. 51–79.

Hinkel, E., and S. Fotos, eds. 2002. *New perspectives on grammar teaching in second language classrooms.* Mahwah, NJ: Lawrence Erlbaum Associates, Publishers.

Hockett, C., ed. 1987. *A Leonard Bloomfield anthology.* Chicago and London: The University of Chicago Press.

Holland, J. 1998. *Emergence: From chaos to complexity.* Reading, MA: Addison Wesley Publishing Company.

Hopper, P. 1988. Emergent grammar and the a priori grammar postulate. In D. Tannen (ed.), *Linguistics in context: Connecting observation and understanding.* Norwood, NJ: Ablex Publishing Corporation. 117–134.

Hopper, P. 1998. Emergent grammar. In M. Tomasello (ed.), *The new psychology of language.* Mahwah, NJ: Lawrence Erlbaum Associates, Publishers. 155–175.

Howatt, A. P. R. 1984. *A history of English language teaching.* Oxford: Oxford University Press.

Hughes, R., and M. McCarthy. 1998. From sentence to discourse: Discourse grammar and English language teaching. *TESOL Quarterly* 32 (2): 263–287.

Hulstijn, J. 1990. A comparison between the information-process and the Analysis/Control approaches to language learning. *Applied Linguistics* 11 (1): 30–45.

Hulstijn, J. 2002. The construct of input in an interactive approach to second language acquisition. Paper presented at the Form-Meaning Connections in Second Language Acquisition Conference, February 22, Chicago, IL.

Hunston, S., and G. Francis. 2000. *Pattern grammar.* Amsterdam/Philadelphia: John Benjamins Publishing Company.

Hymes, D. 1972. On communicative competence. In J. B. Pride and J. Holmes (eds.), *Sociolinguistics.* Harmondsworth, England: Penguin Books. 269–293.

Jaeger, J., A. Lockwood, D. Kemmerer, R. Van Valin, B. Murphy, and H. Khalak. 1996. A positron emission tomographic study of regular and irregular verb morphology in English. *Language* 72 (3): 451–497.

Johnson, K. 1994. Teaching declarative and procedural knowledge. In M. Bygate, A. Tonkyn, and E. Williams (eds.), *Grammar and the language teacher.* Hemel Hempstead, England: Prentice Hall International. 121–131.

Johnston, B., and K. Goettsch. 2000. In search of the knowledge base of language teaching: Explanations by experienced teachers. *The Canadian Modern Language Review*, 56 (3): 437–468.

Johnstone, B., ed. 1994. *Repetition in discourse: Interdisciplinary perspectives.* Volume Two. Norwood, NJ: Ablex Publishing Corporation.

Kauffman, S. 1995. *At home in the universe: Searching for the laws of self-organization and complexity.* Oxford: Oxford University Press.

Keller, R. 1985. Toward a theory of linguistic change. In T. Ballmer (ed.), *Linguistic dynamics: Discourses, Procedures and Evolution.* Berlin: Walter de Gruyter. 211–237.

Kelly, L. 1969. *Twenty-five centuries of language teaching.* New York: Newbury House.

Kelso, J. A. S. 1995. *Dynamic patterns: The self-organization of brain and behavior.* Cambridge, MA: MIT Press.

Klein, W., and C. Perdue. 1997. The basic variety, or Couldn't languages be much simpler? *Second Language Research* 13: 301–347.

Knowles, P. 1979. Predicate markers: A new look at the English predicate system. *Cross Currents*, VI (2): 21–36.

Kramsch, C., ed. 2002. *Language acquisition and language socialization.* London: Continuum.

Krashen, S. 1981. *Second language acquisition and second language learning.* Oxford: Pergamon.

Krashen, S. 1982. *Principles and practice in second language acquisition.* Oxford: Pergamon.

Krashen, S. 1989. We acquire vocabulary and spelling by reading: Additional evidence for the input hypothesis. *Modern Language Journal* 73 (4): 440–464.

Krashen, S. 1994. The input hypothesis and its rivals. In N. Ellis (ed.), *Implicit and explicit learning of languages.* London: Academic Press. 45–77.

Krashen, S. 1998. Comprehensible output? *System* 26: 175–182.

Krashen, S., and T. Terrell. 1983. *The natural approach: Language acquisition in the classroom.* Hayward, CA: Alemany Press.

Lamendella, J. 1979. The neurofunctional basis of pattern practice. *TESOL Quarterly* 13 (1). 5–19.

Lampert, M. 2001. *Teaching problems and the problems of teaching.* New Haven: Yale University Press.

Langacker, R. 1987. *Foundations of cognitive grammar.* Volume 1, *Theoretical prerequisites.* Stanford, CA: Stanford University Press.

Langacker, R. 1991. *Foundations of cognitive grammar.* Volume 2, *Descriptive applications.* Stanford, CA: Stanford University Press.

Lantolf, J., and A. Pavlenko. 1995. Sociocultural theory and second language acquisition. *Annual Review of Applied Linguistics* 15: 108–124. Cambridge: Cambridge University Press.

Larsen-Freeman, D. 1976. An explanation for the morpheme acquisition order of second language learners. *Language Learning* 26 (1): 125–134.

Larsen-Freeman, D. 1982. The "what" of second language acquisition. In M. Hines and W. Rutherford (eds.), *On TESOL '81.* Washington, DC: TESOL. 107–128.

Larsen-Freeman, D. 1991. Consensus and divergence on the content, role, and process of teaching grammar. In J. Alatis (ed.), *Georgetown University round table on languages and linguistics 1991: Linguistics and language pedagogy: The state of the art.* Washington, DC: Georgetown University Press. 260–272.

Larsen-Freeman, D. 1992. A nonhierarchical relationship between grammar and communication. Part 1. In J. Alatis (ed.), *Georgetown University round table on languages and linguistics 1992.* Washington, DC: Georgetown University Press. 158–165.

Larsen-Freeman, D. 1995. On the teaching and learning of grammar: Challenging the myths. In F. Eckman, D. Highland, P. Lee, J. Mileham, and R. Rutkowski Weber (eds.), *Second language acquisition theory and pedagogy.* Hillsdale, NJ: Lawrence Erlbaum Associates, Publishers. 131–150.

Larsen-Freeman, D. 1997. Chaos/Complexity science and second language acquisition. *Applied Linguistics* 18 (2): 141–165.

Larsen-Freeman, D. 2000a. *Techniques and principles in language teaching.* Second edition. Oxford: Oxford University Press.

Larsen-Freeman, D. 2000b. Second language acquisition and applied linguistics. *Annual Review of Applied Linguistics* 20: 165–181. Cambridge: Cambridge University Press.

Larsen-Freeman, D. 2000c. Grammar: Rules and reasons working together. *ESL/EFL Magazine,* January/February: 10–12.

Larsen-Freeman, D. 2000d. An attitude of inquiry: TESOL as science. *Journal of Imagination in Language Learning* 5: 10–15.

Larsen-Freeman, D. 2001. Teaching grammar. In M. Celce-Murcia (ed.), *Teaching English as a second or foreign language*. Third edition. Boston: Heinle & Heinle. 251–266.

Larsen-Freeman, D. 2002a. The grammar of choice. In E. Hinkel and S. Fotos (eds.), *New perspectives on grammar teaching in second language classrooms*. Mahwah, NJ: Lawrence Erlbaum Associates, Publishers. 103–118.

Larsen-Freeman, D. 2002b. Making sense of frequency. *Studies in Second Language Acquisition* 24 (2): 275–285.

Larsen-Freeman, D. 2002c. An index of development for second language acquisition revisited. Paper presented as part of the closing plenary panel, Second Language Research Forum, October 6, University of Toronto.

Larsen-Freeman, D. 2002d. Language acquisition and language use from a chaos/complexity theory perspective. In C. Kramsch (ed.), *Language acquisition and language socialization*. London: Continuum. 33–46.

Larsen-Freeman, D., and M. Long. 1991. *An introduction to second language acquisition research*. London: Longman.

Larsen-Freeman, D., T. Kuehn, and M. Haccius. 2002. Helping students in making appropriate English verb-tense aspect choices. *TESOL Journal*. 11 (4): 3–9.

Leech, G. 2000. Grammars of spoken English: New outcomes of corpus-oriented research. *Language Learning* 50 (4): 675–724.

Leontiev, A. A. 1981. *Psychology and the language learning process*. Oxford: Pergamon.

Levelt, W. 1989. *Speaking: From intention to articulation*. Cambridge, MA: MIT Press.

Lightbown, P. 1991. Getting quality input in the second/foreign language classroom. In C. Kramsch and S. McConnell-Ginet (eds.), *Text and context: Cross-disciplinary perspectives on language study*. Lexington, MA: D.C. Heath and Company. 187–197.

Lightbown, P. 1998. The importance of timing in focus on form. In C. Doughty and J. Williams (eds.), *Focus on form in classroom second language acquisition*. Cambridge: Cambridge University Press. 177–196.

Lightbown, P. 2000. Classroom SLA research and second language teaching. *Applied Linguistics* 21 (4): 431–462.

Lin, L. 2002. Overuse, underuse and misuse: Using concordancing to analyse the use of "it" in the writing of Chinese learners of English. In M. Tan (ed.), *Corpus studies in language education*. Bangkok: IELE Press. 63–76.

Long, M. 1988. Instructed interlanguage development. In L. Beebe (ed.), *Issues in second language acquisition: Multiple perspectives*. Rowley, MA: Newbury House. 115–141.

Long, M. 1991. Focus on form: A design feature in language teaching methodology. In K. de Bot, R. Ginsberg, and C. Kramsch (eds.), *Foreign language research in cross-cultural perspective*. Amsterdam/Philadelphia: John Benjamins Publishing Company. 39–52.

Long, M. 1996. The role of the linguistic environment in second language acquisition. In W. Ritchie and T. Bhatia (eds.), *Handbook of second language acquisition*. San Diego: Academic Press. 413–468.

Long, M. 1997. Construct validity in SLA research. *Modern Language Journal* 8 (iii): 318–323.

Long, M. and P. Robinson. 1998. Focus on form: Theory, research, and practice. In C. Doughty and J. Williams (eds.), *Focus on form in classroom second language acquisition*. Cambridge: Cambridge University Press. 15–41.

Loschky, L., and R. Bley-Vroman. 1993. Grammar and task-based methodology. In G. Crookes and S. Gass (eds.), *Tasks and language learning: Integrating theory and practice*. Clevedon, England: Multilingual Matters. 123–167.

Lyster, R. 1998. Recasts, repetition and ambiguity in L2 classroom discourse. *Studies in Second Language Acquisition* 20 (1): 51–81.

Lyster, R., and L. Ranta. 1997. Corrective feedback and learner uptake: Negotiation of form in communicative classrooms. *Studies in Second Language Acquisition* 19 (1): 37–66.

Lyster, R., P. Lightbown, and N. Spada. 1999. A response to Truscott's "What's wrong with oral grammar correction." *The Canadian Modern Language Review* 55 (4): 457–467.

MacWhinney, B. 1997. Implicit and explicit processes: Commentary. *Studies in Second Language Acquisition* 19 (2): 277–281.

MacWhinney, B., ed. 1999. *The emergence of language*. Mahwah, NJ: Lawrence Erlbaum Associates, Publishers.

McCarthy, M. 1998. *Spoken language and applied linguistics*. Cambridge: Cambridge University Press.

McCarthy, M. 2001. *Issues in applied linguistics*. Cambridge: Cambridge University Press.

McIntyre, P., and R. Clément. 2002. Willingness to communicate among French immersion students. Paper presented at the Second Language Research Forum, October 6, University of Toronto.

McLaughlin, B. 1987. *Theories of second-language learning*. London: Edward Arnold.

McLaughlin, B. 1990. Restructuring. *Applied Linguistics* 11 (2): 113–128.

McLaughlin, B., T. Rossman, and B. McLeod. 1983. Second language learning: An information processing perspective. *Language Learning* 33 (2): 135–159.

Meara, P. 1997. Towards a new approach to modelling vocabulary acquisition. In N. Schmitt and M. McCarthy (eds.), *Vocabulary: Description, acquisition and pedagogy*. Cambridge: Cambridge University Press. 109–121.

Meara, P. 1999. Self organization in bilingual lexicons. In P. Broeder and J. Murre (eds.), *Language and thought in development*. Tubingen: Narr. 127–144.

Meisel, J., H. Clahsen, and M. Pienemann. 1981. On determining developmental stages in natural second language acquisition. *Studies in Second Language Acquisition* 3 (1): 109–135.

Mellow, D., and K. Stanley. 2001. Alternative accounts of developmental patterns: Toward a functional-cognitive model of second language acquisition. In K. Smith and D. Nordquist (eds.), *Proceedings of the third annual high desert linguistics society conference*. Albuquerque, NM: High Desert Linguistics Society. 51–65.

Miller, T., ed. 1997. *Functional approaches to written text: Classroom applications*. Washington, DC: United States Information Agency.

Mitchell, R. 2000. Applied linguistics and evidence-based classroom practice: The case of foreign language grammar pedagogy. *Applied Linguistics* 21 (3): 281–303.

Mohanan, K. P. 1992. Emergence of complexity in phonological development. In C. Ferguson, L. Menn, and C. Stoel-Gammon (eds.), *Phonological development*. Timonium, MD: York Press, Inc. 635–662.

Murday, K. 2000. Reflection. Paper written for the course Dynamical Systems Approach to Language and Language Acquisition, Carnegie Mellon University.

Murphy, C. 1997. The spirit of Cotonou. *The Atlantic Monthly*. 279 (1): 14–16. January.

Myles, F., J. Hooper, and R. Mitchell. 1998. Rote or rule? Exploring the role of formulaic language in classroom foreign language learning. *Language Learning* 48 (3): 323–363.

Nattinger, J., and J. DeCarrico. 1992. *Lexical phrases and language teaching.* Oxford: Oxford University Press.

Newman, F., and L. Holzman. 1993. *Lev Vygotsky: Revolutionary scientist.* London and New York: Routledge.

Nicholas, H., P. Lightbown, and N. Spada. 2001. Recasts as feedback to language learners. *Language Learning* 51 (4): 719–758.

Norris, J., and L. Ortega. 2000. Does type of instruction make a difference? Substantive findings from a meta-analytic review. *Language Learning* 51, Supplement 1: 157–213.

Norton Peirce, B. 1989. Toward a pedagogy of possibility in the teaching of English internationally: People's English in South Africa. *TESOL Quarterly* 23 (3): 401–420.

Nunan, D. 1989. *Designing tasks for the communicative classroom.* Cambridge: Cambridge University Press.

Ohta, A. 2000. Rethinking recasts: A learner-centered examination of corrective feedback in the Japanese language classroom. In J. Kelly Hall and L. Stoops Verplaetse (eds.), *Second and foreign language learning through classroom interaction.* Mahwah, NJ: Lawrence Erlbaum Associates, Publishers. 47–71.

Partington, A. 1998. *Patterns and meanings: Using corpora for English language research and teaching.* Amsterdam/Philadelphia: John Benjamins Publishing Company.

Paulston, C. B. 1970. Structural pattern drills: A classification. *Foreign Language Annals* 4: 187–193.

Pawley, A., and F. Syder. 1983. Two puzzles for linguistic theory: Nativelike selection and nativelike fluency. In J. Richards and R. Schmidt (eds.), *Language and communication.* London: Longman. 191–226.

Peters, A. 1977. Language learning strategies: Does the whole equal the sum of the parts? *Language* 53 (4): 560–573.

Peters, A. 1983. *The units of language acquisition.* Cambridge: Cambridge University Press.

Pica, T. 1983. Adult acquisition of English as a second language under different conditions of exposure. *Language Learning* 33 (4): 465–497.

Pica, T. 1994. Questions from the language classroom: Research perspectives. *TESOL Quarterly* 28 (1): 49–79.

Pickrell, J. 2002. Searching for the tree of babel. *Science News* 161: 328–329.

Pienemann, M. 1998. *Language processing and second language development.* Amsterdam/Philadelphia: John Benjamins Publishing Company.

Pike, K. 1960. Nucleation. *Modern Language Journal* 44 (3): 291–295.

Pinker, S., and A. Prince. 1994. Regular and irregular morphology and the psychological status of rules of grammar. In S. Lima, R. Corrigan and G. Iverson (eds.), *The reality of linguistic rules.* Amsterdam/Philadelphia: John Benjamins Publishing Company. 321–351.

Platt, E. and F. Brooks. 2002. Task engagement: A turning point in foreign language development. *Language Learning* 52 (2): 364–399.

Plunkett, K, and V. Marchman. 1993. From rote learning to system building: Acquiring verb morphology in children and connectionist nets. *Cognition* 48: 21–69.

Prator, C. 1965. Development of a manipulation-communication scale. *NAFSA Studies and Papers,* English Language Series, No. 10, March: 385–391.

Putzel, R. 1976. Seeing differently through language: Grammatical correlates of personality. Ph.D. dissertation, University of California, Los Angeles.

Rea Dickins, P., and E. Woods. 1988. Some criteria for the development of communicative grammar tasks. *TESOL Quarterly* 22 (4): 623–646.

Riddle, E. 1986. The meaning and discourse function of the past tense in English. *TESOL Quarterly* 20 (2): 267–286.

Riggenbach, H., and V. Samuda. 2000. *Grammar dimensions: Form, meaning, and use.* Book 2. Platinum edition. Boston, MA: Heinle & Heinle.

Robb, T., S. Ross, and I. Shortreed. 1986. Salience of feedback on error and its effect on EFL writing quality. *TESOL Quarterly* 20 (1): 83–95.

Robins, R. H. 1967. *A short history of linguistics.* Bloomington: Indiana University Press.

Roediger, H. 1990. Implicit memory: Retention without remembering. *American Psychologist* 45: 1043–1056.

Rogers, M. 1994. German word order: A role for developmental and linguistic factors in L2 pedagogy. In M. Bygate, A. Tonkyn, and E. Williams (eds.), *Grammar and the language teacher.* Hemel Hempstead, England: Prentice Hall International. 132–159.

Rosch, E. 1978. Principles of categorization. In E. Rosch and B. Lloyd (eds.), *Cognition and categorization.* Hillsdale, NJ: Lawrence Erlbaum Associates, Publishers. 28–46.

Rutherford, W. 1987. *Second language grammar: Learning and teaching.* London: Longman.

Rutherford, W., and M. Sharwood Smith, eds. 1988. *Grammar and second language teaching.* New York: Newbury House.

Salaberry, R. 1997. The role of input and output practice in second language acquisition. *The Canadian Modern Language Review* 53 (2): 422–451.

Schachter, J. 1984. A universal input condition. In W. Rutherford (ed.), *Universals and second language acquisition.* Amsterdam/Philadelphia: John Benjamins Publishing Company. 167–181.

Schachter, J. 1986. Three approaches to the study of input. *Language Learning* 36 (2): 211–225.

Schachter, J. 1991. Corrective feedback in historical perspective. *Second Language Research* 7 (2): 89–102.

Schmidt, R. 1990. The role of consciousness in second language learning. *Applied Linguistics* 11 (2): 129–158.

Schmidt, R. 1994. Implicit learning and the cognitive unconscious: Of artificial grammars and SLA. In N. Ellis (ed.), *Implicit and explicit learning of languages.* London: Academic Press. 165–209.

Schmidt, R., and S. Frota. 1986. Developing basic conversational ability in a second language: A case study of an adult learner of Portuguese. In R. Day (ed.), *"Talking to Learn": Conversation in second language acquisition.* Rowley, MA: Newbury House. 237–326.

Schulz, R. 2001. Cultural differences in student and teacher perceptions concerning the role of grammar instruction and corrective feedback: USA-Colombia. *Modern Language Journal* 85 (2): 244–257.

Schwartz, B. 1993. On explicit and negative data effecting and affecting competence and linguistic behavior. *Studies in Second Language Acquisition* 15 (2): 147–163.

Seidenberg, M., and J. Hoeffner. 1998. Evaluating behavioral and neuroimaging data on past tense processing. *Language* 74 (1): 104–122.

Seidlhofer, B. 2001. Closing the conceptual gap: The case for a description of English as a lingua franca. *International Journal of Applied Linguistics* 11: 133–158.

Selinker, L. 1972. Interlanguage. *IRAL* 10 (2): 209–21.

Selinker, L., and S. Gass. 1984. *Workbook in second language acquisition.* Rowley, MA: Newbury House Publishers.

Sfard, A. 1998. On two metaphors for learning and the dangers of choosing just one. *Educational Researcher* 27 (2): 4–13.

Sharwood Smith, M. 1993. Input enhancement in instructed SLA: Theoretical bases. *Studies in Second Language Acquisition* 15 (2): 165–179.

Shirai, Y. 1992. Conditions on transfer: A connectionist approach. *Issues in Applied Linguistics* 3: 91–120.

Simard, D., and W. Wong. 2001. Alertness, orientation, and detection: The conceptualization of attentional functions in SLA. *Studies in Second Language Acquisition* 23 (1): 103–124.

Sinclair, J. 1991. *Corpus, concordance and collocation.* Oxford: Oxford University Press.

Skehan, P. 1994. Second language acquisition strategies, interlanguage development and task-based learning. In M. Bygate, A. Tonkyn, and E. Williams (eds.), *Grammar and the language teacher.* London: Prentice-Hall International. 175–199.

Skehan, P. 1998. Task-based instruction. *Annual Review of Applied Linguistics* 18: 268–286. Cambridge: Cambridge University Press.

Smith, L., and E. Thelen, eds. 1993. *A dynamic systems approach to development: Applications.* Cambridge, MA: MIT Press.

Spada, N., and P. Lightbown. 1993. Instruction and the development of questions in the L2 classroom. *Studies in Second Language Acquisition* 15 (2): 205–221.

Stauble, A., and D. Larsen-Freeman. 1978. The use of variable rules in describing the interlanguage of second language learners. *Workpapers in TESL.* UCLA. 72–87.

Stevick, E. 1959. "Technemes" and the rhythm of class activity. *Language Learning* 9 (3): 45–51.

Stevick, E. 1996. *Memory, Meaning & Method.* Second edition. Boston: Heinle & Heinle.

Suh, K. H. 1992. Past habituality in English discourse: "Used to" and "would." *Language Research* 28 (4): 857–882.

Swain, M. 1985. Communicative competence: Some roles of comprehensible input and comprehensible output in development. In S. Gass and C. Madden (eds.), *Input in second language acquisition.* Rowley, MA: Newbury House. 235–253.

Swain, M. 1995. Three functions of output in second language learning. In G. Cook and B. Seidlhofer (eds.), *Principles and practice in applied linguistics.* Oxford: Oxford University Press. 125–144.

Swain, M. 1998. Focus on form through conscious reflection. In C. Doughty and J. Williams (eds.), *Focus on form in classroom second language acquisition research.* Cambridge: Cambridge University Press. 64–81.

Swain, M., and S. Lapkin. 1995. Problems in output and the cognitive processes they generate: A step towards second language learning. *Applied Linguistics* 16 (3): 371–391.

Swain, M., and S. Lapkin. 1998. Interaction and second language learning: Two adolescent French immersion students working together. *Modern Language Journal* 82 (3): 320–337.

Takahashi, E. 1998. Language development in social interaction: A longitudinal study of a Japanese FLES Program from a Vygotskyan approach. *Foreign Language Annals* 31 (3): 392–406.

Talyzina, N. 1981. *The psychology of learning.* Moscow: Progress Publishers.

Tan, M., ed. 2002. *Corpus studies in language education.* Bangkok: IELE Press.

Tarone, E. 1979. Interlanguage as chameleon. *Language Learning* 29 (1): 181–191.

Tarone, E. 2002. Frequency effects, noticing, and creativity: Factors in a variationist interlanguage framework. *Studies in Second Language Acquisition* 24 (2): 287–296.

Terrell, T. 1991. The role of grammar in a communicative approach. *Modern Language Journal* 75 (1): 52–63.

Tharp, R., and R. Gallimore. 1988. *Rousing minds to life: Teaching, learning, and schooling in social context*. New York: Cambridge University Press.

Thelen, E. 1995. Time-scale dynamics and the development of an embodied cognition. In R. Port and T. van Gelder (eds.), *Mind as Motion*. Cambridge, MA: MIT Press. 69–100.

Thewlis, S. 2000. *Grammar dimensions: Form, meaning, and use*. Book 3. Platinum edition. Boston, MA: Heinle & Heinle.

Thornbury, S. 2001. *Uncovering grammar*. Oxford: Macmillan Heinemann.

Todeva, E. 1998. Non-traditional focus on form activities in Japanese EFL classes: Collaborative dictoglosses. *NUCB Journal of Language, Culture and Communication* 1 (1): 47–58.

Tomasello, M., ed. 1998. *The new psychology of language*. Mahwah, NJ: Lawrence Erlbaum Associates, Publishers.

Tomasello, M., and C. Herron. 1988. Down the garden path: Inducing and correcting overgeneralization errors in the foreign language classroom. *Applied Psycholinguistics* 9 (3): 237–246.

Tomlin, R., and H. Villa. 1994. Attention in cognitive science and second language acquisition. *Studies in Second Language Acquisition* 16: 183–203.

Truscott, J. 1996. Review article: The case against grammar correction in L2 writing classes. *Language Learning* 46 (2): 327–369.

Truscott, J. 1998. Instance theory and Universal Grammar in second language research. *Second Language Research* 14 (3): 257–291.

Truscott, J. 1999. What's wrong with oral grammar correction. *The Canadian Modern Language Review* 55 (4): 437–455.

Vande Kopple, W. 1997. Using the concepts of given information and new information in classes on the English language. In T. Miller (ed.), *Functional approaches to written text: Classroom applications*. Washington, DC: United States Information Agency. 216–229.

van Geert, P. 1994. *Dynamic systems of development*. London: Harvester-Wheatsheaf.

Van Lier, L. 2002. An ecological-semiotic perspective on language and linguistics. In C. Kramsch (ed.), *Language acquisition and language socialization*. London: Continuum. 140–164.

VanPatten, B. 1996. *Input processing and grammar instruction in second language acquisition*. Norwood, NJ: Ablex Publishing Corporation.

VanPatten, B. 2002. Processing instruction: An update. *Language Learning* 52 (4): 755–803.

VanPatten, B., and T. Cadierno. 1993. Input processing and second language acquisition: A role for instruction. *Modern Language Journal* 77: 45–57.

Vigil, F., and J. Oller. 1976. Rule fossilization: A tentative model. *Language Learning* 26 (2): 281–295.

Vygotsky, L. 1978. *Mind in society: The development of higher psychological processes*. Cambridge, MA: Harvard University Press.

Vygotsky, L. 1989. *Thought and Language*. Cambridge, MA: MIT Press.

Waldrop, M. 1992. *Complexity: The emerging science at the edge of order and chaos*. New York: Simon and Schuster.

Waugh, L. 1997. Roman Jackobson's work as a dialogue: The dialogue as the basis of language, the dialogue as the basis of scientific work. *Acta Linguistica Hafniensia* 29: 101–120.

White, L. 1987. Against comprehensible input. *Applied Linguistics* 8 (2): 95–110.

White, L. 1991. Adverb placement in second language acquisition: Some effects of positive and negative evidence in the classroom. *Second Language Research* 7: 133–161.

White, L. Forthcoming. *Second language acquisition and universal grammar.* Cambridge: Cambridge University Press.

Whitehead, A. N. 1929. *The aims of education.* New York: MacMillan.

Widdowson, H. G. 1979. *Explorations in applied linguistics.* Oxford: Oxford University Press.

Widdowson, H. G. 1990. *Aspects of language teaching.* Oxford: Oxford University Press.

Widdowson, H. G. 1996. *Linguistics.* Oxford: Oxford University Press.

Wilkins, D. A. 1976. *Notional syllabuses.* London: Oxford University Press.

Williams, J., and J. Evans. 1998. What kind of focus and on which forms? In C. Doughty and J. Williams (eds.), *Focus on form in classroom second language acquisition.* Cambridge: Cambridge University Press. 139–155.

Williams, R. 1977. *Marxism and literature.* Oxford: Oxford University Press.

Willis, J. 1996. *A framework for task-based learning.* London: Longman.

Wolfe-Quintero, K., S. Inagaki, and H-Y Kim. 1998. *Second language development in writing: Measures of fluency, accuracy & complexity.* Honolulu, Hawaii: University of Hawaii Press.

Wong Fillmore, L. 1976. The second time around. Ph.D. dissertation, Stanford University.

Wray, A. 2002. *Formulaic language and the lexicon.* Cambridge: Cambridge University Press.

Yang, L., and K. Ko. 1998. Understanding preservice teachers' responses to unexpected questions. Paper presented at the 32nd Annual TESOL Convention, March 19, Seattle, Washington.

Yu, C-H. 1994. Abduction? Deduction? Induction? Is there a logic of exploratory data analysis? Paper presented at the Annual Meeting of the American Educational Research Association, New Orleans, Louisiana.